THE GEORGE GUND FOUNDATION
IMPRINT IN AFRICAN AMERICAN STUDIES

The George Gund Foundation has endowed
this imprint to advance understanding of
the history, culture, and current issues
of African Americans.

Named in remembrance of

the onetime *Antioch Review* editor

and longtime Bay Area resident,

the Lawrence Grauman, Jr. Fund

supports books that address

a wide range of human rights,

free speech, and social justice issues.

Freedom Train

The publisher and the University of California Press Foundation gratefully acknowledge the generous support of the George Gund Foundation Imprint in African American Studies.

The publisher and the University of California Press Foundation gratefully acknowledge the generous support of the Lawrence Grauman, Jr. Fund.

Freedom Train

BLACK POLITICS AND THE STORY OF
INTERRACIAL LABOR SOLIDARITY

Cedric de Leon

UNIVERSITY OF CALIFORNIA PRESS

University of California Press
Oakland, California

Library of Congress Cataloging-in-Publication Data

Names: Leon, Cedric de, author.
Title: Freedom train : black politics and the story of interracial labor
 solidarity / Cedric de Leon.
Description: Oakland : University of California Press, 2025. | Includes
 bibliographical references and index.
Identifiers: LCCN 2024048631 (print) | LCCN 2024048632 (ebook) |
 ISBN 9780520410244 (cloth) | ISBN 9780520410251 (paperback) |
 ISBN 9780520410268 (ebook)
Subjects: LCSH: Labor unions, Black—United States—History. | Labor
 movement—United States—History. | African American labor union
 members—United States—History. | Black people—Civil rights—
 History.
Classification: LCC HD6870.5 .L36 2025 (print) | LCC HD6870.5
 (ebook) | DDC 331.88089/96073—dc23/eng/20250106
LC record available at https://lccn.loc.gov/2024048631
LC ebook record available at https://lccn.loc.gov/2024048632

GPSR Authorized Representative: Easy Access System Europe,
Mustamäe tee 50, 10621
Tallinn, Estonia, gpsr.requests@easproject.com

34 33 32 31 30 29 28 27 26 25
10 9 8 7 6 5 4 3 2 1

For the UMass 57

Contents

Illustrations

Abbreviations

ABB	African Blood Brotherhood
AFL	American Federation of Labor
AFL-CIO	American Federation of Labor-Congress of Industrial Organizations
AFSCME	American Federation of State, County and Municipal Employees
AFT	American Federation of Teachers
ANLC	American Negro Labor Congress
BSCP	Brotherhood of Sleeping Car Porters
CBTU	Coalition of Black Trade Unionists
CIO	Congress of Industrial Organizations
CORE	Congress of Racial Equality
CPUSA	Communist Party USA
DPOWU	Distributive, Processing and Office Workers Union
DRUM	Dodge Revolutionary Union Movement
ERP	Employee Representation Plan
FE	United Farm Equipment Workers of America
FTA	Food, Tobacco, Agricultural, and Allied Workers Union
HERE	Hotel Employees and Restaurant Employees Union

HTUC	Harlem Trade Union Council
ICC	Interstate Commerce Commission
ILD	International Labor Defense
ILGWU	International Ladies Garment Workers Union
ILWU	International Longshore and Warehouse Union
IUE	International Union of Electrical, Radio and Machine Workers of America
IWW	Industrial Workers of the World
JCNR	Joint Committee on National Recovery
LNPL	Labor's Non-Partisan League
Mine Mill	International Union of Mine, Mill and Smelter Workers
MOWM	March on Washington Movement
NAACP	National Association for the Advancement of Colored People
NALC	Negro American Labor Council
NIL	National Industrial League
NLC-USA	Negro Labor Committee-United States of America
NLVC	Negro Labor Victory Committee
NMU	National Maritime Union
NNC	National Negro Congress
NNLC	National Negro Labor Council
NTUC	National Trade Union Conference for Negro Rights
PWOC	Packinghouse Workers Organizing Committee
RWDSU	Retail Wholesale and Department Store Union
SNYC	Southern Negro Youth Congress
SWOC	Steel Workers Organizing Committee
TSLU	Tobacco Stemmers and Laborers Union
TUEL	Trade Union Educational League
TULC	Trade Union Leadership Council
TUUL	Trade Union Unity League
TWIU	Tobacco Workers International Union

TWU	Transport Workers Union
UAW	United Auto Workers
UE	United Electrical, Radio and Machine Workers of America
UMWA	United Mine Workers of America
UNIA	United Negro Improvement Association
UOPWA	United Office and Professional Workers of America
UPWA	United Packinghouse Workers of America
USW	United Steel Workers
WP	Workers Party

1 *Black Vanguard*

August 28, 1963, began inauspiciously. Organizers of the much-anticipated march for jobs and freedom had promised the press a major protest, yet reporters were the only people standing on the National Mall in Washington. Turning to Bayard Rustin, the event's lead organizer, the reporters asked, "Where are the people?"[1]

Rustin, like any organizer worth their salt, was wondering much the same thing. For six months, the leadership and staff of the march had been lining up sponsors, mobilizing the grassroots, and arranging transportation for what they hoped would be a historic protest. Some signs pointed in that direction. News of the event caused such a stir that travel agencies across the country were asking if they might be hired to arrange transportation. A month before the march, the nation seemed to be running out of buses. On July 30, Al Lowenthal of the International Union of Electrical, Radio and Machine Workers of America (IUE) warned all local IUE presidents to reserve their transportation immediately as chartered buses were at a premium. By August 20, Rustin would write to supporters that "charter service between Washington and New York . . . has been exhausted," and that marchers should request a special two-day permit from the Interstate Commerce Commission (ICC) to carry passengers across state lines. Anticipating the traffic, the New Jersey Turnpike

Authority was coordinating with Rustin to direct automobiles and buses to different rest stops and to arrange for extra supplies to be made available along the route.[2]

But there were worrying signs, too. Despite repeated attempts to charter trains and buses for southern activists, as late as August 18 organizers had not secured sufficient transportation for even the leading representatives of the Student Nonviolent Coordinating Committee (SNCC). In a letter to SNCC leader Stokely Carmichael, Courtland Cox of the march's administrative committee stated frankly, "I have gone to great lengths to inquire as to the possibilities of providing transportation for the people from the Southern areas, let me tell you partner ain't nothing happening." Suspicious that this might be a racist conspiracy to prevent a mass caravan from the South, organizers lodged a formal complaint with the ICC and asked US Congressman Leonard Farbstein to push for a full-scale investigation.[3]

Their internal numbers were also worrisome. At last count, on August 22, six days before the protest, the number of people committed to attending the march was 67,080, well shy of the 100,000 that Rustin had promised. The numbers were sufficiently problematic that Rachelle Horowitz, the staff person in charge of transportation, would write to Rustin, "Don't be alarmed by the seeming decrease in estimate."[4]

And so, looking out into the gray and muggy morning of August 28, Rustin had to stall. He whipped out a document, glanced at his pocket watch, and told the press smoothly, "It's all coming according to schedule." Horowitz recalls that when the reporters left them, she asked Rustin, "What were you looking at?" He said, "A blank piece of paper."[5]

In hindsight, Rustin had little to worry about, for within hours, the National Mall would be occupied by over 200,000 people. The March on Washington for Jobs and Freedom became what many of its organizers hoped it would be: an epoch-defining blow to the forces of white supremacy and institutionalized Jim Crow segregation. That the march was a watershed in the Black Freedom Struggle is by now a well-known fact. What is less well-known is that the prime mover of the march was the Black labor movement.[6]

A former Youth Communist League and antiwar activist, Bayard Rustin worked as deputy to A. Philip Randolph, president of the Brotherhood of Sleeping Car Porters and the Negro American Labor Council (NALC). Now largely forgotten, NALC was an independent Black labor organization formed in 1959 to integrate the institutionalized labor movement. Randolph had poached Rustin from A. J. Muste's War Resisters League to plan the march. NALC also served as treasurer of the event, housing the small donations that poured in from across the country and redistributing money to local councils in need of support, especially for transportation.[7]

Due largely to Black labor's efforts but also in part to UAW president Walter Reuther, head of the industrial department of the American Federation of Labor and Congress of Industrial Organizations (AFL-CIO), 40,000 marchers, or one-fifth of the total audience, were union members. Though that in and of itself is impressive, in fact, organized labor was meant to be the featured constituency. At their last internal count, 31,225 labor activists were confirmed passengers on chartered transport going to the march, roughly half of the anticipated total. Indeed, the March on Washington was led and organized as much by Black labor activists as it was by either SNCC or Dr. Martin Luther King, Jr.'s Southern Christian Leadership Conference (SCLC). To those involved at the highest levels, this would have been a simple statement of fact, for the march was understood chiefly as a protest against racial exclusion from the labor market and unions—hence its name, "The March on Washington for *Jobs* and Freedom." As Tom Kahn, a friend to Stokely Carmichael and Bayard Rustin, would write, "the original plans . . . focused on the need to draw national attention to the economic crisis confronting the masses of unskilled and semiskilled Negro workers." Only later would the march be seen as a tactic to defeat the anticipated Senate filibuster of the Civil Rights Act.[8]

Indeed, within the world of organized labor, the march was part of an escalating standoff between NALC and the National Association for the Advancement of Colored People (NAACP) on the one hand, and the International Ladies Garment Workers Union (ILGWU) and the AFL-CIO on the other. The conflict emerged out of the ILGWU's practice of segregating Black and Puerto Rican members into the worst jobs, and intensified with the AFL's continued unwillingness to punish local and state affiliates for excluding Black people from meetings, membership, and elected office. The widespread persistence of Jim Crow unionism, combined with accelerating deindustrialization (then called "runaway shops"), created a crisis of unemployment in the Black community. This was corroborated by a series of blockbuster reports from the US Commission on Civil Rights, the New York City Youth Board, and others, all with the same message: racial segregation in the labor movement concentrated Blacks in menial occupations and the growing ranks of the unemployed. Accordingly, in the years just prior to the march, NALC, the NAACP, SNCC, and the SCLC called AFL-CIO president George Meany to account for not doing enough to curb employment discrimination.[9]

The March on Washington for Jobs and Freedom generated such immense pressure on the labor movement that in the following months the AFL-CIO and its affiliates agreed to do more to fight racial discrimination in their ranks. Even the state federations of Alabama and Mississippi lobbied in favor of the Civil Rights Act and resisted attempts by Senate Dixiecrats and Republicans to dilute the legislation. By June 1964, the so-called "Negro-Labor Alliance" was confident enough to threaten a national one-day strike on the anniversary of the march if the Senate blocked the bill's passage. The Senate would pass the Civil Rights Act that same month.[10]

Though the historical evidence suggests that independent Black labor organizations (that is, those unaffiliated with unions or labor federations) pushed for their own inclusion in the US labor movement, the story of interracial solidarity as most scholars tell it centers on white activists. White-led unions were either racially exclusionary toward Black people, thereby undermining interracial solidarity, or racially inclusive, thereby fostering it. Evelyn Nakano Glenn, for example, notes that the American Federation of Labor's focus on organizing white skilled tradesmen "excluded unskilled and semiskilled workers," adding, "because women and black workers were concentrated in unskilled and semiskilled jobs, they were among those excluded." Other scholars have challenged this point of view, arguing that progressive trade unionists have championed the organization of Black workers. Thus, in their canonical book *Left Out*, Stepan-Norris and Zeitlin emphasize the "racially egalitarian impact of Communists and their allies on the policies of the UAW [the United Auto Workers], UPWA [the United Packinghouse Workers of America], and other internationals," noting that Communist-led unions were more likely to have a guarantee of membership equality and a Black officer or executive board member than their non-Communist counterparts.[11]

While the existing research has helped us to understand the conditions that enable and constrain interracial solidarity, it nevertheless suffers from at least two limitations. First, scholars tend to look for interracial solidarity in unions, even though Black people in this period were unlikely to be union members. By comparison, independent or unaffiliated labor organizations receive much less attention. Second, and as a consequence of the preoccupation with unions, Black workers typically show up as minor or passive actors in their own history. We know relatively little about instances in which Black workers played the leading role.[12]

Nor is this problem exclusive to the disciplines of sociology and labor studies, of which I am a practitioner. Historians have done a better job of centering the experience and leadership of Black workers, but even they contend that labor history "has a race problem." In 1989, Nell Irvin Painter famously wrote that the field was guilty of "the deletion of black workers." Similarly, David Roediger observed that "even as the issue of race is raised . . . the Black worker enters the story of American labor as an actor in a subplot which can be left on the cutting-room floor, probably without vitiating the main story." More recently, Jenny Carson's research on Black women laundry workers has pointed out that historians continue to frame Black workers as the passive victims or beneficiaries of powerful white-led industrial unions.[13]

This book challenges scholars and activists to think differently about the cause of interracial labor solidarity, which I define here as a vision of working-class comradeship based on the principles of inclusive membership, representative leadership, and the struggle for economic and racial justice. If we are interested in illuminating the role of Black labor activists, then we must shift our focus from unions, where white workers have historically predominated, to what we might call "subaltern" organizations, where Black workers were the leading figures.

Widening our aperture in this way allows as to ask a different question: what conditions *within the Black community* advanced the cause of interracial labor solidarity? I ask this question because Black people were, and indeed saw themselves as, the vanguard of that struggle. Though progressive whites assisted, it was Black workers and their organizations who continually pressed for their own inclusion in white-led unions. Black labor activists in the middle of the twentieth century referred to themselves as the "Freedom Train," harkening back to the Underground Railroad that spirited the enslaved to freedom.

My answer to this question centers on Black politics. African peoples have challenged their exploitation from their ocean passage to these shores and up through slavery, so it is fitting that their challenge to racial exclusion from unions coincided with the birth of the US labor movement, beginning with their fight to integrate the National Labor Union in the 1860s.[14] But the politics that would come to define the modern struggle for interracial solidarity emerged from the primordial soup of early twentieth-century Harlem. The key actors were the Brotherhood of Sleeping Car Porters and the African Blood Brotherhood, which respectively became the basis of Black labor's centrist and left factions. It was also out of this ferment that a form unique to the struggle of Black labor emerged, namely, an ideologically diverse coalition in which Black organizations put aside their differences to pool their resources and demand political, social, and economic citizenship.

The energy that propelled the Freedom Train forward was the conflict and consensus among organizations within Black civil society. This is what I mean by "Black politics." If a key task of this book is to demonstrate the agency of Black people, then I should point out that the story I tell is slightly different from other accounts with the same goal. This is not only a story of unified collective struggle, but also one of messiness, internal division, intrigue, and betrayal. I want to suggest that such fractiousness does not diminish Black agency. If anything, evidence of internal conflict enhances it. What appears in these pages suggests that Black folk were invested enough in the cause of interracial labor solidarity to debate the correct course of action and sometimes form a united front. Both the consensus *and* conflict in Black civil society add important details to the claim that Black people were agents of their own liberation. Indeed, as I seek to demonstrate, an unintended consequence of these internal debates was tactical innovation, and the successive shifts in tactics applied ever greater pressure upon the state and organized labor to integrate unions. This may seem a counterintuitive finding to some. It is not uncommon for activists to deflect charges of racism, sexism, and homophobia in social movement spaces as divisive, destructive, and ultimately disloyal. The story of Black labor activists provides an important counter to that argument, for it was precisely their ability to navigate conflict in their own organizations and in the wider movement that forced white labor leaders to confront the problem of the color line. The supposed weakness of internal division was in fact a strength.

Throughout the course of the twentieth century, these factions split and consolidated to form successive and sometimes competing independent Black labor organizations. Note that this history overlaps with, but is distinct from, the now well-documented class and generational conflicts within the Black community.[15] Chief among these groups were the centrist faction, led historically by A. Philip Randolph on the one hand, and on the other, the left faction led by successive cadres like Cyril Briggs of the African Blood Brotherhood, John P. Davis and Thelma Dale of the National Negro Congress (NNC), and Ernest Thompson and Vicki Garvin of the National Negro Labor Council (NNLC). The broken remnants of these struggles would come together briefly in the NALC. Though I imply that the centrist faction was more conservative than the left, it is important to bear in mind that both factions were more progressive on the question of race than the mainstream labor movement.

This political fault line—centrist and left—was salient within and between independent Black labor organizations themselves. By "left," I refer to those organizations that were internationalist in orientation, whether in their commitment to the international communist movement or Black anticolonial politics. The left faction condemned capitalism as a system of economic, racial, and colonial domination and looked with suspicion upon organized labor as class collaborationist and racist. The "centrist" faction, by contrast, oriented toward the United States primarily and was critical of capital only insofar as it excluded Black people from the workforce. Centrists were more comfortable than their left counterparts in engaging with the bureaucracy of organized labor. They oscillated between liberal and progressive politics, sometimes working with the left, and other times participating in outright red-baiting.

The rest of Black civil society tended to fracture and unite along this same fault line. Whenever Black labor's two great factions joined forces, so, too, did the NAACP, the National Urban League, the Black clergy, press, and intelligentsia. Whenever the factions divided, most followed the centrists; Black artists and intellectuals, who tended to lean leftward, were the exception. This is not to say that Black labor's centrist faction could always count on the unwavering support of the Black community: in the early years of the Brotherhood of Sleeping Car Porters, for instance, A. Philip Randolph had a notoriously toxic relationship with elements of the Black press. By and large, however, the factional divide held for the time period in question.

In support of these big-picture claims of Black leadership and factionalism, I want to make three additional points. First, white workers and trade unionists were inconsistent advocates of interracial solidarity. Some of the earliest unions in the United States were formed explicitly to keep Black labor out of the formal labor market. This was in part the legacy of slavery, for white planters hired out enslaved Black artisans to shops, shipyards, and factories across the country at cheaper rates than what it might have cost to employ white workers. As a result, before the Civil War the enslaved dominated the skilled trades as far north as New York City. Because of slavery's long shadow, many white labor leaders, even those deemed relatively progressive on racial issues, struggled after the Civil War to maintain interracial discipline on the ground and ultimately surrendered to their racist members. This was true especially of the AFL, the country's preeminent union federation, but also of other late nineteenth-century organizations like the National Labor Union and the Knights of Labor. Likewise, the Congress of Industrial Organizations (CIO) struggled with racial animus in their failed attempt to organize industrial workers in the South.[16]

The second point concerns the leadership of Black women and the importance of gender inequality alongside the entwined struggles for racial and economic justice, what Black feminists call "intersectionality." Black women, with varying results, insisted upon centering their triple oppression at the hands of patriarchy, capitalism, and white supremacy. The work of the National Negro Labor Council in the 1950s was the high point of that political project. In those years, Vicki Garvin and Viola Brown rose to high office in the NNLC and made the integration and promotion of Black women in the labor movement and the workplace a centerpiece of their organizing. While the fight for gender equity was more muted during the heydays of the National Negro Congress (1936–1947) and the Negro American Labor Council (1959–1968), one cannot understand the development of those organizations without reference to Black women either. For example, Thelma Dale and her all-woman staff led the NNC through the Second World War and saved it from a divisive sectarian conflict. Black women also threatened to derail the NALC's founding convention if A. Philip Randolph and the all-male leadership refused to make room for two women vice presidents. Thus, although it would be a mistake to suggest that independent Black labor organizations embraced intersectionality with any kind of consistency, neither would this history be complete without documenting the ways in which women demanded a seat at the table.

The third point has to do with the state. If Black people make their own politics, they do not do so under conditions of their own choosing. Jim Crow unionism was underpinned by a political economy that Cedric Robinson famously called "racial capitalism," which relied upon the segregation and super-exploitation of Black workers on the most precarious rungs of the labor market. Solidarity across the color line was an existential threat to such a system. Accordingly, a throughline from 1917 to 1963 was the state's repression and surveillance of independent Black labor organizations, who comprised the vanguard of interracial labor solidarity. In this, the Cold War and other intermittent outbursts of red-baiting were particularly devastating. To the rabid hunters of alleged communists, the surest sign of a Red was their defense of Black people. This often earned radicals the gratitude of the Black community, but it rained down hell upon the left. Red Scares destroyed Black organizations and Black lives. The Federal Bureau of Investigation (FBI) surveilled dozens of Black labor activists and turned them into informants on their own people. Simultaneously, Black FBI agents infiltrated Black organizations and reported their daily movements to the US government.[17]

The role of the state brings us organically to the historical evidence that appears in this book. Because interracial labor solidarity is an existential threat to both capital and the state, some of my data comes from law enforcement records. A great deal is now known of the FBI's surveillance of Dr. King and the Black Panthers, but my research suggests that the US Justice and State departments were spying on Black labor activists well before the 1960s. Indeed, many of my primary sources for the 1910s and 1920s come from US intelligence on Cyril Briggs, Claude McKay, A. Philip Randolph, and Marcus Garvey. I have had to read these intelligence reports "against the grain." That is, instead of reading for the whereabouts and seditious speech of Black activists, as intelligence officers did to build the government's case against them, I looked for the formation of independent labor organizations and the relationships among them. Anti-Black racism has important methodological consequences, including for data collection and analysis.

One might then logically ask whether the need to find data from unseemly sources like the FBI is due to a corresponding lack of more palatable sources and evidence. The answer is somewhat complicated. On the one hand, there are very few secondary sources on this topic. Though a small number of historians of the Civil Rights Movement and the Communist Party make mention of the National Negro Congress of the 1930s and 1940s, there is in fact only one book devoted to the NNC, Erik Gellman's *Death Blow to Jim Crow*. Similarly, although the National Negro Labor Council was the leading Black labor organization of the 1950s, it is the focus of only one master's thesis and one published biography, both by the same author, Mindy Thompson Fullilove. On the other hand, having collected and analyzed the sheer quantity of primary data that appears in this book (which is a mere fraction of the total collected), my sense is that the historical evidence exists, but too few have bothered to look for it. The W. E. B. Du Bois Library in Amherst, the Library of Congress in Washington, DC, the Schomburg Center for Research in Black Culture in Harlem, and the Walter Reuther Library at Wayne State University in Detroit, among others, have excellent collections for those who want to follow up on this research.[18]

While we are on research methods and data, I want to address two more methodological questions preemptively. First, why have I chosen to study national organizations instead of one or two local unions, as professional historians and sociologists often do? For example, why not do a deep dive into Black-led unions like Local 9 of the Industrial Workers of the World (IWW), Food, Tobacco and Agricultural Workers Union (FTA) Local 22, the Black caucus of the United Steel Workers (USW), or the Black Communists of Alabama? There are three reasons why I did not go in that direction. To begin, scholars have already done a magnificent job of excavating the histories of these local struggles. By comparison, we know less about the historical development of successive national struggles to integrate the labor movement. Next, research on these larger groups reveals that local and national struggles were not mutually exclusive. For instance, as the political scientist Michael Goldfield writes, the National Negro Congress supplied the organizers who recruited Black workers into the steelworkers' union in places like Pittsburgh, Birmingham, Chicago, and Gary. Most importantly, I did not want to give the impression that Black labor's efforts were small exceptions to the larger rule that white people were the leading advocates of interracial solidarity. As we will see, Black activists established extensive mass organizations with local councils in every region of the country. That is the story that I believe has yet to be told.[19]

The second question has to do with my identity as a Filipino scholar. People sometimes ask why I study Black workers, given my background. I often respond to this question with a query of my own: would you ask me this question if I were studying *white* workers? The answer of course would be, "No." Studying white workers and white-led unions is the unspoken norm in labor studies. Nobody thinks twice when a graduate student says they want to write a dissertation comparing two white-led unions that few have ever heard of. My position is that everyone should study Black labor history. If more people did, then a study comparing independent Black labor organizations might have been written in 1965 instead of 2024. I also have intellectual and political reasons for writing this book. As I read through the vast scholarship on race and labor in the United States, I was troubled to find that very few authors wrote about Black workers. If interracial solidarity in theory could alleviate unemployment and raise the standard of living in the Black community, then surely some Black workers must have played an active or a leading role in fighting for racial inclusion in the labor movement. I wondered what their names were, which organizations they established, and how much they achieved. Politically, I happen to believe that the revitalization of the labor movement today will depend in part on the leadership of Black workers. Black labor has been vital to all the major upsurges in US labor history, from the rise of the Knights of Labor in the 1880s and industrial unionism in the early twentieth century to the public-sector organizing wave of the 1960s. If we are to see the rebirth of the labor movement in our lifetime, then Black people, as ever, will be a part of it. One of the reasons I wrote this book was to learn from our Black predecessors in the movement and obtain clues for how to organize in our own time.

. . .

This discussion brings us to the moving intellectual spirit behind this book: the work of W. E. B. Du Bois. In his magisterial work, *Black Reconstruction in America*, Du Bois overturned the widely held belief that Abraham Lincoln and the Republican Party were responsible for both the northern victory in the US Civil War and the Reconstruction amendments to the US Constitution that abolished slavery, established the principle of equal protection under the law, and prohibited discrimination in voting. Du Bois insisted that the decisive turning point in the Civil War was the defection of enslaved Black labor from the South to the North. This "general strike" of the Black worker transformed the Confederacy's workforce into an armed resistance that crippled southern supply lines and ultimately enabled the Union to prevail. In addition, Du Bois reminds us that Black people were the fiercest advocates of Radical Reconstruction, not only as citizens, but also as elected leaders in local, state, and federal government.[20]

The implications of *Black Reconstruction* are many, but there are two interrelated claims that bear special mention. First, Black people were agents of their own liberation. As much as they relied upon the moral courage of white allies in the abolition movement, Black folk also organized themselves and were the drivers of Reconstruction. Second, we must look beyond elites to "subaltern" voices for the sources of social change. By centering the experience and activism of women, workers, people of color, and other marginalized groups, we stand to achieve a fuller picture of our collective history. This ethic, what we might call the subaltern imperative, was central to Du Bois's intellectual and political project.

In recent years, we have witnessed a renaissance of Du Boisian sociology, led by Aldon Morris. Early in Morris's career, sociologists believed that the success of the Civil Rights Movement in the 1960s was due mainly to the support of white elites like Presidents Johnson and Kennedy and the resulting fracture in a power structure that had once turned a blind eye to Black suffering. Breaking with this school of thought, Morris demonstrated that in fact the rapid spread of the Civil Rights Movement across the South was due to the institution of the Black Church, which formed the crucial node in local clusters of civil rights activism. It was the internal resources of the Black community—not the external support of sympathetic whites—that fueled the cause of Black liberation. In a similar move of intellectual history, in his 2015 book *A Scholar Denied*, Morris argued that Du Bois—not Robert Park at the University of Chicago—was the father of American sociology. Several other sociologists have followed in Morris's footsteps since 2015, and this book is another in this tradition.[21]

Historians and other labor studies scholars have provided additional inspiration for what appears in these pages. Though the field of labor studies continues to lionize white activists, an intrepid few have established a critical scholarly literature that foregrounds the monumental contribution of Black people to the labor movement. Those whose work has been most influential to the writing of this book include Philip S. Foner, Mindy Thompson Fullilove, Erik Gellman, Glenda Elizabeth Gilmore, Robin D. G. Kelley, Robert Rodgers Korstad, Earl Lewis, and Mark Solomon. For them, as for me, Black workers are not a sideshow in the march for economic democracy, but the main event.[22]

Where this book differs theoretically from the aforementioned sociologists and historians is in conceiving of the "subaltern" not as a group, but as a terrain of struggle—what some sociologists call a "field." Often when we elevate subaltern voices, we follow the career of one social movement or organization over time. The cause of interracial labor solidarity from 1917 to the 1963 March on Washington, by contrast, is a story of successive battles among organizations with competing political dispositions in the same social space, which I refer to here as Black labor.

Hopefully by this point, you are convinced that what I offer is an important contribution to our collective knowledge as a society, but for those of you who are still wondering why any of this matters, let me add a few more words. As with other aspects of American history and society, the role of Black people in the labor movement has been systematically erased or ignored by workers, trade unionists, and scholars alike. It is an intrinsic good to reveal to the world and each other the contribution that our Black sisters and brothers have made to the multiracial labor movement we have today.

Moreover, since the #RedforEd strike wave of 2018 and the surge in worker organizing during the COVID-19 pandemic, reporters and other observers have begun to ask whether the labor movement is back after a generation of decline. Public support for unions is at its highest point since 1965; petitions for National Relations Labor Board elections are up 58 percent; and workers have posted surprising victories at iconic brands like Starbucks, Amazon, and Trader Joe's. The newest research on labor movement revitalization offers several explanations for how workers and their unions have achieved such victories and may achieve more: workers are organizing pro-union super-majorities in the workplace; a militant minority of progressive workers has infiltrated the labor movement, most famously in the field of education; workers, not staff organizers or union bureaucrats, are finally taking the lead; and unions are at last prioritizing racial and gender equity in addition to economic justice. Though most of these explanations acknowledge the importance of race, relatively few insist that Black people must *lead* the labor movement in order for it to be a more successful version of itself. Nor is it common to suggest that Black labor should publicly confront the still largely white-led labor movement for perpetuating racial inequality, as NALC and its predecessors did.[23]

Finally, and in a related vein, this book demonstrates that internal conflict can be a resource instead of a liability in movement building. The ongoing tension between the centrist and left factions of Black labor and the clash that tension engendered in the wider labor movement produced tangible gains in the cause of interracial solidarity. For example, the Negro-Labor Alliance of the 1960s, which sought to resolve the racial tensions in unions and end workplace discrimination, touched off a historic wave of public-sector organizing. The Memphis sanitation workers' strike of 1968, during which Dr. King was assassinated, encouraged other Black public-sector workers to organize in Florida, Virginia, and South Carolina. In 1962, about 10 percent of public employees belonged to unions; by 1973, 23 percent did. The public-sector wave remains what sociologist Dan Clawson called the last major "upsurge" in US labor history. What this suggests is that social movement activists should not shy away from race or other potentially divisive issues, but rather take the plunge, confident in our collective capacity to survive the mess and emerge stronger for the experience.[24]

. . .

The rest of this book unfolds in five chapters. Chapter 2, "The Brotherhoods," sets the stage for the advent of the great labor organizations of the 1930s to 1960s. The chapter begins in Harlem, arguably the capital of Black radicalism in the United States from the 1910s to the 1920s. It tells the stories of A. Philip Randolph and Cyril V. Briggs, leaders of the Brotherhood of Sleeping Car Porters (BSCP) and the

African Blood Brotherhood (ABB). It was these organizations that gave rise to two distinctive factions in the emerging Black labor movement. Moreover, the primordial soup of Harlem civil society of which the brotherhoods were a key ingredient simultaneously gave rise to the forms that future coalitions between the factions would take in the years to come.

Chapter 3, "The Congress and the March," begins with the first truly national mass organization of Black labor, the National Negro Congress (NNC), founded in 1936. The NNC was a big-tent coalition of Black civil society organizations, but its leaders reflected the legacy of the Brotherhoods. The NNC president was A. Philip Randolph, who was then still the leader of the Brotherhood of Sleeping Car Porters and a player in the conservative American Federation of Labor. The longest-serving national secretaries of the NNC were John P. Davis, a leftist intellectual and lobbyist with ties to the Communist Party, and Thelma Dale, a Communist Party member and leader in the Southern Negro Youth Congress. The NNC, through its local chapters, supplied the staff and rank-and-file leaders who organized Black workers in steel, meatpacking, auto, and tobacco. Despite these important victories, the internal tensions in this coalition would split it in two. Ever suspicious of the Russian Bolsheviks, Randolph charged that Communists had come to dominate the NNC. He left the Congress in 1940, taking with him the NAACP, the Urban League, and the Black clergy. In 1941, Randolph formed a new organization, the March on Washington Movement (MOWM). The MOWM concentrated its efforts on integrating the defense industry. In perhaps the most dramatic moment in the MOWM's history, Randolph warned President Franklin D. Roosevelt that if he did not find a way to outlaw racial discrimination in defense jobs, 100,000 Black people would descend on the nation's capital.

Chapter 4, "The Council and the Committee," discusses a similar factional conflict. After the state destroyed the NNC by turning some of its top leaders into FBI informants, its youngest cadres, especially Ernest Thompson, Vicki Garvin, Coleman Young, and Ewart Guinier, founded the National Negro Labor Council in 1951. The NNLC established local councils in every region of the country. Their primary responsibilities were to pressure large corporations like Sears Roebuck and General Electric to hire and promote Black women and push white-led labor unions to pledge support for local Fair Employment Practice Commissions (FEPC). With the March on Washington Movement more or less defunct by 1950, Randolph moved into high gear to head the NNLC off at the pass. Hoping to steal the NNLC's thunder, Randolph brought liberals, trade unionists, and reformed socialists together under the umbrella of the Negro Labor Committee-USA. Though the committee launched a vicious red-baiting attack on the NNLC with the blessing of organized labor, it failed to gain traction among the Black rank and file, while its more radical counterpart prospered. Ultimately, it was once again the state that destroyed the NNLC. The House Un-American Activities Committee and later the US Attorney General demanded that the NNLC defend itself against charges of disloyalty and subversion. Rather than put the organization and its local leaders through an endless legal battle, the national leadership disbanded.

Chapter 5, "The March Triumphant," tells the story of the Negro American Labor Council (NALC), the main organizational force behind the 1963 March on Washington for Jobs and Freedom. Though the organization was officially anti-Communist, its staff, leadership, and rank and file included several prominent progressives like Bayard Rustin, Cleveland Robinson, Horace Sheffield, and Vicki Garvin. The centrist and left factions of Black labor thus gathered under the same roof despite the acrimony of the 1950s. Today the march's cosponsors—the NAACP, the National Urban League, etc.—are more well-known, but in fact NALC had to cajole some of these other groups to support the protest. The Urban League, for instance, a key institution of the Black middle class, initially declined to participate for fear that it might jeopardize their relationships on Capitol Hill. In the end, Black civil society accepted NALC's leadership and agreed to exert maximum pressure on the labor movement to integrate unions and the labor market. As mobilization around the march picked up steam, it soon became clear that it could also force the passage of the civil rights bill making its way through Congress. By means of the march, NALC succeeded not only in starting what would become a historic upsurge in union organizing, but also in passing the most consequential civil rights legislation since Reconstruction.

Chapter 6, "Freedom Is a Constant Struggle," is about the aftermath of the March on Washington. It begins with two successive victories in which the Negro-Labor Alliance remained largely intact: the 1968 Memphis sanitation workers' strike and the 1969 Charleston hospital workers' strike. The chapter continues with the re-emergence of the conflict between the left and centrist factions of Black labor. The Dodge Revolutionary Union Movement (DRUM) rose up in 1968 to challenge the pattern of racial exclusion in the UAW as well as the union's cozy relationship with the Big Three automakers. The Coalition of Black Trade Unionists (CBTU) carried on the struggle at the national level. In its early years, CBTU was at odds with the AFL-CIO's A. Philip Randolph Institute, which was then directed by none other than Bayard Rustin. The clash between the centrist and left factions thus continued into the late twentieth century. The chapter ends with lessons from the history of independent Black labor organizations. The first is that the struggle for economic justice cannot be separated from the fight for racial and gender equity. The second is that the labor movement consists of other organizations besides unions, who can help lead the struggle to re-establish democracy both in the workplace and society at large.

. . .

As I write this book, after the "Hot Labor Summer" of 2023, the UAW's successful "Stand Up" strike against the Big Three automakers, and the landmark framework for a master contract with Starbucks Workers United, it is the left faction of Black labor that is in the ascendant. Though it is not housed in a national organization, there are Black-led independent unions, most famously Amazonians United, so named for their struggle to organize the logistics giant Amazon. For the most part, however, the organic revolt among Black workers is spread out among numerous unions. The triple scandal of anti-Black police violence, deepening economic inequality, and Trumpism is the daunting backdrop against which this new generation of Black labor activists have taken the field.

Of course, this is not the first time that Black workers have confronted long odds. Despite the terror of lynchings, near total exclusion from the formal labor market, and a widening Red Scare, Black people in the 1910s and 1920s began to organize and innovate. The impetus for this wave arose from the founding of the Brotherhood of Sleeping Car Porters and the African Blood Brotherhood. Though the leaders of both organizations had been activists in the Harlem Socialist Party, each went in decidedly different directions. The Porters, under the leadership of A. Philip Randolph, slowly but surely made its way into the American Federation of Labor. Indeed, their most important campaign, apart from organizing the Pullman Company, was to gain admission to the AFL as a chartered affiliate. The ABB were best known for their advocacy of Black self-defense, most famously in the Tulsa race riots, but over time they became ever more enmeshed in the Communist Party, which in 1920s Harlem was known as the Workers Party. It was this divergence among former socialists that gave birth to the centrist and left factions of Black labor. The movement of the brotherhoods toward the AFL and Communist Party, respectively, is the subject of the next chapter.

2   *The Brotherhoods*

Of all the minor accidents of history, among the more consequential for the US labor movement was the sacking of A. Philip Randolph and Cyril V. Briggs in 1917. But for their dismissal—Randolph from the New York waiters' union and Briggs from the venerable Black paper, the *Amsterdam News*—they might not have gone on to lead Black labor's two great factions. As it was, Randolph would become president of the Brotherhood of Sleeping Car Porters (BSCP), while Briggs would head the African Blood Brotherhood (ABB).

Randolph began his career in labor by establishing an employment bureau with his friend and co-conspirator, Chandler Owen. Owen was the spirited and stocky counterpoint to Randolph's shy, serious, and upright persona. The two met while Owen was a law student at Columbia University, and Randolph an undergraduate at City College. Together they consumed the radical texts of the times, especially Karl Marx, and debated their meaning in public forums. When they decided to start the employment bureau in Harlem, they envisioned helping unskilled Black workers from the South transition to a new life in New York City. They called their joint enterprise "the Brotherhood."[1]

Randolph must have seen himself in the workers he served, for he, too, was an expatriate of the South. Asa Philip Randolph was born on April 15, 1889, in Florida, the son of James and Elizabeth Randolph and younger brother to James, Jr. For most of his childhood, the family lived in Jacksonville, which NAACP president James Weldon Johnson, a Jacksonville native, called "a good place for Negroes." Black people were elected officials in town government; over a third of the local police were Black, and the police commissioner himself was Black. This is not to say that whites were satisfied with the status quo, for they eventually imposed their will on the town through a combination of poll taxes and gerrymandering. Nor did it mean that the Randolphs lived a middle-class existence. Randolph's father was the minister of a local African Methodist Episcopal (AME) congregation consisting mainly of sharecroppers. Since his flock could not contribute much in the way of cash, the family ran a number of side businesses, cleaning clothes and supplying meat and firewood to the residents of Jacksonville's Oakland neighborhood.[2]

The critical mass of Black folk in Jacksonville did mean that white people did not always get their way. Once when he was nine years old, Asa (as he was called back then) watched as a white mob attempted to lynch a Black man for allegedly harassing a white woman. Leaving his wife on the porch with a shotgun to watch over the boys, James, Sr., assembled a group of his friends and held off the mob by standing vigil outside the jail where the victim was being held. Randolph was to say that he learned a valuable lesson from that moment: Black people need not be helpless victims but could act in their own self-defense.[3]

What they lacked in money, the Randolphs more than made up for with sheer intellect and Black pride. James, Sr., and Elizabeth exposed their sons to the work of Black revolutionaries like Nat Turner and Toussaint L'Ouverture. They insisted that Asa and James, Jr., walk to where they needed to go rather than endure the humiliation of segregated streetcars. At home they read Shakespeare and Keats alongside Frederick Douglass and AME ministers; the brothers held contests on who could better pronounce and explain the meaning of the words they read. In general, mastery of the English language was paramount in the Randolphs' two-story rented home, and this translated to their superlative performance in school.[4]

James, Jr., and Asa were the best students at the Cookman Institute, Florida's first high school for Black people. There they drilled each other on the elements of a classical liberal arts education: Greek, Latin, ethics, drama, and music. Indeed, Asa showed considerable talent as an actor. But it was his seriousness that fellow pupils remembered most. His classmates called him "Old Asa." One recalled, "He was over-earnest. Dogged diligence—that's Randolph." Another remembered that Asa and his brother "never raised hell like some of us. . . . They were two of the most handsome boys at Cookman, but they were not the kind of fellows girls would pick to go out and have a good time with. Morally, they were beyond reproach."[5]

As more affluent Cookman students went off to college, Randolph, who was habitually poor, had to make money before he could pursue his passion for literature and acting in New York City. He made it to the Big Apple in April 1911. In between odd jobs to make his rent of a $1.50 a week for a shared room in Harlem, he acted in several local productions of Shakespeare. His fellow actors were impressed and thought he might make a career on the stage, but James, Sr., overruled those ambitions. Out of deference to his father, Randolph shifted his attention to politics. At City College (which was then still tuition-free), he changed his course of study from public speaking and drama to history, philosophy, and political science. He organized a current events forum and volunteered in a local political campaign for alderman. As if to complete his transformation from actor to activist, he began asking those he met to call him by his middle name, Philip.[6]

It was during this time that Randolph met Lucille Green. Green was the owner of a hair-straightening salon and a protégé of C. J.

Walker, a black woman mogul in the same industry who traveled in a chauffeur-driven limousine. Green had been trained as a teacher and possessed a sharp mind. She pushed him out of his comfort zone: whereas he took her to lectures and shows, she took him to sparkling soirées. Their marriage was a vital turn of events for the budding activist's career, as Lucille provided the financial security he needed to pursue a precarious life in the labor movement. As Randolph would say, "We were on an uncharted sea. Chandler and I had no job and no plan for the next meal. But I had a good wife. She carried us."[7]

Randolph's first encounter with a union helped him navigate the unknown waters of organized labor. In January 1917, William White, president of the Head Waiters and Side Waiters Society of Greater New York, recognized Randolph and Owen from their soapbox speeches on Harlem streetcorners. White asked if they might be willing to publish a newspaper, the *Hotel Messenger*, for the union. In exchange, he offered them an office at 486 Lenox Avenue and a desk that was large enough to share. Crucially, White also allowed them to hold political meetings there, and the office soon became a regular haunt for the leading lights of the Harlem left, including Lovett Fort-Whiteman, a Texan who would become the first Black Communist in America; Wilfred A. Domingo, a Jamaican-born nationalist and socialist; Hubert Harrison, a socialist from St. Croix who was dubbed the "Black Socrates" of Harlem; and Cyril V. Briggs, the fearless editor of the *Amsterdam News*. Those were heady times, and the young Randolph, feeling himself a member of the Black avant-garde, changed his nom de plume again, this time to "A. Philip Randolph."[8]

The halcyon days of the *Hotel Messenger* would come to an end in August, 1917, however, a mere eight months after the newspaper began publication. A group of side waiters stormed up to the union offices, complaining that the head waiters were selling them uniforms at exorbitant rates and accepting kickbacks from the uniform company. Seemingly unconcerned by any gratitude they might owe to

William White, the coeditors ran a story exposing the head waiters' scheme for the racket that it was. White, who owed his position primarily to the support of the head waiters, denounced and fired his editors.⁹

The incident ended Randolph's employment with the waiters' union, but it also began his fateful career as founder and coeditor of *The Messenger*. The magazine, which Randolph and Owen started just two months after their dismissal from the waiters' union, was shockingly anti-racist and unapologetically socialist for its time. Randolph would call it "the first voice of radical, revolutionary, economic and political action among Negroes in America." In an editorial titled "The Cause of and Remedy for Race Riots," for example, Randolph identified the various actors responsible for stoking labor competition between whites and Blacks. He blamed capitalists who imported "Negro laborers . . . to take the jobs of white workers" and "the short-sighted position of organized white labor," which framed Black labor as a threat instead of an ally. As a remedy, Randolph argued that "Black and white workers must unite in the same unions, ask for the same wages, same hours and the same working conditions," adding optimistically that in the Industrial Workers of the World (IWW) and American Federation of Labor (AFL), "there has been a movement from the competition of black and white workers to the unionism of black and white workers." As a partisan of the so-called right wing of the Socialist Party, Randolph evinced a commitment to electoralism and democracy that would come to characterize his future critique of the left or communist wing of the party. Anticipating the schism to come, Randolph urged democratic deliberation. "Fight the difference out on its merits," he urged. "Then take a clean, straight vote. If the Left Wing wins, let us yield to the majority. If the Right Wing wins, let us do likewise. Don't have a split. Stay in the party and fight for the change within!" Finally, it is worth noting that Randolph remained a staunch advocate of "physical force in self-defense." Recalling his childhood memory of the foiled lynching, Randolph urged armed conflict when necessary, characterizing such activity as "the determination to respond unflinchingly when the occasion calls to fight the battles of life." Nor did these alarming pronouncements scare readers off. At its high point, *The Messenger* had a readership of 26,000; it was the most widely read radical Black magazine in the country. The combination of its reach and content would lead the US Department of Justice to declare in 1919 that *The Messenger* was "by long odds the most able and the most dangerous of all the Negro publications."[10]

It was because of his reputation as a leading voice in Black civil society that a group of porters working for the Pullman Company approached Randolph with a proposal. The Pullman Company rented luxury sleeping cars to railroads across the country, and it was the porters' job to serve sleeping car passengers. Porters turned down beds, shined shoes, hung and pressed clothing, and more than occasionally nursed incapacitated passengers after an evening of drinking. Because passengers found themselves in compromising positions, it was critical, the employer reasoned, that workers be anonymous to their clientele, and no one was more anonymous than a Black manservant. In a formal labor market where Black people were systematically excluded, in part because of white unions, the Pullman Company offered porters a chance at a decent living. Indeed, porters were greatly admired in the Black community for precisely this reason. However, the working conditions were brutal and the pay low. Porters were paid a mere $67.50 plus tips for four hundred hours of work a month and were required to purchase their own uniforms, food, and blacking for shining the shoes of passengers. This is to say nothing of hours of unpaid "preparatory time" in advance of receiving passengers on board. Porters worked long shifts, laboring for the length of cross-country trips, only to have to pull double shifts without advance notice or extra pay. While patrons slept in comfortable berths, porters had no place to lay their heads. Perhaps most galling, passengers called porters "George" after the name of their employer, George Pullman, a practice from the days of slavery. This would give rise to a favorite slogan of the union to come: "Service not Servitude."[11]

For these reasons and many more, Pullman porters had been trying to organize a union since 1909. One recurring problem was that the boss fired anyone who talked union. The porters resolved to circumvent the problem by hiring someone who was not a porter and therefore could not be dismissed for organizing. The person they hoped to hire was A. Philip Randolph.

· ● ·

Cyril Valentine Briggs was born on the Caribbean island of St. Kitts on May 28, 1888, just one year before Randolph. Briggs was the son of Marian M. Huggins, a Black woman, and Louis E. Briggs, a white plantation overseer from Trinidad. His parents never married and had no other children. Briggs spent most of his childhood on the neighboring island of Nevis. Though he could pass as white, Briggs embraced his Black identity, a fact that would feed his nascent Black nationalism. Even as a child, he refused to cross Nevis's strict color line, preferring instead the company of the island's Black community. Like Randolph, Briggs was exceptionally gifted as a student and won a scholarship to continue his studies, but he declined the award. Briggs was then an avid reader of Robert Ingersoll, the American politician, whose agnosticism and progressive opinions on women's equality and abolitionism made him something of a radical in those days. Having endured years of a narrow colonial education, Briggs resolved to leave his home for New York City, where he believed he could freely cultivate his political views. He arrived in Harlem in 1905.[12]

If Harlem attracted migrants from the American South like Randolph, it also attracted a considerable West Indian population. Immigrants who had experienced the severe class and racial stratification of the Caribbean tended to blend anticolonial politics with a hostility toward capitalism; for them, colonialism and capitalism were one. West Indian radicals like Otto Huiswoud of Surinam, Arthur P. Hendricks of British Guiana, and Hubert Harrison of St. Croix joined their African American counterparts—Randolph, Owen, and Randolph's future collaborator Frank Crosswaith—in the interracial AD 21st Socialist Party. Together, this nucleus of incipient Harlem cadres urged Black people to embrace socialism, even though the wider American Socialist Party had not yet embraced them. Others would join the party as a result of their efforts, including the fiery orator Richard B. Moore, the teacher and organizer Grace B. Campbell, and the aforementioned Fort-Whiteman and Domingo. Eventually the organization would split, with Huiswoud, Moore, and Campbell of the party's left wing forming the Communist Party of America, and Randolph, Owen, Crosswaith, and Harrison remaining, at least in the short term, with the Socialist Party. The source of the schism in Harlem was the continuing inability of white socialists to understand, let alone embrace, the racial politics of their fellow Black members.

It was for this reason that Briggs never followed his fellow West Indians into the Socialist Party, though he publicly agreed with their critique of capitalism as far as it went. Early in his political career, Briggs was above all a Black nationalist and was for a time on good terms with another famous West Indian of that political stripe, Marcus Garvey of the United Negro Improvement Association (UNIA). However, whereas Garvey tended toward Black separatism, advocating a return migration to Africa, and only flirted with leftist politics, Briggs was focused on Black self-determination in the United States and openly admired the 1917 Bolshevik Revolution in Russia for its avowed anticolonialism. Briggs's politics were underpinned by a variety of unlikely ideological currents. More important to his early political development than the Bolshevik Revolution was the Easter Rising in Ireland. As a former British subject himself, Irish Republicanism hit closer to home. Briggs explained, "It should be easily possible for Negroes to sympathize with the Irish fight against tyranny and oppression, and vice-versa, since both are in the same boat and both victims of the same Anglo-Saxon race." Briggs was also, strangely, a fan of US President Woodrow Wilson, whose commitment to national self-determination on the world stage seemed a friendly framework for Black self-determination.[13]

In addition to his identification as a "race man," another defining characteristic of Cyril Briggs was his stutter. His dear friend of many years Harry Haywood recalled that Briggs's speech impediment was so severe that "it often took him several seconds to get out the first word of a sentence." Wilfred A. Domingo said, "it was impossible to understand him or even to hold a conversation with him." The stutter was apparently less severe when he was angry. For instance, when Garvey accused Briggs of being a white man masquerading as Black, Briggs reportedly climbed a stepladder and denounced him for an hour without stammering once.[14]

Because of his speech impediment, Briggs would never become the front man of the radical causes he espoused. Instead, he became a talented polemicist behind the scenes. In 1912, he landed a job as the editor of the premier Black newspaper of the time, the *New York Amsterdam News*. As a journalist, Briggs was consistently radical. Even when President Wilson himself made it exceedingly difficult to speak out against America's involvement in World War I, he managed to do so anyway. One censor observed that Briggs had a "peculiar talent for saying the most fervently patriotic things in the most irritating unpatriotic manner." Again, his antiwar stance was not so much inspired by the contemporaneous Bolshevik Revolution, but by his own abiding hatred for British imperialism and his related commitment to Black self-determination. Briggs's writing for the *Amsterdam News* blended these long-held beliefs in race pride and solidarity with an emerging embrace of working-class partisanship. For example, in an editorial titled "Security of Life for Poles and Serbs, Why Not for Colored Nations?," Briggs advocated for a separate Black state within the United States, justifying the ceding of one-tenth of American territory as reparations for the generations of unpaid work done by Black labor. By most accounts, the *Amsterdam News* eventually fired Briggs for his sneaky diatribes against the war, though in an interview Briggs claimed that he resigned. The US Department of Intelligence, he said, had placed increasing pressure on the newspaper to censor his editorials, which "condemned Jim Crow in the army and the use of the Negro Regiment as stevedores."[15]

Be that as it may, like Randolph's dismissal from the *Hotel Messenger*, Briggs's departure from the *Amsterdam News* opened up new vistas. In 1918, he began editing his own newspaper, the *Crusader*, which would become one of the orienting voices in Black journalism in Harlem, alongside Garvey's *Negro World* and Randolph and Owen's *Messenger*. Over time, the *Crusader* would travel back and forth along the spectrum between the others, eventually settling on a unique vision of Black-led revolutionary socialism.

Though his analysis varied in this early period, Briggs focused reliably on the question of Black labor. For instance, in an April 1919 editorial he compared the federal government's deportation of foreign radicals with the recent deportation of Black steelworkers from Pennsylvania to the South. He explained the linkage between the two in this way: "The capitalists who would bring the Negro North during a crisis and then shuffle him back willy nilly to the old hateful conditions and to Lynch Law—all of which were cited in the argument to make him leave the South—are the same capitalists who would send out of the country all workers who dare to talk against the system." In

July of the same year, Briggs would write, "With no race are the interests of Labor so clearly identified with racial interests as in the case of the Negro race." Briggs traced this alignment of interests to a complex process: "Parasitic Capital Civilization with its Imperialism incubus . . . is squeezing the life-blood out of millions of our race" not only in the United States, but also "in Africa and the islands of the sea." Briggs thus oscillated between insisting that the capitalists alone were the root cause of Black labor's misery in the April editorial, and insinuating in July that capitalism and imperialism were independent partners whose coupling robbed Black people of their vitality. The distinction may seem semantic, but in a political milieu defined by the poles of Black nationalism and socialism, the difference would have been palpable. One editorial leaves room for a separate, albeit aligned, anticolonial project and set of racial interests, and the other is a more straightforward socialist project with only class interests to account for.[16]

Briggs and his cohorts, chief among them Grace Campbell, W. A. Domingo, Otto Huiswoud, and Richard B. Moore, would attempt to use the *Crusader* as a vehicle for starting a secret mass organization. In the October 1919 issue, Briggs began the effort with a tiny advertisement buried on page 27:

Mr. CYRIL V. BRIGGS, Editor of
THE CRUSADER
announces the organization of
The African Blood Brotherhood
for African Liberation and Redemption.
Membership by enlistment. No dues, fees or assessments. Those only need apply who are willing to go the limit!

Write or call at
299 Seventh Avenue, New York. U.S.A.[17]

Here Briggs evinces a Black nationalist politics (not a call to class struggle), and, hearkening back to the armed resistance of the Easter Rising, announces that the African Blood Brotherhood is a militant organization with no time for half-measures. This fifty-two-word signal, no bigger than an inch on the page, would launch Black labor's left faction.

. . .

Secretiveness also marked the beginning of the International Brotherhood of Sleeping Car Porters, the nucleus of Black labor's centrist faction. The Pullman Company was thorough in its attempts to bust the porters' union. It had an entire network of stool pigeons to inform on pro-union workers. Their public relations strategy was also impressive, in a diabolical way. After George Pullman died in 1897, the company chose Robert Todd Lincoln, Abraham Lincoln's son, as its president. Surely the Great Emancipator's own progeny would treat Black workers fairly, and indeed in his testimony before Congress in 1915, he said, "I fully recognize . . . the right of the employees to organize." Perhaps most sophisticated of all, the employer established the so-called "Employee Representation Plan" (ERP), a company union, whose board consisted of equal numbers of managers and workers. The ERP gave the appearance of a responsive employer but in practice did little to improve the lives of workers except to ply their representatives on the board with fine wine, cigars, and women.[18]

But as sophisticated as union-busting can be, it can never fully squelch worker resistance. Three of the five men who comprised the union organizing committee had been involved in the ERP: Ashley Totten, Roy Lancaster, and William H. Des Verney. Despite their best efforts, however, one intractable problem remained: the company's extensive network of spies ensured that the boss could fire any worker just as soon as they started organizing. It occurred to Totten (when he himself was fired for union activity in 1925) that the union required someone who was not an employee of the company.[19]

It just so happened that A. Philip Randolph had given a speech in front of the Pullman Porters Athletic Association of New York at around the time of Totten's dismissal. Immediately after the speech, Des Verney approached Randolph to discuss the idea of organizing the porters, and the two agreed to continue the conversation. On August 25, 1925, Randolph brought with him the former porter S.E. Grain and the socialist Frank R. Crosswaith to meet in secret with Des Verney, Lancaster, and Totten at Des Verney's home in New York City. Randolph ran the meeting as if it was all his idea to begin with, so that none of the porters themselves could be implicated.[20]

This was a pattern of practice that would characterize the Brotherhood's early years. Stealth was paramount. The union inducted members in a secret ceremony where initiates learned the Brotherhood's confidential rules of conduct. When a porter saw Randolph walking down the street, he was meant to cross to the other side. The Brotherhood had a password, "solidarity," for it was, according to the induction ritual, "the *Key* to freedom of all oppressed and exploited races and classes." As with other underground organizations of the time, the union had a secret signal: the left hand clenched in a fist facing downward, which "denotes that the Brotherhood realizes that only through a fight can justice and freedom be achieved." The porters' wives were central to these precautions. An organized network of women collected dues at social gatherings, distributed union literature, and stood in for their husbands at meetings where it was thought there might be a company spy.[21]

Where they did not need stealth was in Randolph's pen. The Chief (as they called him) could pour the members' fury and injured pride into his editorials for the *Messenger*. Members would then distribute the newspaper to brethren across the country as they rode the rails. In his September 1925 editorial, just weeks after the porters hired him as their national organizer, Randolph wrote,

> Despite the long, devoted, patient and heroic service of the Pullman porter to the Pullman Company, despite the fact that the fabric of the company rests upon his shoulders, despite the fact that the Pullman porter has made the Company what it is today, the Company . . . treats him like a slave. In very truth, the Pullman porter has no rights which the Pullman Company is bound to respect. So far as his manhood is concerned, in the eyes of the Company, the porter is not supposed to have any.

Here, Randolph expressed what so many porters felt. Just as American civilization was built upon the backs of Black people, so, too, was the Pullman Company's wealth. And though slavery was supposed to have ended and they were now free, the boss treated them as if nothing had changed. Randolph went so far as to allude to the US Supreme Court's language in the 1857 Dred Scott decision, language that most every African American knew well: that Black people had "no rights which a white man was bound to respect."[22]

Because the company's system of labor control had psychological, as well as physical, effects akin to slavery, Randolph and the rank-and-file leadership believed that they needed to break the habits of mind that would lead porters to side with the boss out of fear or self-interest. For example, naming the union as one of "sleeping car porters" instead of "Pullman porters" was meant to conjure in the workers' minds that they were members of a profession instead of employees of a company. The notion that they were a brotherhood, they hoped, would disabuse the workers of the idea that they were individuals looking out only for themselves. As Randolph explained, "The purpose was to get the men convinced of the fact that they were brothers and have a common interest, each one, in helping make it possible for all porters to have a better life." Finally, Randolph used the figure of the Uncle Tom, the slaveowner's hated Black lieutenant on the plantation, to urge workers to think for themselves. In a bulletin to the workers, for instance, Randolph wrote,

> The Company thinks that you are such complete slaves that you Think White and Act White, that is, do whatever a White Man says, believing it to be the Gospel Truth and will oppose the Brotherhood because white Pullman Officials tell Black Stool pigeons to advise you Against your own Welfare. But the day of that Spineless type of Uncle Tom Negro is going rapidly. The Brotherhood is proving that all Negroes are Not for Sale . . . that Negroes could build up an organization in this Country with their own money, brains and spirit, which the white man hasn't got money enough to Buy.[23]

In this passage, Randolph sought to deprogram the workers by shocking them into the realization that believing the boss was equivalent to siding with the slaveowner, as the Uncle Tom had once done. The opposite of this kind of thinking, one which Randolph encouraged workers to see as a monumental achievement, was to build an organization with their own resources—their "money, brains and spirit"—that the company, unlike the slaveowner, could not buy.

In less than a year, these efforts began to bear fruit. As bosses often do during an organizing drive that is gaining traction, the Pullman Company made minimal but still significant concessions. The workers won an 8 percent wage increase, a change in the time sheet used to account for hours worked, and a general improvement in worker treatment. Such victories, Randolph asserted in the program of their first annual convention, "have taken many unions ten and fifteen years to achieve."[24]

Just before the end of its second year, the Brotherhood had organized a majority of the approximately twelve thousand Pullman porters and maids across the country; this led to a rapid escalation in the union's standoff with the company. Organizing a majority of the workers qualified the union to present their case to the US Mediation Board on July 10, 1927, under the terms of the Railway Labor Act. The Mediation Board recognized the Brotherhood as the workers' representative and recommended that a body consisting of members from the company, the union, and the public arbitrate the dispute and come to an agreement. Though the Brotherhood agreed to arbitration, indeed campaigned and pinned their hopes on a mediated negotiation, the boss rejected it.[25]

The next step under the law was for the union to threaten a strike that could disrupt interstate commerce and thereby prompt the President of the United States to convene an Emergency Board to mediate the dispute. The Brotherhood conducted a strike vote, and the members voted overwhelmingly in support of the job action—six thousand in favor and fifty against. The key for the bosses, meanwhile, was to prevent an Emergency Board from being empaneled, which they did by convincing US officials that the situation was not urgent. It is unclear what the company did to achieve this result, but the government's decision was suspicious given the fact that the Mediation Board had recently recommended emergency arbitration for a strike of only six hundred white railroad workers. Be that as it may, the Brotherhood had just one road open to them once the US government declined to designate the Pullman dispute an emergency: to strike at high noon on June 8, 1928.[26]

· • ·

The ideological confusion of the early *Crusader* (and by association the African Blood Brotherhood) was in part due to its affiliation with the Hamitic League. The League was the brainchild of George Wells Parker, an Afrocentric from Omaha, Nebraska. Parker offered to financially support the newspaper in exchange for publishing his arti-cles, which centered largely on the claim that Africa was the cradle of civilization. Cyril Briggs, who was broadly in agreement with Parker's politics, needed the resources and so affiliated the newspaper with the League, announcing in December 1918 that the *Crusader* was the "Publicity Organ of the Hamitic League of the World." However, as Briggs grew ever more preoccupied with the ABB and drew closer to the Communist Party from the fall of 1919 onward, this relationship be-came untenable. Parker's cohorts made antisemitic comments in their articles that would have been anathema to party members, many of whom were Jewish. Briggs schemed to contradict the work of his busi-ness partner with editorials on the importance of interracial solidarity. By the end of 1920, the *Crusader* at last disaffiliated, and the Hamitic League disappeared from the newspaper's masthead.[27]

From that point forward, Briggs and the ABB developed a unique ideological vision that blended Black liberation with revolutionary socialism. That vision had three tenets, each of which reoccurs the-matically from 1920 to 1921. The first was that communism was not the invention of Europeans but a long-standing practice in the conti-nent of Africa before the advent of colonial capitalism. In his October 1920 editorial "Africa for the Africans," Briggs wrote, "Those who have studied the Negro peoples of Africa are aware that wherever these peoples have had opportunity for independent development their peculiar race-genius has led them into the sphere of what in the European world are today known as Socialism and Communism, both having been in practical application in Africa for centuries be-fore they were even advanced as theories in the European world." Six months later, in his April 1921 editorial on "The Salvation of the Ne-gro," he reiterated this claim by referring to the ancient "Communis-tic States of Central Africa" and "our Communist African forefa-thers." In both pieces, Briggs married Black nationalism with socialism by framing the latter as native to African culture.[28]

The second tenet addressed the question of Black self-governance. In "Africa for the Africans," Briggs urged "government of the people of Africa by the people of Africa and *for* themselves and the glory, advancement and protection of the entire Negro race," in contrast to "the present system of government of Africa by and in the interest of European capitalists" [emphasis in original]. In "The Salvation of the Negro," Briggs put more meat on the bones of this idea by theorizing the Black state's relationship to Socialism. Black and white people "might live together in peace and inequality" in a "Socialist Co-operative Commonwealth," he reasoned, "but the Negro has been treated so brutally in the past by the rest of humanity that he may be pardoned for now looking at the matter more from the viewpoint of the Negro." Rather than put African-descended peoples at the mercy of a worldwide socialist system, Briggs offered a Black nationalist counterweight: a strong Black state. He wrote that the best hope for the race was a balance between two bodies: "salvation for all Negroes through the establishment of a strong, stable, independent Negro State (along the lines of our own race genius) in Africa or elsewhere; and salvation for all Negroes (as well as other oppressed peoples) through the establishment of a Universal Socialist Co-operative Commonwealth." The socialist commonwealth was to be the global framework within which Black national independence would most likely thrive, but it did not mean total absorption into Marxism or the Communist movement. On the contrary, the Black embrace of socialism would be based on the national aspirations of the African diaspora.[29]

Third and perhaps most importantly for our purposes, Briggs offered a strategic solution to the ever-present conflict between white and Black workers. Just as the Negro State was meant to stand at some remove from the Socialist Commonwealth, likewise Black workers would not lose themselves in a movement of the international working class. Instead Black labor must act independently as an organizational wedge to break apart the coalition of white labor and capital, in hopes that white workers might see that their interests lie with other workers. Thus, in a July 1921 editorial Briggs wrote, "There are schisms in the white race which, by encouraging, we can ultimately benefit ourselves." At the same time, this did not mean that Black people should uncritically accept the hand of friendship from white workers. The "acid test of white friendship," Briggs cautioned, was "whether that person is willing to see the Negro defend himself with arms against aggression, willing even to see Negroes killing his own (white) people in defense of Negro rights." Within this wedge strategy, then, white workers must accept the prerogative of Black self-defense. Through each of the above tenets—the African origins of Communism, the Black state, and an independent Black labor movement—Briggs aligned revolutionary socialism with Black nationalism.[30]

Though the ABB aspired to be a mass movement with paramilitary capabilities, it was in practice a propaganda organization with about 3,500 members in the United States, Africa, and the West Indies (estimates range from as low as 2,500 to as high as 50,000). These members, in turn, organized approximately fifty posts in total with the strongest ones at their New York headquarters (called "Post Menelik"), the West Virginia post consisting mainly of Black miners, and the Tulsa, Oklahoma, post consisting primarily of Black ex-servicemen from World War I.[31]

True to its militant ethos, the ABB was organized like a top-down quasi-military operation, modeled after the Irish Republican Army. An article in the June 1920 issue of the *Crusader* reveals that its "sole purpose" was "the liberation of Africa and the redemption of the Negro race." Like the Brotherhood of Sleeping Car Porters, it was for a time a secret organization. The same article states that it had "a ritual of its own, with degrees, pass-words, signs, etc., and a formal initiation ceremony when a solemn oath is taken." Membership was purely voluntary, but the local post could approve or reject any application as they saw fit. The governing authority in the ABB was the "Supreme Council" or "War College" of five leaders, including the "Paramount Chief" Cyril Briggs. The council controlled the appointment and tenure of the "commanders" of the local posts and directed the policies, activities, and movements of the organization. When issued in the form of "instructions," the word of the council was law, whereas "suggestions" were recommendations to which local posts should give respectful consideration. Despite its hierarchical structure, the ABB had a system of democratic elections. The membership elected the local secretaries, treasurers, chaplains, and international officers; the leadership, in turn, was subject to the rulings and decrees of the Supreme Council.[32]

The ABB platform consisted of six planks. The first was consistent with Briggs's commitment to Black self-defense and called for "Armed resistance against lynchings." The second aligned with Briggs's long-standing Black nationalism: it demanded "Self-determination for the Negro" in states where they were the majority. The next two planks centered on civil rights, namely, the right to vote in in the American South and a general struggle against Jim Crow segregation. The fifth spoke to the question of interracial solidarity, calling for Black people to be organized into unions and demanding an end to racial exclusion from the white-led labor movement. The sixth and final plank reflected the ABB's international orientation: it declared itself "against Imperialism in Africa and the West Indies" and urged a "world struggle for a free Africa."[33]

The Brotherhood's big break as an organization came paradoxically with a horrific tragedy: the Tulsa Race Riots of 1921. Home to what some have called "Black Wall Street," Tulsa, Oklahoma, was the site of one of the most infamous anti-Black pogroms in US history. Its origins will be familiar to students of race riots elsewhere, for this one, like so many others, began with the allegation that a Black man, Dick Rowland, had assaulted a white woman in an elevator. The local white press, which was jealous of the wealth that Black people had built in the local oil industry, incited a mob to burn Black Wall Street to the ground. Seemingly in an attempt to cover their tracks, the white press then pinned the blame on the Tulsa post of the African Blood Brotherhood. The *New York Times* repeated this lie. Both Briggs and the commander of the Tulsa post denied that the ABB had started the riot but admitted that their members, many of whom were veterans, had taken up arms to defend the Black community. Indeed, the counter-offensive of seventy-five well-armed Black men was succeeding until the white militia took to the sky to firebomb them. The Tulsa post commander wrote,

> The white mob and their police allies failing to dislodge the Negro fighters, the white militia was called out. Upon their arrival on the scene, they instantly directed their attacks upon the Negroes, and acted in the capacity of a vanguard for the howling white mobs who greeted their appearance with glee, and confidently lined behind them for the assault upon the embattled Negroes. But not even the militia reinforcements to our enemies proved able to drive out the Negro fighters until their bombing aeroplanes began circling above the Negro lines and dropping bombs upon them. These aeroplanes were the ones that dropped incendiary bombs upon the Negro section and started the fire that wiped it out.

Briggs, too, speaking for the entire Brotherhood, defended the Tulsa membership's actions. Pointing out that "the Tulsa riot was fomented by the malicious misrepresentation by the Tulsa white press," Briggs wrote that "there is no need to answer the charge that the ABB fomented the riot." But, he added, "As to whether the Tulsa Post of the A.B.B. had any part in organizing and directing Negro defense once the riot had started—that is another matter." "The A.B.B.

is organized not for aggression," Briggs wrote, "but for protection of otherwise defenceless Negroes."[34]

The ABB's work in Tulsa earned them the respect of the Harlem masses. Whereas the Brotherhood had hosted gatherings of a few hundred people before the riot, a crowd of two thousand turned out for an ABB rally at Harlem's Palace Casino on June 12, 1921. Membership applications flooded in, and the Brotherhood, in turn, made it easier for prospective recruits to begin the convoluted seven-degree process of initiation. From that point forward, the ABB ceased to be an underground organization, at least in the North. In the June 1921 issue of the *Crusader*, Briggs referred to the newspaper as the official organ of the African Blood Brotherhood and printed the organization's constitution for the first time. Not coincidentally, Communists in the Workers Party (WP), with whom the ABB had been collaborating, also became an aboveground organization. Indeed, the Brotherhood sent Briggs and another delegate to the first Workers Party convention in December 1921.[35]

The WP's comprehensive program on the question of Black labor reflected the ABB's growing influence in Communist circles. William Z. Foster, head of the party's Trade Union Educational League, called the program "the most advanced resolution on the matter ever adopted by any Marxist party in the United States up to that time." Briggs defended his involvement in the Workers Party when Marcus Garvey used his attendance at the December convention as proof that Briggs was a subversive. Briggs justified the Brotherhood's deepening relationship with the WP in two ways. First, the party's program was an unprecedented statement on the question of Black labor. The program, which Briggs quoted at length, read,

> The Workers Party will support the Negroes in their struggle for liberation, and will help them in their fight for economic, political and social equality. It will point out to them that the interests of the Negro

workers are identical with those of the white. It will seek to end the policy of discrimination followed by organized labor. Its task will be to destroy altogether the barrier of race prejudice that has been used to keep apart the black and white workers, and weld them into a solid union of revolutionary forces for the overthrow of their common enemy.

The Workers Party thus spoke to nearly every frustration and demand that the emerging centrist and left factions of the Black labor movement had articulated. These included Black workers' exclusion from organized labor, the mutual antagonism between the white and Black fractions of the working class, and the need for interracial solidarity. Perhaps most important of all, the party acknowledged and pledged support for Black people's autonomous "struggle for liberation." Having printed these words for all of Black civil society to read, Briggs wrote unapologetically in response to Garvey, "the African Blood Brotherhood sent fraternal delegates to said convention. Sure, we sent delegates! And what of it?" Second, Briggs referred to the WP's substantial economic resources, resources that the ABB then severely lacked. The Brotherhood's finances were so bad, in fact, that the *Crusader* would cease publication later that year. Briggs asked, "Is it not worthwhile to have the support of a party . . . which has eleven daily newspapers . . . a membership of over 50,000 in the United States . . . several million dollars worth of property in printing plants, buildings, etc., . . . [and] fraternal organizations in affiliation which count a membership of over 200,000?"[36]

More and more, the ABB entered the ambit of the international Communist movement, and for a time the benefits seemed to go both ways. Briggs could feel that the Brotherhood was having an impact on the greatest international mass movement of the age and would gain much-needed resources to continue the Black liberation struggle. At the same time, the white leaders of the WP could say that they were making inroads into the Black working class. By the end of 1922, the party would come to think of the Brotherhood as a party auxiliary.

.　•　.

At around the same time that Briggs was becoming a communist, Milton Price Webster was becoming a union organizer. Webster had been a Pullman Porter for eighteen years. He had a long human resources rap sheet of various and sundry derelictions, but the most important, and the very last, occurred on February 2, 1921, when the boss "discovered he was holding meetings during [a] layover" and talking against the company union. Given Pullman's long history of firing labor organizers, it came as no surprise that Webster soon had a run-in with a "special officer" at the Pullman Company's Chicago West district. Knowing what was coming, Webster quit rather than give the boss the satisfaction of terminating him.[37]

Webster went on to lead the Chicago local of the Brotherhood of Sleeping Car Porters. Having quit the company, he could not be fired for organizing. In this, he shared Randolph's immunity, but that is as far as the likeness went. Whereas Randolph was lanky and frail, Webster was barrel-chested and paunchy. If Randolph was dignified and charming, Webster was rough and imposing. And while the Chief reigned over the Brotherhood as its voluble editor and spokesman, his lieutenant ran the Brotherhood as its chief operations officer and muscle.[38]

When it came time to strike, Webster was therefore in his element. He predicted that 85 percent of the workers in Chicago would walk out and was even having trouble keeping them from striking before the June 8, 1928, deadline. Other hubs were ready, too. Ashley Totten, one of the union's founding members, said that the Brothers in Kansas City had a stockpile of sawed-off shotguns and knives to meet the bosses' counter-offensive. The workers in Oakland had their own soup kitchens at the ready and staged rallies where workers vowed to lie on the tracks so that no train could leave the city. Moreover, the would-be strikers had timing on their side: both the Republican and Democratic national conventions would be happening in a matter of days and families were about to head out on vacation.[39]

The problem, as with all labor disputes, was that the bosses were preparing, too. Randolph was aware that the Pullman Company was putting in place a massive apparatus to outlast the union. For example, he disclosed to the *New York Herald Tribune* that "the Pullman Company . . . has already begun to fight our strike threat by firing brotherhood men on the club cars and employing Chinese and Filipino porters." In addition, the employer prepared temporary encampments of replacement workers at railroads across the country and engaged the services of the Pinkertons, the notorious antiunion paramilitary group. The company made provisions to station police at the New York and Pennsylvania yards in case of trouble and demanded that all employees say, as they clocked out, whether they planned to strike or continue working.[40]

To make matters worse, the union's leaders—whether intentionally or not—were sending mixed messages. On the one hand, they told the press that some seven thousand porters were ready to strike. Roy Lancaster, secretary-treasurer of the union, told the *New York Times* that "a country-wide strike of Pullman porters is inevitable within a short time if the Pullman Company does not recognize the Brotherhood of Sleeping Car Porters." On the other hand, Randolph implied that the Brotherhood might be bluffing. Because the union's strategy was to trigger a government Emergency Board that could force a settlement on the company, Randolph told the membership that voting in favor of a strike did not indicate their intention to actually walk off the job. Instead, he framed it as a tactic to bring the boss to the negotiating table. Randolph wrote, "A strike vote IS NOT A

STRIKE. . . . It does not follow that Pullman porters will strike because they take a strike vote. The Telegraphers Union on the Burlington Railroad took a strike vote but did not strike. The United States Mediation Board stepped in and effected a settlement" [emphasis in original].[41]

As any seasoned organizer will point out, these competing signals can create problems for the union. First, it can telegraph to the company that the workers do not intend to follow through on the strike threat. Second, it can communicate to the workers that they and their families should not prepare to make the ultimate sacrifice, namely to refuse to work for as long as it takes until the employer gives them what they want. Edward P. Morrow, a Mediation Board official, reported that the Pullman Company was not impressed with the workers' strike force. On the morning of June 4, Morrow wrote to his superior, "They do not believe that any real strike threat is threatened by Randolph or those associated with him. They do not believe that Randolph can induce any considerable number of employees to leave their service, but is taking a fake strike vote in order to induce the Board to believe that large numbers of porters will go out of the service." Though the employer was clearly planning for a major job action, Morrow accepted this assessment uncritically. He instructed John Merrinan, the secretary of the board, to send two letters, one to Randolph and the other to the Pullman Company. To Randolph, he wrote, "it is the judgment of the board that an emergency . . . does not exist in this case." Simultaneously, Merrinan sent a copy of the board's decision to the railroad with a cover letter that read, "*I take pleasure* in herewith forwarding for the information of your Company a copy of a letter which I have been instructed to send today to Mr. A. Philip Randolph" [emphasis added].[42]

Randolph and the leadership accused Morrow of racial bias. The Mediation Board had only recently declared an emergency for a group of six hundred white railroad workers; for the board to declare that a much larger strike of Black workers was not an emergency was, in their eyes, a travesty of justice. Ashley Totten wrote to the Board sarcastically congratulating them on "the very splendid work" they were doing "to adjust grievances of white workers on the railroad." Randolph wrote to Morrow, "No union . . . can present any greater evidence of a threat of interruption . . . than the Brotherhood presented; namely, an overwhelming strike vote, with date and hour of strike fixed and announced." He continued, "Certainly, the Board has no right to go behind the strike vote of the porters and assume that the porters would not strike, that the votes didn't mean what they say, because the Company said so." Though it is probable that something was amiss, what is certain is the board's unwillingness to declare an emergency when seeing a battlefield in which power alone—the bosses' Pinkertons and replacement workers against the members' solidarity—would decide the question.[43]

It was now up to the union leadership whether to double down on their threat or fold. Historians debate what happened next, but the events of the ensuing days hinged on a telegram from the president of the American Federation of Labor, William Green. Green wrote to Randolph saying that the union was not yet strong enough to take on an employer as well-resourced as the Pullman Company. "A strike at this time would play into the hands of the Pullman Company," Green wrote, adding that the union should instead engage in a "campaign of education and public enlightenment regarding the justice of your cause and the seriousness of your grievances."[44]

Based on this advice, the union leadership called off the strike on the very day it was supposed to start, June 8, 1928. Milton Webster, leader of the Chicago local, wrote, "It is almost certain . . . that if we actually interrupted commerce . . . they [the Board of Mediation] would have assumed a 'hand off' policy which would have meant that we would have been face to face with the millions of dollars of the Pullman Company. . . . Had we walked into the trap, the organization would have been seriously crippled." Another leader, C. L. Dellums, agreed, but mainly because of the union's uneven strength across the country. He wrote, "There was no question we were going to win in Oakland. We were also going to win in Kansas City, where Totten was. New York and Chicago would have made one hell of a showing, and they might have won. But the rest of the country would have been wiped out, and that way the whole union couldn't have won."[45]

While the leadership were convinced of the wisdom of their actions, outside observers attacked Randolph's retreat as a sellout. Communists in particular were withering in their criticism, saying that the Brotherhood's leaders "have forsaken the policy of militant struggle in the interest of the workers for the policy of class collaboration with the bosses and bluffing with the strike." For years afterward, the Communists continued to harken back to the events of June 1928. In 1931, the Black Communist paper, *The Liberator*, wrote, "The chances of success were very bright. . . . The rank and file of the porters were very militant. The Randolph leadership and the AF of L called the strike off, betraying Negro workers in the interest of the labor fakers." The attitude in some quarters of organized labor was no more forgiving. For example, Rienzi B. Lemus, leader of the Brotherhood of Dining Car Employees, wrote in the Socialist *New York Age*, "This milk-fed cornerlogist, Piffle Randolph, is a millstone about the necks of Pullman employees which if not disengaged, will carry them into the depths of the sea of oblivion." Nor did criticism come only from the outside. In the years after the union's confrontation with the Company, the members voted with their feet. The Brotherhood's membership rolls shrunk precipitously from an all-time high of 4,632 workers in 1928 to 2,368 in 1929, and 1,091 in 1931.[46]

Randolph fought back, but in private he was devastated. Against the Communists, he mounted a spirited defense, calling the charges of a sellout "the sorriest nonsense and silliest tommyrot which could only emanate from crack-brained fanatics or low grade morons." To the members he sounded a note of optimism and framed June 1928 as a victory. He wrote,

> For the first time in the history of Black Americans, a strike vote was taken and the date and hour set for the walk-out of the porters. The strike was postponed, however, upon the intervention of William Green, President of the American Federation of Labor. The organization is stronger now than ever before. It purchased its own home at 239 West 136th Street, in November, 1928. This is the first National Negro Labor movement in America. It is the pride of the race. Long live the Brotherhood!

In the proverbial backstage of public life, however, Randolph admitted that calling off the strike was "next to the saddest moment" of his life. The saddest had been losing his brother James to diphtheria just five months earlier. James had been completing his bachelor's degree at City College in New York and was set to enter graduate school at the University of Berlin when the disease poisoned his heart and destroyed his digestive system. Randolph, who had always looked up to his older brother, was still grieving the loss when he and his colleagues pulled the plug on the nationwide job action. On top of this personal tragedy, tensions emerged within the union leadership. His right-hand man, Milton Webster, became worried that leaders were losing touch with the largest swaths of the membership in places like Chicago, St. Louis, and Boston. Accordingly, Webster manuevered to strip Randolph of much of his authority and displaced New York as the union's power center. For a time, it seemed as though Randolph had only one friend left in the world: the president of the American Federation of Labor.[47]

. . .

With the *Crusader* now defunct, Cyril Briggs found himself on the hunt once again for new employment. In March 1922, he accepted a job at the national office of an organization called the Friends of Soviet Russia. In the fall, he became organizer for the Yorkville Branch of the Workers Party. Seemingly to fill the void left in the life of their friend, Grace Campbell, Otto Huiswoud, and Richard B. Moore helped Briggs start the *Crusader News Service*, a twice-weekly digest that fed news stories to the Black press.[48]

Though the African Blood Brotherhood still existed, the Harlem post was in practice one of the few remnants of the once international organization. More than that, the Supreme Council of the ABB was also the leadership of the West Harlem Branch of the Workers Party. Huiswoud was the Brotherhood's delegate to the WP as well as the organizer of the WP branch. In addition to being the ABB's Paramount Chief, Briggs was now also the party's recording and financial secretary in West Harlem. Moore and Campbell joined Claude McKay on the branch's Propaganda and Educational Committee.[49]

Over the next several months, the ABB's leadership oscillated between rebuilding their organization and furthering the Workers Party's organizing among trade unions. Huiswoud went on a summer recruitment tour for the ABB, and Briggs fundraised for a project to establish twenty-five cooperatives and a death benefit for members of the Brotherhood. But according to FBI surveillance, in the fall and winter the ABB was also cultivating its relationship with the party. In September, undercover agent Earl E. Titus reported that he took copies of the *Crusader News Service* to William Z. Foster's Trade Union Educational League (TUEL). In November, Briggs was himself visiting unions and distributing ABB and party literature so that, in his words, Black workers would get "both ends of it." In order to systematize their trade union work, the Brotherhood divided up unions by sector. For example, because Briggs was a newspaper man, the ABB assigned him the task of organizing the printing trades. On

November 27, 1923, Agent Titus would report to his superiors that "Briggs read a communication from the supreme council that the ABB and the Workers Party, Harlem Branch, had joined together by agreement for the purpose of getting a place for an office and for a forum to meet jointly for the good of both organizations."[50]

As the WP and ABB grew closer, they became part of an early effort to bring together Black civil society organizations across ideological differences. That effort, called the United Front Conference, would preoccupy Briggs and his comrades from 1923 to 1925. Work began in late 1922, with Cyril Briggs's colleague, William Monroe Trotter, who was editor of the radical *Boston Guardian* and secretary of the National Equal Rights League (NERL). For over a decade, Trotter fearlessly documented anti-Black racism in the trade union movement. As early as 1910, long before African Americans had made inroads in organized labor, he reported, "White men assaulted colored workmen because they were given machinists' work to do." On another occasion, "A negro laborer who recently was sent to the lock and dam from Alexandria, VA., was set upon by a party of white laborers yesterday afternoon and badly beaten." Trotter joined the ABB's inner circle, not surprising given their mutual interest in the question of Black labor. Titus places Trotter at Grace Campbell's home in August 1923 and notes that he was in correspondence with Campbell over sensitive matters related to the organization of the United Front Conference.[51]

It was Trotter who urged NERL president Dr. Matthew A. N. Shaw to call a conference of Black leaders after conservatives in the US Congress defeated what would have been landmark antilynching legislation. The United Front Conference, which took place in New York City on March 23–24, 1923, was remarkable in at least two respects. First, the United Front was a "Concordat" or agreement of "Six Leading Civil Rights Organizations" with widely divergent ideologies, including the African Blood Brotherhood, A. Philip Randolph's "The Friends of Negro Freedom," the NAACP, NERL, the National Race Congress, and the International Uplift League. The Concordat's co-signers were a Who's Who of the Black political scene, including Trotter, W. A. Domingo (for the ABB), Randolph's colleague George Schuyler, NAACP executive secretary James Weldon Johnson, and Howard University dean Kelly Miller signing for the National Race Congress. Second, the six organizations agreed to put aside their differences in a form that independent Black labor organizations would imitate again and again, up to and including the March on Washington for Jobs and Freedom. "Knowing the strength of the forces opposed to justice and fair play for Americans of African descent," the concordat read, the undersigned members "realized that these forces must be met by the closest co-operation and the most harmonious relationship possible among all the agencies working for the civil and citizenship rights of Negro Americans."[52]

In the new year, Harlem's Black Communists began laying the groundwork for a follow-up gathering to the United Front Conference, the so-called "Negro Sanhedrin" or Supreme Council, to be held in February 1924 in Chicago. At a meeting of the Workers Party held on January 18, 1924, Harlem's Black cadres stated that the ABB and WP expected to be well represented at the assembly and that the two groups were working quietly to spread their propaganda. The goal, they said, was to ensure that Black workers would be able to join the labor movement. Earl Titus reported their endgame in this way: "To get colored people to think, and join our party, and in that way . . . we will be able to join any trade union in this, or any other country, who are Communists." As evidence that Black people would be able to join left-led unions, one speaker said, "Look at Claude McKay in Soviet Russia today, he is one of our group, and he is received with open arms, and there is no discrimination." Their excitement for the Sanhedrin would turn out to be unfounded, however, as the cadres placed their trust in Kelly Miller, who they suspected of unspoken left sympathies. Far from being "a Communist in his heart," as the cadres put it, however, Miller blocked nearly every attempt of the party to influence the direction of the Sanhedrin.[53]

The Howard University dean began orchestrating a power grab as early as the United Front Conference itself. It was Miller who suggested that the New York assembly was merely a prelude to a "Negro Sanhedrin." Then, when the six organizations agreed to appoint a steering committee based in Harlem with Briggs as its chair, Miller—who was chair of a "Committee on Arrangements" to organize conference logistics—unilaterally declared that the steering committee was no longer necessary. In doing so, Miller shifted the Sanhedrin's center of gravity from New York to Washington and took control of the program. The result was that of the Sanhedrin's 250 delegates from twenty states and sixty-one organizations, most represented Black middle-class groups. The ABB and WP were in the minority, along with a handful of Black-led unions. And while Briggs, Huiswoud, Trotter, and Randolph were all on the program, none of them was on the speakers list. The conference turned primarily on the themes of individual self-help, not of organizing Black labor or challenging the color line in the trade union movement.[54]

Nevertheless, the conference marked the Workers Party's debut in Black civil society. Even if Black Communists did not realize their hopes for the Sanhedrin, they did unveil a left vision of liberation for all to see. This was evident in the resolutions that the party tried to pass against overwhelming opposition. By this point international communism had moved into its so-called "second phase," when its affiliates joined coalitions including partners whose ideologies did not line up with theirs. Accordingly, though the WP proposed nonstarters like making the Internationale the Sanhedrin anthem, they made their top priority an issue upon which all Black organizations could agree: the inclusion of Black workers in unions. They placed before the Sanhedrin the urgent need of a massive migrant workforce from the South that was vulnerable to exploitation without organization. They urged the assembly to initiate a union organizing drive among Black people and to put the influence of the Black press behind it. This, for them, included the establishment of sharecropper unions in the South. When Miller's cohorts maneuvered to table these issues for an inscrutably named "Commission on Permanent Results" to consider, Otto Huiswoud rose to protest the move and demanded that the Sanhedrin address the issues of Black workers, who, he reminded them, comprised 95 percent of their people. In the end, Miller relented and agreed to a watered-down version of the party's resolutions. These included a call to end racial discrimination in unions and a commitment to promote trade unionism among Black people. At the subsequent meeting a year later in Washington, Miller's faction would bar the WP from attending, but such maneuvering was all for naught as it would be the Sanhedrin's last convention.[55]

Having failed to influence the Sanhedrin and its middle-class leadership, the party resolved to establish an organization of their own, the American Negro Labor Congress (ANLC). The stated goals of the ANLC were uncontroversial in Black Communist circles. It sought to forge a united front of Black organizations that would end racial discrimination in organized labor, turn the Black masses away from bourgeois leadership, and train Black people to lead the American working class in a struggle against imperialism and capitalism. Despite their best intentions, however, the Congress ended up isolating itself from the Black community, in part because they dismissed the legitimate concerns of the ABB.[56]

The first warning signs appeared in the conceptual and planning phases of the first ANLC conference, to be held in October 1925 in Chicago. The WP ordered that the ABB disband and that the ANLC take over as their official voice in the Black community. As part of this organizational transition, the leadership replaced Briggs with Lovett Fort-Whiteman, who was more well-known in the international movement. Former ABB activists Otto Huiswoud and Richard Moore warned of a sectarian "fiasco." They advised not to "place the stamp of our Party conspicuously upon the Congress," because a strong association with Communism would invite criticism from trade union officials, thus "killing the movement from its very start."[57]

Fort-Whiteman and his allies in the party did not listen. Communist organizers hit the streets of Chicago's South Side talking to people about the international class struggle and abstruse examples thereof like the travails of the Moroccan Rif people. The program of the ANLC convention featured radical speakers from abroad such as C. T. Chi of the Chinese Students Alliance. The party even mandated that Communist unions and other affiliates send public telegrams of support for the upcoming conference.[58]

As Briggs and Huiswoud predicted, organized labor reacted poorly. AFL president William Green criticized the ANLC for making Black people think that "all their grievances will be remedied by overturning the government of the United States and establishing a Soviet Republic." Green's broadside came with a threat: the AFL would revoke the charter of any union who participated in the ANLC. Though Randolph supported the United Front Conference in 1923, in 1925 he turned his considerable editorial powers against the ANLC, because he believed that the party sought to infiltrate the Brotherhood of Sleeping Car Porters. To his members, he wrote, "We cannot temporize with the Communist menace. It's a sinister and destructive crowd. . . . We shall kill this reptile at the very outset." The one-two punch of the House of Labor and the only Black-led union of national significance ensured that even intrigued trade unionists would think twice about attending the ANLC.[59]

The rest of Black civil society was more sympathetic, if varied. Some support was unqualified. Howard University economist Abram L. Harris said that the ANLC was a healthy response to the color bar in organized labor, while the *Baltimore Afro-American* wrote that the

Congress was a legitimate expression of Black workers' aspirations. The support of other Black organizations was more equivocal. The editor of the National Urban League's magazine *Opportunity* wrote that the AFL's opposition was rich given their systematic exclusion of Black workers. While indicating their support for the practical aims of the ANLC, however, they explicitly opposed the underlying Communist agenda. Similarly, the *Chicago Defender* wrote that although they did not align ideologically, they understood how the brutality of Jim Crow segregation might have given rise to the ANLC.[60]

If there were any doubts that Communists were behind the operation, Lovett Fort-Whiteman obliterated them on the ANLC's opening night. A Russophile given to fits of extravagance, Fort-Whiteman offered the audience of five hundred people a Russian ballet. While not an obvious choice for a working-class revolutionary organization, the real problem was that the ballerinas were white Southerners. One dancer reportedly looked out at the Congress and used colorful language to indicate that she was not going to perform, whereupon a Black audience member used equally colorful language to demand that the ANLC throw the ballerinas out of the building. One disaster followed another. Fort-Whiteman introduced a play by Pushkin, a playwright of African descent who was the finest in all of Russia. The audience seemed relieved to have the ballet behind them, until the actors begin saying their lines—in Russian. Fort-Whiteman did redeem himself somewhat. He ended the evening with a fiery speech on the purpose of the organization. He said, "The aim of the American Negro Labor Congress is to gather, to mobilize, and to coordinate into a fighting machine the most enlightened and militant and class conscious workers of the race." These words seemed to enliven the group as they retired for the day, but the following morning, the audience shrunk to a crowd of less than a hundred.[61]

It became clear at that point that only thirty-three accredited delegates had come. Apart from the Chicagoans, almost everyone came from industrial cities in Ohio and Pennsylvania. Only three delegates hailed from the South: a dockworker from Texas, a freight handler from Louisiana, and a Black woman who led the 250-strong Montgomery, Alabama post of the ABB. Though the party had demanded that ANLC organizers recruit Black sharecroppers to attend, none came. On the positive side, most delegates were Black working women and men.[62]

The second-day assembly met in a hall decorated with the imagined likenesses of Black revolutionaries, past and present. Beneath the portraits of Denmark Vesey, Nat Turner, and Toussaint Louverture and a banner of Black and white hands clasped in solidarity, the group heard speeches from a Mexican immigrant miner and a Chinese student who had suffered at the hands of Japanese and British imperialism. Until the AFL dissolved the color line in organized labor, the ANLC promised to organize "inter-racial committees between black and white trade unionists." The group also resolved to fight for "full social equality," demanded an end to anti-miscegenation laws as well as segregation in public spaces, and connected their fight to international struggles, struggles in which they believed the Soviet Union would be their fiercest ally.[63]

Similar to the prognostications about the ANLC, the postmortem was mixed. Robert Minor, a white Communist who was chair of the WP's Negro Commission, was effusive in his praise. He called the Congress a "splendid foundation" that broke the hold of the Black bourgeoisie on their social underlings. The white press redbaited the whole affair. *Time* magazine called Lovett Fort-Whiteman "The Reddest of the Blacks," and not in a good way. Other white journalists accused Communists of "Bolshevizing the American Negro" and said that the ANLC was "directed by the Communist Internationale in Moscow as part of its worldwide propaganda among backward and 'oppressed' colored races.'" In the pages of the NAACP's *Crisis* magazine, however, W. E. B. Du Bois defended the Congress. He insisted that Black people had the "right . . . to investigate and sympathize with any industrial reform, whether it springs from Russia, China or the South Seas."[64]

In the end, the true test of any mass organization is the ability to connect with workers. By this metric, the ANLC was a disappointment. The Congress started a decent newspaper, the *Negro Champion*, edited by Cyril Briggs, whose words reportedly jumped off the page. In one letter to the editor, an avid reader from Alabama wrote, "I understand that all of the city young people are in unions and are getting higher wages and are perfectly satisfied with life. . . . How should we go about organizing?" But by January 1926, only one branch of the ANLC existed. It was in Chicago, and it had only fifty members.[65]

And yet, the ANLC was hardly an exercise in futility. The Black left learned something from the Chicago fiasco. They discovered that they could not do this alone and that imposing their particular vision of Black liberation was a sure way to prevent an effective coalition. In this sense, the United Front Conference of 1923 did far better. There, Black civil society came together across the political spectrum to press for the integration of the US labor movement. The unfortunate follow-up to that conference, the Negro Sanhedrin, seems to have frustrated Black Communists to such a degree that they became determined to establish a Black organization in their own image, without the meddling of middle-class actors like Kelly Miller. Their next major effort would be much more successful, but not before A. Philip Randolph went on his own odyssey in the American Federation of Labor.

.   .   .

Randolph strode into a meeting of the AFL executive council in Washington on the morning of October 19, 1928. The council consisted of the presidents of the major international unions, leaders like

Arthur Wharton of the International Association of Machinists, and of course, the president of the AFL himself, William Green. Randolph was there to persuade the council that it should grant the Brotherhood of Sleeping Car Porters an international charter. Becoming an affiliate of the mainstream labor movement instead of remaining an independent union, he reasoned, would help the Brotherhood gain recognition from the Pullman Company.[66]

Randolph began his remarks by recounting the events prior to and immediately following the postponement of the June 8 strike. He said that in the weeks leading up to the appointed date, "the spirit and enthusiasm of the members was at a high watermark," but that while "wiser counsel prevailed and the strike was called off there was a slump in the morale of our organization and a corresponding slump in the dues-paying membership." He then admitted that his every effort now, including his appeal for an AFL charter, was "to regain that morale."[67]

Having explained the purpose of his presence there, Randolph then worked to preempt the objections that others had made of his leadership and of the union as a whole. The most important of these was the charge that he and his membership were radical malcontents. To this, he said, "our organization is not representative of any wild-eyed, foolish or irresponsible radicalism, but it is capable of initiating a sense of responsibility" and "can cooperate with the company by way of service efficiency." As to the specific charge that Randolph was a Communist, he held up a copy of the Workers Party's own organ, the *Daily Worker*, which vilified him for his alliance with President Green. He said, "The fact that I am not [a Communist] is established by the Communists themselves." This was a critical point to make, as the Pullman Company for years had said that it was willing to negotiate, but not with a radical like Randolph.[68]

A second objection was the thinly veiled racist charge that the Brotherhood was somehow incapable of running a union of their own.

For example, the company charged that the union did not employ a bookkeeper. Randolph dignified this insult with a tedious discussion of the union's compliance with the best practices of white people. He said, "We have our auditing done by Stuart Chase of the Labor Bureau, Inc. I have brought copies of his financial statement. This will show that we have a definite accounting system. We have a bookkeeper in our office. The work is systematically done." He also turned back the insinuation that he was running the union on his own, saying that apart from himself "there is a General Secretary-Treasurer, there are two assistants, field organizers, and we have a division of organizers, for instance in Chicago, St. Louis, and several other places where the districts are large. We have regional zone supervisors to see that the records are being properly kept by the organizers."[69]

A third and equally damaging objection was bureaucratic in nature—namely, that other unions like the Hotel Employees and Restaurant Employees Union (HERE) had jurisdiction over the work of the sleeping car porters and that the Brotherhood had no right to represent them. Randolph denied HERE's claim to the porters on ideological grounds. He said, "The porters themselves are opposed to going into the hotel group. There is a growing sense of race consciousness, of race pride. Among negroes there has been a continued stream of progress. Every year growing numbers of negroes are coming out of colleges and universities and this spirit of progress is reflected in every profession and sphere of life." When Wharton asked Randolph whether "in the event of their getting a charter" the porters would accept as president "a man of the white race with unquestioned standing and knowledge of the labor movement," Randolph replied that they would be opposed to white officials. He explained, "They feel their progress entitles them to assume responsibility in the administration of their own affairs."[70]

Randolph's appeal seemed to go over well. At the end of the meeting, the executive council directed President Green to gather all relevant information on the Brotherhood's local unions, including the number of members in each. The council also agreed to arrange a conference with President Edward P. Fiore of HERE at the AFL's upcoming annual convention in New Orleans, where they hoped Fiore would relinquish his claim over the sleeping car porters. The outcome of that conference, while not ideal, nevertheless put Green on record as being favorable toward Randolph. Fiore continued to claim jurisdiction over the porters, but Green expressed his doubts. At a meeting after the conference, he recalled, "I pointed out that they had not been able to organize these men in their organization and that time has proven it is unworkable and impracticable." President M.S. Warfield of the Order of Sleeping Car Conductors, who represented the white engineers on Pullman cars, concurred. He, too, said that "the American Federation of Labor should give a charter to the porters."[71]

If the Brotherhood seemed on the verge of an international charter in 1928, the years following proved that the AFL's systematic exclusion of Black labor was no mere rumor. In February 1929, three months after the conference with President Fiore in New Orleans, the AFL executive council voted to incorporate the porters not as a duly recognized international union but as a "Federal Labor Union." Among its various uses, the AFL employed this designation when it wanted to bring Black locals into the federation. It was, in other words, the mechanism through which organized labor maintained a segregated movement. For the next six years, Randolph continued to apply for an international charter, and for six years, the AFL denied his application.[72]

In a dirty double-cross, President Warfield of the Sleeping Car Conductors went as far as to try to steal the porters from the Brotherhood. After initially supporting Randolph's bid for an international charter, Warfield later insisted that the porters and conductors belonged in the same union—his union. Warfield's rationale was that the Pullman Company was combining the work of conductors and porters. To a meeting of the AFL executive council in 1934, he said, "There is no way we can control that unless we have jurisdiction over them. If the porters were granted a separate charter there would be two international unions in one company, each trying to negotiate an agreement for men doing the same work." This convinced the council. They again denied Randolph's application for an international charter and ordered President Green to discuss with the conductors "the conditions under which these men will be organized and the Federal Labor Unions turned over to them." In one fell swoop, the AFL voted to undo all the work that the Brotherhood of Sleeping Car Porters had done since 1909 to organize their union.[73]

As if this were not bad enough, Warfield then put a plan in place that would have segregated the conductors from the porters. In his appeal to overturn the AFL's decision, Randolph shared a circular, dated November 12, 1934, in which Warfield informed his white members of the impending merger. Warfield described the porters' application cards for union membership in this way: "The employees' portion gives a brief sketch of the nature of the porters' organization. It shows that it will be entirely separate from our own. Of course, they will not send delegates to our conventions. They will hold their own if they so desire. We are simply acting as their attorney when questions arise concerning wages, working conditions, or grievances." In union parlance, this meant that the porters would pay dues in exchange for legal advice but never be full citizens of the union. Indeed, Warfield appears here to be soothing his white members' anxiety about rubbing shoulders in the same conventions with Black people.[74]

Randolph was not without allies in his attempt to appeal the AFL's decision. John L. Lewis, who was then president of the United Mine Workers of America (UMWA) and an AFL vice president, questioned Warfield's authority to represent the porters. For example, he asked

Warfield whether "it was fair trade union policy to ask the men to accept membership and representation under the foremen who control them." Lewis also pointed out that the very constitution of the conductors' union contained an explicit color bar.[75]

It was not Lewis who engineered the Brotherhood's counterattack, however, but Randolph himself. At the August 1935 meeting of the AFL Executive Council in Atlantic City, Randolph revealed that the porters had been busy. The Brotherhood had worked with the US Mediation Board to hold an election under the Railway Labor Act, in which the conductors' and porters' unions were on the ballot. In Atlantic City, Randolph announced that the porters had voted overwhelmingly in favor of the Brotherhood to represent them and that furthermore, a representative of the Pullman Company, L. S. Hungerford, had agreed to meet on July 29, 1935 to negotiate over working conditions.[76]

The fact that the Brotherhood had won a free and fair election and brought the intransigent Pullman Company to the bargaining table proved to be the decisive turning point in the saga. At the end of 1935, the AFL leadership decided that a "charter would be issued but that conferences be held of the proper parties to see if we could overcome objections." At the council's instruction, Randolph sent Warfield a letter asking him to surrender his jurisdiction over the porters and maids and reminding him of how the Brotherhood came to represent the workers in the first place. He wrote,

> The Brotherhood won this right by virtue of the fact that it has secured the membership of the large majority of the Pullman porters and maids, embracing now more than six thousand out of the 9,000 in the Pullman service. As an old trade union man, I am confident that you recognize the logical and natural authority which inheres in an organization which has won the allegiance of the majority of workers of any class or craft.

Having received no reply from Warfield, the AFL leadership adopted the following resolution: "That the Executive Council carry out its former decision and issue a national charter to Pullman porters and maids." With that, the Brotherhood became the first ever fully chartered Black-led union in US labor history.[77]

. . .

The story of the two brotherhoods—the African Blood Brotherhood and the Brotherhood of Sleeping Car Porters—evinces four clear patterns, and a fifth, more nascent. The first pattern is that white activists were inconsistent in their support of interracial solidarity. For example, even if we concede that William Green and John L. Lewis were allies, the American Federation of Labor and its affiliates in the Hotel Employees and Conductors unions repeatedly undermined Randolph's application for a full charter. White Communists, while generally more supportive of Black labor, also undermined an interracial coalition with the labor movement by imposing their sectarian vision of Black liberation on the American Negro Labor Congress.

The second pattern is that Black people were the vanguard of racial inclusion in the labor movement. This was not an obvious reaction to their systematic exclusion. Black civil society was uniformly resentful of organized labor's racism, which is why some, like Marcus Garvey, embraced Black separatism from white society. Nevertheless, Black activists made their advocacy of interracial solidarity known in publications like the *Messenger* and *Crusader*, in the organizations that they founded such as the United Front Conference, and in their battles with white trade unionists. In each case, it was Black labor that pressed for interracial solidarity, sometimes in concert with, and at other times over the objection of, their white comrades. Even when whites proved receptive, they did so in part because Black activists made them see reason. For instance, after years of insisting that the "Negro question" was a parochial matter of the American working class, the Workers Party embraced a platform taken straight out of the pages of the *Crusader*. Similarly, after an eight-year saga in which Randolph applied over and over again for an AFL charter, it was ultimately the Brotherhood of Sleeping Car Porters who engineered an election and brought the bosses to the table in 1935, and in so doing convinced the federation to incorporate them as an international union.

This is not to say that Black people were of one mind on how to achieve interracial solidarity, and this is the third pattern. While Randolph, Briggs, and other members of the Harlem left once ran in the same social circles, they eventually broke into two factions. On the left was the ABB, whose exponents believed that interracial solidarity must be accomplished in concert with the international Communist movement. Randolph headed the centrist faction and came to believe that Black liberation could be achieved within the mainstream US labor movement. The two factions clashed publicly, especially in their opinions of the American Negro Labor Congress and the postponement of the porters' June 8 strike. This clash, which I call "Black politics," is further evidence of Black people's agency in the cause of interracial solidarity. It suggests that they were not only active in the struggle for their own liberation, but also invested in the cause to such an extent that they disagreed bitterly over how to achieve it.

The fourth pattern is the effort of the state to surveil the nascent Black labor movement. Much of the data that appears in this chapter comes from intelligence reports by agents like Earl E. Titus, who posed as a Black Communist to infiltrate the ABB. US intelligence officers were laying the groundwork for the repression of Black labor activists in the years to come. They reported on the activities of Randolph, Briggs, McKay, Garvey, and many others on a daily and even hourly basis, amassing the evidence they would need to subvert and ultimately destroy Black labor organizations in the future.

A fifth pattern was only just emerging in this period, namely, the role of Black women. Women were by no means the focus of the Brotherhoods' political programs, but without them the two organizations would have suffered. Randolph's wife, Lucille Green, was the breadwinner of the family and enabled her husband to carry on his political work. Because of the Pullman Company's extensive network of spies, the porters' wives were pivotal to collecting dues and spreading propaganda secretly among the workers. This is to say nothing of the fact that a sizable minority of the union's members were maids. And lest we forget, Grace Campbell was a leading figure in the African Blood Brotherhood, part of the latter's inner circle along with Otto Huiswoud, Richard B. Moore, Cyril Briggs, and Claude McKay.

Though these five patterns sometimes worked to undermine the cause of interracial solidarity, none could prevent a coalition of Black labor from taking hold. We cannot discount the fact that as young men and women the leading lights of Harlem civil society gathered in the offices of the *Messenger* to debate the issues of the day. It is no stretch to suggest that the leaders of the two factions came of age together. Moreover, these very same actors proved in 1923 that they could sign a concordat at the United Front Conference, putting aside their ideological differences.

The complex tensions and solidarities of this earlier period would give rise to two of the most significant organizations in Black labor history: the National Negro Congress (NNC) in 1936 and the March on Washington Movement (MOWM) in 1941. These would represent respectively the left and centrist factions of Black labor during the Great Depression and its aftermath. Like the African Blood Brotherhood before it, the NNC had ties to the Communist Party; indeed, the NNC was in part a product of the ABB's and the WP's failed efforts to mobilize the Black community. Its primary objective was to organize Black workers into militant industrial unions. The March on

Washington Movement was self-consciously anti-Communist. Its purpose was to pressure the state into eliminating employment discrimination in the defense industries through direct action. The next chapter explains why these two seemingly complementary movements—movements that in fact shared leaders in common—became hostile to one another at the onset of the Second World War.

3   *The Congress and the March*

Cyril Briggs was fired again in October 1933. Like his dismissal from the *Amsterdam News*, this marked a new beginning for Black labor, but one in which he ceased to be a relevant player. The country was then in the throes of the Great Depression, and the focus of Communist Party activity was on cultivating interracial class solidarity through a combination of legal action and industrial unionism. As his persistent Black nationalism was a distraction from these other priorities, the Communists relieved him of his post as editor of their Harlem newspaper, the *Liberator*. Briggs accepted his reassignment to the staff of the *Daily Worker*, but from that point forward, he would no longer be the focal point of the Harlem left.[1]

In the early years of the Depression, the party was developing a new model of mobilization: rather than push a pure Communist agenda on their own as they did with the ANLC, they worked with other organizations on issues of broad appeal to the Black community. The first high-profile experiment in this regard took place in March and April of 1931 and involved the trial of nine Black teenaged boys in Scottsboro, Alabama. White authorities charged the defendants with raping two white women aboard a train based on the flimsiest of evidence. A hostile Southern jury convicted the boys and sentenced them to death. The party's legal arm, the International Labor

Defense (ILD), sent attorneys to represent the accused and began organizing mass protests in Harlem. A crowd of seven hundred attended their initial meeting at St. Luke's Hall on April 24. The next day, five thousand Harlemites arrived at Lenox Avenue and 140th Street to show their support. When a large contingent of white Communists joined in solidarity, the New York police descended on the protest and behaved with their customary brutality. The Communists' public support of the Scottsboro Nine even in the face of violence earned them the allegiance of the Harlem streets and built bridges with religious and other local organizations that had been previously disconnected from the party.[2]

The next experiment in the party program involved a nineteen-year-old Black cadre named Angelo Herndon. Herndon was a soldier in the Communists' bid to organize the American South. In the summer of 1931, he turned out nearly a thousand unemployed workers, both Black and white, at the Fulton County Commissioner's offices to demand relief. Two weeks later, the police arrested Herndon on the basis of a pre-Civil War insurrection law. Benjamin Davis, Jr., a Black Harvard-trained lawyer from the ILD, became lead attorney on the case. Despite Davis's best efforts to convince a hostile white jury that the Georgia insurrection law was unconstitutional, the jurors returned a guilty verdict and recommended a prison sentence of up to twenty years. Like the Scottsboro case, this travesty of justice brought together a diverse coalition of dissenters. In Atlanta, the campaign to free Angelo Herndon gained the support of Reverend J. Raymond Henderson, the city's most prominent Black Baptist minister; the socialist Mary Raoul Millis; and the historian C. Vann Woodward. Nationally, the Herndon case became a cause célèbre. The progressive magazines *The New Republic* and *The Nation*, came out in support of the jailed activist. In 1935, when the party was in the midst of collecting two million signatures on behalf of their young comrade, A. Philip Randolph himself wrote in the *New York Age* that while he did not share the "Communist views of Herndon," he saw the verdict as a "dangerous threat to Negro Americans." The only way to achieve justice in this case, he wrote, was "for Negroes to develop a united front in church, fraternal society, social, political, professional and labor organizations and join with white radical and liberal movements that are fighting for the downtrodden and the oppressed."[3]

The CP's third experiment was to organize unskilled industrial workers into the mainstream labor movement. The party had formed separate Communist industrial unions for years in the Trade Union Unity League (TUUL), but in 1934 they began infiltrating existing unions like John L. Lewis's United Mine Workers of America (UMWA). In industries and regions where Black workers were disproportionately concentrated, Black rank-and-file activists, both women and men, were the core of the local Communist leadership, though white organizers like Clyde Johnson were also pivotal to these efforts. Coal mining in the South is a good example. In 1933, the labor movement had scored a pyrrhic legislative victory with the passage of the National Industrial Recovery Act (NIRA). The act recognized the workers' right to organize but provided no mechanism of enforcement; it was also ostensibly colorblind, but its industry "codes" set lower minimum wage rates in regions and occupations where Black workers predominated. When the UMWA accepted lower wages for Southern coalminers, 60 percent of whom were Black, Black Communists launched an unauthorized wildcat strike of 20,000 workers. The party then filled the coal camps with pamphlets calling for an end to the segregation of Black miners into the most menial positions, causing an additional 14,000 workers to join the strike. Violence quickly followed. Four workers, three Black and one white, died in the initial struggle. The strike built to another violent confrontation on September 16, 1934, when deputies opened fire on a rally of 2,500 people, killing another three workers.

When the workers struck again in 1935, the regional coal operators surrendered.[4]

. . .

The man who replaced Cyril Briggs as the standard-bearer of the Black left in this new period of interracial mass mobilization was John P. Davis. Davis was born in 1905, the same year that Briggs arrived in Harlem as a young man from the Caribbean. He was the third child of a Black middle-class family, newly settled in Washington, D.C. Davis's father, William, was a clerk in the federal civil service. Like other Black labor leaders, Davis was an excellent student. He attended Dunbar High School, Washington's elite academy for Black students, and won a scholarship to Bates College in Maine.[5]

He shared with Randolph a love for the creative arts that gave way to a career in politics. Hoping to train as a writer, Davis went to New York in the 1920s to become part of the Harlem Renaissance. But after obtaining a master's degree in literature from Harvard and then a teaching position at Fisk University, he made a fateful return to Cambridge, this time for a law degree. On this second stint at Harvard, he became embroiled in the social activism of the Great Depression and worked on the Scottsboro case with the radical lawyers of the ILD. His fellow traveler on the left was another Black Harvard student, Robert C. Weaver.[6]

After graduating from law school, he returned to Washington, D.C., to take part in the promise of the New Deal, but what he saw concerned him. Davis attended a congressional hearing on the National Recovery Administration (NRA) in June 1933 and found that he was the only Black person in the room. If these proceedings were meant to kickstart and sustain the economic recovery, then the absence of people like him spelled doom for Black workers. Rising immediately to the moment, Davis dragooned Robert Weaver into starting a two-person operation that they called the National Industrial League (NIL). Weaver and Davis went to every congressional hearing on the national recovery, testifying to any legislator who would listen that the federal government was putting the Black worker at a disadvantage in industries such as timber, textiles, and coal. In so doing, they said, the Roosevelt administration was undercutting the buying power of Black workers and thus the capacity of Americans to reverse the crisis of underconsumption that was the Great Depression.[7]

The NIL died in late summer 1933 when the Roosevelt administration co-opted Weaver and other young Black intellectuals who were making a name for themselves in Washington. Clark Foreman, a liberal white Southerner who was an adviser on Negro Affairs in the Department of the Interior, hired Robert Weaver as his assistant, leaving Davis as the lone voice of the NIL. It was also around this time when Mabel Byrd became the only Black woman staffer in the NRA's research division. Through her work, Byrd confirmed that the NRA was drawing up industrial codes that paid Black workers less than their white counterparts for the same work. When she proposed a research trip to conduct field work in Southern cities, her white boss dismissed it. When Byrd then proposed a new rule that would classify racist wage differentials as an improper application of New Deal legislation, the bureaucracy fired her.[8]

Though the NIL's tenure was short, Davis had cultivated strong relationships with Black civil society for as long as it lasted. The main financial support behind the League was Walter White, president of the NAACP. Black newspapers also showed their appreciation of Davis and Weaver's work. By exposing the scandalous wage differentials in NRA codes, the League had even won a few wage gains for Black workers, though they lost most of their appeals because of the Democratic Party's allegiance to the Southerners in their caucus. With Weaver's departure, Davis built on these connections and forged a coalition of the NAACP, Randolph's Brotherhood of Sleeping Car Porters, the Elks (a Black fraternal organization), and twenty other organizations. He called the new group the Joint Committee on National Recovery (JCNR).[9]

The JCNR continued the work of the NIL as gadfly to the National Recovery Administration, but the broad coalition at its back gave Davis the authority to speak on behalf of the entire Black community for the first time. At an NRA hearing a few months after the JCNR's founding, Davis said, "I am here as the chosen representative of 22 national organizations. The long established character of these organizations is beyond question. Embraced in the membership of one or more of them you will find several million of your Negro fellow Citizens. The Joint Committee on National Recovery exists for the purpose of integrating Negroes in the recovery program of the federal government."[10]

Davis moved beyond the racist wage differentials that were the bread and butter of the NIL to speak more expansively about the causes of Black people's subordination in the labor market, especially their exclusion from unions. "White labor has denied us admission to their unions, and robbed us of the opportunity of joining with them to bargain collectively," he said, adding, "I say to them today that every stumbling block put in our way is a knot in the noose which will be used by unscrupulous employers to hang black and white workers alike." Consistent with his growing ideological allegiance to the Communist Party, Davis offered the labor movement a reason to join Black workers against their common enemy. He said, "The time has come when white labor should no longer be crucified because of cheap Negro labor. . . . Large sums of money have been expended by a group of Southern manufacturers to propagandize among Negro workers, urging them to protest high code wages on the ground that they would be displaced by white workers." Davis thus pinned the blame for the low wages of all workers not only on the implicit bias of

NRA officials, but also on Southern capital, who sowed division among the working class.[11]

When Davis was not in Washington, he worked as a social scientist. He and his wife Marguerite De Mond, who was a staffer for the Association for the Study of Negro Life and History, used their own money to finance the JCNR's research trips to the South. Doing what Mabel Byrd envisioned but could not do before she was fired, Davis toured the most impoverished Southern communities, collecting copious amounts of data on the exploitation of Black workers. Together with Charles Hamilton Houston, who would become the architect of the NAACP's legal challenge to segregation, Davis produced comprehensive reports on racist wage differentials in the steel and shipping industries among others. The analytic throughline was once again the exclusion of Black workers from the labor movement. For instance, in his evaluation of racial inequality among longshoremen, he wrote, "the unorganized groups to which those low wages are offered will be in no position to refuse. White labor, organized as it is, will be in a position to force higher wages than those offered in the code. But Negro labor, in its unorganized state, will have to be content to accept these low wage levels." Because of his tireless work on the exclusion and exploitation of Black labor, Davis, while still in his twenties, had become one of the most widely respected experts on Black workers and unions.[12]

But perhaps the JCNR's most lasting contribution to the development of the Black labor movement was its conference at Howard University on "The Position of the Negro in Our National Economic Crisis." Before the Communist Party could coin the term "Popular Front" to name their coalitional strategy, Davis and his allies would make the concept a reality in May 1935. The purpose of the conference was to bring together the leaders of Black civil society and develop a collective strategy for challenging the ongoing degradation of Black labor during the Depression. Speakers ran the gamut of the political spectrum, and it was precisely this ideological diversity that gave the conference its life and staying power.

Davis was the conference's principal organizer and gave the opening address. True to his billing in the Communist Party as a possible successor to Cyril Briggs, Davis announced that the days of the existing economic system were numbered. He said, "Capitalism is only a few hundred years old; as feudalism is dead, so may it die." Briggs echoed the speech of Howard University's progressive political scientist Ralph Bunche, who criticized the New Deal for representing "merely an effort to refurbish the old individualistic-capitalistic system and to entrust it again with the economic destines and welfare of the American people." After reporting on the scourge of wage inequality, Davis again pointed to the labor movement as an underlying cause. He said, "The American Federation of Labor, the Railroad Brotherhoods, and others, since their inception have followed the policy of Jim Crowism based upon the premise that Negroes are unorganizable." Davis signaled that a possible solution to this problem was to harness the growing militance of the Black working class. "We have seen tens of thousands of Negro workers both agricultural and industrial risk their lives in strike struggles for better labor conditions," he said, and proposed that their principal concern be "The problem of achieving solidarity of Negro and white workers."[13]

W. E. B. Du Bois likewise dwelled on the issue of racial exclusion from the labor movement. He said, "Not only has the attempt of American Negroes to join the ranks of [the] white labor movement been discouraging for more than a century, the welcome which they are accorded is questionable." Ever the sociologist, he posed the problem in data-driven terms. Speaking of the rate of union membership nationally, he said, "If we take the less than 5,000,000 who are organized, the overwhelming majority of them will not allow the Negroes to join their ranks under any circumstances, and most of the rest have only allowed Negroes to intrude when the power of Negro labor was such that they did not dare oppose its competition." Though some unions were inclusive, he observed, "Their total number must be less than half a million. With such workers, Negro labor ought by all means to unite." Unlike Davis and Bunche, however, Du Bois believed that given the likely toll of state violence, "one of the worst things that Negroes could do today would be to join the American Communist Party." Because Communists believed "in immediate, violent and bloody revolution," he said that war and bloodshed would be "a silly program even for white men," but for Black men, it would be "suicide."[14]

A significant break in the discussion of organized labor occurred with the speech of Mary Anderson, a Swedish-born labor activist who was then director of the Women's Bureau in the US Department of Labor. Her speech, "The Plight of Negro Domestic Labor," shifted the conversation toward Black women. Noting that the latter comprised over a million domestic workers in the United States, Anderson stated with alarm that they were much more likely to be unemployed than white women. Various studies estimated that between one-half and three-fourths of all unemployed domestic workers were Black women, numbers wholly out of proportion with their representation in the domestic labor force and the population at large. Moreover, whereas more than half of all white women were eligible for unemployment relief under the New Deal, only between 10 and 15 percent of Black women were. This, Anderson insisted, was a crisis within a crisis, and "Any sound program of recovery must somehow include restoration of purchasing power to this substantial proportion of our working population."[15]

But the speaker who made the biggest impact on the conference and shaped its aftermath was none other than A. Philip Randolph. Though he covered the same ground as the previous speakers, including an indictment of the racial blind spots of organized labor and the New Deal, he ended with a vision for addressing the social and economic degradation of Black labor. In addition to a policy of "destruction" that must tear down the "discrimination, segregation and Jim Crowism in the trade unions," the group should also a develop "a program of construction." Randolph sketched out that program, beginning with two interrelated axioms. The first of these was that Black people could not rely upon whites to embrace interracial solidarity. "Even if the A.F. of L. and the national and international unions believed thoroughly in the organization of Negro workers, they could not be depended upon to do the job themselves," he said. Consequently, the second axiom was that if "the problem of Negro workers is organization," then "this is the task of Negroes themselves. Nobody else will organize Negro workers but Negro workers." Having laid out the basic predicament, Randolph called for a Black labor coalition consisting of organizations drawn from every corner of Black civic life. He said, "The paramount and big question before the Negroes today of all strata is the development of a long-range program for the organization of Negro workers in the trade unions, either in or out of the A.F. of L., for the purpose of developing economic power to improve their lot in terms of wages and hours of work and for the larger objective of industrial and political democracy."[16]

After all was said and done, the participants at the Howard conference decided that the utmost need was to coordinate Black labor, political, religious, and fraternal groups through a centralized body, which they called the National Negro Congress (NNC). The group appointed John P. Davis National Secretary and assembled a board consisting of Lester Granger and Elmer Carter of the National Urban League; Alain Locke of Howard University; the Black clergymen James A. Bray, R.A. Carter, and W.J. Wells; M.O. Bousfield of the Rosenwald Fund (the charitable foundation of Sears and Roebuck Company), and A. Philip Randolph of the International Brotherhood of Sleeping Car Porters. The first meeting of the congress was scheduled to begin on Valentine's Day 1936. On the eve of the meeting, over eight hundred delegates representing nearly six hundred organizations and more than five thousand visitors were set to attend, but one problem remained: they did not have a president.[17]

. . .

The winter of 1936 was not kind to A. Philip Randolph. Though he had seemingly won his battle with the Pullman Company, the campaign was taking a toll on his body. He lay bed-ridden at home, sick with a variety of ailments. Randolph had a 103-degree fever, busted tonsils, a respiratory infection, and chronic laryngitis. His doctor at Mount Sinai Hospital in New York recommended a tonsillectomy and cautioned him against abusing his vocal chords further. It was a wonder that he could speak at Howard University at all, for he was then on the cusp of the union election that recognized the Brotherhood as the porters' rightful representative. Whatever the state of his health, his stature by 1936 was unquestioned. He was far and away the most respected Black trade unionist in America and a leader upon whom a wide array of Black leaders could agree. John P. Davis said as much, and Randolph's very own enemies agreed. Claude McKay of the Harlem Workers Party was to say of him:

> More than any other Negro leader, he has a comprehensive understanding of the vast conquests of modern industry and the grand movement of labor to keep abreast of it. And he is aware that the Negro group is in a special position and has a special force. His outlook remains unblurred by passion and prejudice. He takes a long, balanced view of men and affairs. He could not be tagged with radical, chauvinist, nationalist, or reactionary labels . . . He believes that the mainspring of the Negro group lies within himself.

It was no surprise to anyone that Reverend Adam Clayton Powell, Jr., Harlem's venerable religious leader and politician, approached Randolph to lead the NNC. Randolph turned him down.[18]

The reason he gave Powell was his health, but it was more complicated than that. Although the Brotherhood had won their election and at long last brought the Pullman bosses to the bargaining table, they were still embroiled in a difficult contract campaign. Looking forward from that moment, there was no end in sight to negotiations. Moreover, the rank-and-file leaders of the union were not thrilled at the prospect of Randolph splitting his time between the porters and some untested outside organization. Recall that after the postponement of the 1928 strike, Milton Webster of the Chicago local was concerned that Randolph had become aloof from the lives of the members. The result was that the power center of the union shifted away from New York to its busiest hubs like Boston, St. Louis, and Chicago. Politically speaking, taking on the presidency of the NNC was not wise.[19]

There were, however, several realities that tended to overshadow the Brotherhood's internal needs. One was the Great Depression. The economic crisis, now seven years old, had slowly but surely sucked the financial life out of even the most established Black organizations, including the NAACP, the National Urban League, and the Black Church. With membership support and philanthropic dollars (including from the Pullman Company) drying up, organizations that had once relied heavily on white elites now relied increasingly on the Black community. This unprecedented shift in resource dependency made them less tethered to Black middle-class respectability politics and opened them up to an alternative mass program like that of the National Negro Congress. Without a deliberate strategy to split Black civil society from white elites, this predisposition might have been wasted. The Sleeping Car Porters sought to engineer this split with all deliberate speed. For example, in Chicago, the

Ida B. Wells Club and other Black women's organizations, together with attorney Charles Wesley Burton, gradually built up a community reservoir of good will that yielded dividends in the Depression years. Though the Brotherhood's local membership fell precipitously from 1,000 to 250 when the economic crisis set in, the union's new backers in the Young Women's Christian Association and the Baptist Church, among others brought them back from the brink.[20]

Another factor eclipsing the internal needs of the Brotherhood had to do with Randolph's own vision for the union. For Randolph, who retained at least some of his commitments to Democratic Socialism, the Brotherhood was not just a labor organization, but the vanguard of the Black working class—the tip of the spear in the struggle for liberation. The National Negro Congress would fulfill this vision by bringing together the support of hundreds of Black organizations and a membership of millions. If there were any organization he wanted to lead apart from the Brotherhood itself, it was the NNC. And so, when Charles Burton followed up on Powell's earlier offer of the NNC presidency and assured him that he need not go to Chicago to assume his post at the first meeting of the congress, Randolph accepted.[21]

It was a good thing, too, that the ailing Randolph did not attend, for the inaugural meeting of the National Negro Congress began on a freezing February day. Eight hundred delegates from twenty-eight states converged on the Eighth Regiment Armory in Chicago's Bronzeville neighborhood. Like the participants of the Howard conference several months earlier, the delegates came from across the ideological spectrum. Speaking for the left were Harlem Workers Party chief James Ford and Howard University professor Ralph Bunche. The Reverend Adam Clayton Powell, Jr., spoke on behalf of the Black clergy. Lester Granger promoted the National Urban League's plan for labor education among Black workers. There, too, were the Black community's cultural icons, people like Richard Wright, Arna Bontemps, Langston Hughes, and Augusta Savage. So star-studded was the lineup that one delegate said, "I have never seen so many 'big shots' together in my life." The *New York Age* wrote that it was "the most complete cross section of Negro life in the United States gathered under one roof." Nor was this lost on the residents of Chicago's historic Black neighborhood. Those who could not fit inside the Armory huddled in their thousands around outdoor loudspeakers to hear what their leaders had to say.[22]

Given the NNC's potential to mobilize the political will of the Black community, Randolph was determined to put his stamp on the proceedings and provide organizational direction, albeit in absentia. Charles Wesley Burton, who had persuaded the union leader to accept the presidency, read Randolph's speech aloud. It was clear by his somewhat conciliatory tone that the NNC's first president sought to give credit to previous attempts at Black unification while simultaneously suggesting that the times called for new tactics and strategy. He said that while

> the fight for civil and political liberties for the Negro peoples . . . has been brilliantly waged by the NAACP and the ILD, the gravity and complexity of the problems of civil and political liberties, accentuated and widened by the evil of fascist trends in America, demands that new tactics and strategy be employed to meet the situation. . . . The maneuvering and disposing of the forces of Negro peoples and their sympathetic allies against their enemies can only be effectively worked out through the tactics and strategy of the united front.

Randolph thus drew a line in the sand between two great forces. On the one side was fascism, including the white supremacists who had spurred the ILD and NAACP to action in the first place. On the other side was Randolph's united front: an alliance of Black and white progressive forces, who must put aside their differences to guard against the incursions of the far right.[23]

He then explained why it was vital that the NNC not succumb to the influence of any one organization but rather learn to rely upon the strengths and resources of all the members of the united front. "The task of overcoming the enemies of democratic institutions and constitutional liberties is too big for any single organization," he said, for "it requires the united and formal integrating and coordinating of the various Negro organizations, church, fraternal, civil, trade union, farmer, professional, college and what not, into the framework of a united front . . . backed by the embattled masses of black and white workers." Nor was this united front to be an aloof organization, inured to the halls of power, but rather a mass organization—one that organized workers at the grassroots. The NNC would be in the streets and in the workplace; its tactics would be "executed through methods of mass demonstration, such as parades, picketing, boycotting, mass protest, the mass distribution of propaganda literature, as well as legal action." But finally, balanced against the demands of unity and mass action, Randolph insisted that Black people must *lead* the united front. He argued for a break with the tactics of the Black middle class, who had grown accustomed to leaning on enlightened whites for support and in doing so failed to challenge the system of white supremacy which their allies could not help but support. He said, "the Negro problem should not place their problems for solution down at the feet of their white sympathetic allies which has been and is the common fashion of the old school Negro leadership, for, in the final analysis, the salvation of the Negro, like the workers, must come from within."[24]

Edward Strong, a youth delegate to the NNC, echoed these sentiments. Strong was born in Texas in 1914 and moved with his family to Michigan twelve years later. A former member of the youth division of the Flint NAACP, he relocated to Chicago during the Depression, where he worked with legendary organizers like Ella Baker and James Jackson to organize a National Youth Conference in Chicago in 1933 that pledged to fight white supremacy, popularize Black culture, and unite white and Black students in struggle. Strong helped John P. Davis organize the first NNC meeting in Chicago and became a protégé of the elder organizer. In his speech to the congress, Strong said that the philosophy of the old Black intelligentsia was "no answer to the problem" and that the panaceas they offered were "antiquated." With the Depression, Strong continued, "an ever increasing number of young Negroes understand our basic problems to be economic" and these problems "cannot be solved by the Negro alone, but through the cooperative efforts of all people, searching for industrial freedom." He then proposed a relationship between Black youth and the congress that would have alarmed the outmoded Black leadership in the room. He said, "an all inclusive youth movement" would "put a stick of dynamite under the industrial barons that rule this country," and the congress would be "the medium through which Negro youth will unite with all forces working for peace, freedom, and progress."[25]

After several such speeches, the congress voted on and passed a series of resolutions that underlined the meeting's focus on organizing the Black working class. These resolutions, which represent the political will of the body, provide further evidence that the delegates intended to establish a mass organization that could press for interracial solidarity in the wider labor movement. Noting that "Discrimination is practiced against Negro workers in the trade unions . . . thus compelling these workers to remain unorganized and work for lower standards," the congress resolved to establish "Negro Labor Committees for the special purpose of organizing the unorganized Negro workers, and . . . education to end discrimination in any form within the A.F. of L." Moreover, the congress instructed the incoming executive committee to inaugurate a "trade union committee to carry out the decision pertaining to the organization of Negro labor into the unions of the A.F. of L." The combined infrastructure of a governing trade union committee and local councils would be part of a "nationwide drive to organize Negro workers," with a focus on key industries in which Black people predominated. The NNC came out publicly in support of industrial unionism, which sought to move beyond organizing workers narrowly by trades (from which Black workers were excluded anyway) to organizing entire industries wall-to-wall, regardless of skill. Thus, the congress observed that "The industrial union offers a more effective solution of the problems of race discrimination in the labor movement since such unions include all workers in a given industry, skilled and unskilled." Accordingly, the delegates voted to work with John L. Lewis and the Committee on Industrial Organization, which would later leave the AFL to form a competing labor federation, the Congress of Industrial Organizations (CIO).[26]

By virtue of the strategic sectors they chose, the delegates emphasized the role of Black women in working-class struggle, continuing a theme from the Howard University conference. The NNC prefigured what we today call "intersectionality" by observing that "the Negro Women of America are subjected to three-fold exploitation as women, as workers and as Negroes and are forced through discrimination into the most menial labor under the worst conditions without organizational protection." The delegates even went so far as to lift up Black women's reproductive labor in the home. "The Negro mother," they observed, "must bear the greatest brunt of economic crises," explaining, "we housewives, Negro and white, see very little" of the "returning prosperity" of the late 1930s, "for wages are stationary . . . but prices of food continue to creep upward; and relief is being cut and countless families are living on starvation diet." Presented by Nellie Hazell of the Negro Democratic League of Philadelphia, the delegates voted unanimously in favor of a resolution that "a national movement be instituted under the direction of the National Negro Congress to organize the Domestic Workers, who include 85%

of all Negro women workers." Such a movement would also encourage the organization of Black housewives and the formation of interracial women's leagues against the high cost of living.[27]

Thus, the NNC was unique not only because of the breadth of the coalition that came together, but also because the coalition looked to the Black worker to lead the liberation of the race. Previously, it had been middle-class organizations that advocated on behalf of African Americans, and the most illustrious of these were the NAACP and the National Urban League. At the NNC, by contrast, each speech and resolution focused on the plight of Black working women and men, their exclusion from the ranks of organized labor, and the urgency of interracial solidarity to meet the present economic crisis. So focused was the conference on the Black working class that it opened the NNC to charges of being a Communist front in the weeks following. For example, Kelly Miller, the failed middle-class leader of the Negro Sanhedrin, criticized the NNC for being too "leftward" and "revolutionary" and implied that Randolph and the Communist James Ford had cooked up the congress as a subversive plot to overthrow the social order. Because of the NNC's "failure to denounce Communism," Miller declared the congress "a lamentable failure."[28]

Having been a persistent critic of Communist partisanship for years, Randolph took umbrage at the charge of a conspiracy and struck back. He defended the Communists as a "legitimate political party" that "need make no apology" for its existence. Then, calling red-baiting a "regular indoor sport" for those who seek to "condemn those who aggressively fight for human and race rights," he reminded his audience that Jesus Christ and his disciples were nailed to the cross and "persecuted as Communists." He ended by saying, "If we Negroes are so yellow, so cringing . . . and childish to permit the 'red label' to halt our march toward the true status of men . . . God help us!"[29]

The CP's own internal records confirm Randolph's account over Miller's. Having suffered through the embarrassing crucible of the

ANLC, the CP was deliberate in not seeking "mechanical control" of the congress. And so, apart from distributing leaflets, making a speech or two, and contributing a modest amount of money toward the cost of the conference, the party was content for now to remain in the background. Communist leaders believed, as Randolph did, that the "proletarian elements" of the Black community must lead the effort. With the left and centrist factions agreed on this vital point, Davis set about making it so.[30]

· · ·

On June 10, 1936, roughly four months after the first congress, Davis shared his plan to organize Black steel workers with the AFL's Committee for Industrial Organization. Davis shared several of these plans with the AFL, each with the same formula: a rundown of the economic conditions of Black workers in a given industry, a summary of what the NNC had already done to organize those workers, an appeal to the AFL to finance a national campaign, and an outline of next steps.[31]

It just so happened that John Brophy, Director of the AFL industrial committee, was also thinking of collaborating with the NNC. In a letter dated June 11, 1936, Brophy asked Adolph Germer, a former Socialist Party leader turned AFL field representative, to arrange a visit of the NNC leadership to the Midwest, "because . . . their good will is very important in both the steel and auto organizing campaigns that are in prospect." Brophy reported that Davis had been in his office the previous day (perhaps to hand-deliver his plan to organize steel) and said that the National Negro Congress was holding a meeting in Cleveland on June 19–20. While in Cleveland, Davis buttonholed Van Bittner of the Steel Workers Organizing Committee (SWOC) at the Hollenden Hotel and persuaded him to start a campaign that would organize 85,000 Black workers. Davis argued that such a step was necessary to avoid the racial divisions that led to the defeat of the steel strikes in 1919. Eventually Bittner asked Davis to do "a careful survey of Negro trade unionists in the Great Lakes area," with the goal of putting them on staff as SWOC organizers. Davis recommended three at the outset—Henry Johnson, Eleanor Rye, and Leonidas McDonald—to organize the Chicago-Northwest Indiana steel corridor. Davis would recruit seven organizers for the region in total. He would also write the literature that SWOC used to recruit Black steel workers. So involved was he in the steel campaign that Bittner invited Davis to all of SWOC's closed-door meetings.[32]

Johnson, Rye, and McDonald—the so-called "triumvirate"— succeeded beyond even Davis's wildest dreams. Before organizing for the NNC, Eleanor Rye had been a volunteer leader in the Women's Auxiliary of the Brotherhood of Sleeping Car Porters in Chicago and was working on staff at the furriers' union. Her role in the steel campaign was to reach Black workers through their wives. Working with BSCP Women's Auxiliary president Helena Wilson and SWOC organizer Minneola Ingersol, Rye was able to conduct organizing conversations in workers' homes, as opposed to open meetings. Rye used these intimate one-on-one conversations—the building blocks of any good campaign—to recruit effective rank-and-file organizing committees, which in turn built to successful mass meetings in places like the Metropolitan Community Church in Chicago's Bronzeville neighborhood. From there, Rye brought Black women out of the home and into the regular meetings at SWOC lodges. Despite pulling second and third shifts as a wife and mother, Rye, in addition to being an excellent organizer, was also the campaign's communications chief. She cultivated strong relationships with reporters and generated positive news coverage in the Black press that helped to propel the campaign.[33]

Leonidas McDonald and Henry Johnson, who were SWOC's lead organizers in South Chicago and Gary, Indiana, respectively, also developed vibrant member-led organizing committees. By early 1937, they had organized more than half of all Calumet steel workers, comprising 115 separate SWOC lodges, and won strikes at Wilson & Bennet Company and half a dozen other South Chicago plants. Perhaps the most infamous campaign involved the Memorial Day Massacre at Republic Steel, in which eight thousand Black workers walked off the job. The police killed ten strikers, including Lee Tisdale who died of infected bullet wounds after being in jail for days without treatment. Upon hearing of the tragedy, the workers resolved to fight fire with fire and bring guns to the next picket. Joe Cook, a rank-and-file leader and veteran of the 1919 steel strikes, reportedly lifted a picket sign and said, "Men, this is our gun. So long as you keep our ranks united, they can't beat us—so hold that line!" For six weeks, Cook and his compatriots never once permitted a scab to cross. On July 8, 1937, Republic Steel and the workers settled. Due to heroic efforts like these, the NNC organized thousands of Black steel workers in South Chicago and Indiana, who, in turn, joined interracial SWOC lodges with relatively little backlash from white members. When former US President Barack Obama and others say that they once worked with steel workers in the Southside of Chicago, they are speaking about the unions that the NNC built. George Kimbley, a Black organizer in Gary at the time, wrote to John P. Davis with pride of the "tireless [work] of our Congress" and the "bonds of . . . unity between black and white workers." One reporter would write of NNC organizers Rye, Johnson, and McDonald that their work in the Chicago region "advanced race relations at least ten years."[34]

Nor was the Chicago-Gary corridor the only region that the NNC organized. Leading NNC and SWOC officials organized a joint meeting on February 7, 1937, in Pittsburgh to coordinate logistics for campaigns in the South and across the Midwest. SWOC official Philip Murray assured the audience of Black steel workers that he would not permit racial discrimination on the campaign. Also in attendance were Davis and four Black organizers: Henry Johnson of Gary; Maude White of Cleveland; William E. Hill of Pittsburgh; and Joseph Howard of Birmingham, Alabama. Erik S. Gellman, historian of the NNC, writes that after the Pittsburgh conference, follow-up meetings in the steel industry "grew like mushrooms."[35]

And so, when the National Negro Congress met in Philadelphia at its second annual meeting in 1937, the mood was one of forward momentum. In his introductory remarks, John P. Davis said, "Under the banner of the Committee for Industrial Organization we have won new victories; tens of thousands who heretofore have not been a part of organized labor have gained increases in pay, shorter hours at work and improved living conditions." The resolutions committee of the second NNC therefore urged continuing pressure on the white-led labor movement to support the organization of Black workers. The assembly resolved, "That the National Negro Congress go on record in calling upon both the A.F. of L. and the C.I.O. to cement the unity of the Labor Movement to further the gains in the organizing of the unorganized workers and particularly the unorganized Negro worker in the United States." President A. Philip Randolph echoed these sentiments with his characteristic flair, saying, "On the far flung battle lines of steel, it marshalled militant black men to march in the van with the C.I.O. to chalk up an enviable record in bringing workers into the field of industrial organization." He also looked forward to emerging campaigns in other industries, saying, "The Congress has brought eager and aggressive black youth to grapple with the problem of the organization of the tobacco workers in Virginia. . . . And it enlisted Negro organizers to C.I.O. forces to organize the automobile industry."[36]

Indeed, in addition to inaugurating the steel campaign, Davis traveled to Detroit and helped form the Black nucleus of the United Auto Workers (UAW). In a retrospective interview, local NNC leader C. LeBron Simmons said, "Davis came to Detroit to seek people, I don't know how he got my name, but he came to my office and asked me would I be interested in helping to find the organization that wanted to go all out in the struggle for the freedom of black folks. So I said yes." Simmons recalled bringing together a group of activists who included James Walker, Paul Kirk, Vera Vandenberg, and perhaps most famously Coleman Young, who would go on to be an officer in the left-led National Negro Labor Council in the 1950s and later mayor of Detroit. Simmons, who was an attorney and served as president of the Detroit NNC, said that the NNC blended civil rights activism with union organizing. For example, when Black people attempted to move in to the Sojourner Truth housing projects, white residents rioted, overturning cars and trucks and physically assaulting Black people in the surrounding neighborhood. Simmons and the Detroit NNC defended the prospective Black residents in court with a coalition of white progressives in the Civil Rights Congress and the "benign support" of the NAACP. Noting that "the National Negro Congress was instrumental in helping to organize the CIO," Simmons went as far as to say of the UAW that "we had been the forbears of the union." He said, "I know some of the very people who had been the leaders and who had walked on the picket line with me, on the picket lines at Budwheel, at Chevrolet Gear and Axle, and at Chevrolet, and Kelsey-Hayes in this city." By far the Detroit NNC's most consequential victory was in organizing the Ford Motor Company. A group of militant Black unionists that included Shelton Tappes, Coleman Young, and John Conyers, Sr., had been organizing Ford workers for five years when the NNC hosted a conference in April 1941 that proved decisive. The speakers were John P. Davis, NAACP chief Walter White, and most significantly, the Black artist and radical Paul Robeson. By all accounts, the event was the final galvanizing moment that pushed the union to victory.[37]

Though the youth arm of the NNC did the lion's share of organizing, Davis conducted the strategic research and obtained modest institutional backing for the Southern tobacco campaign. In another proposal to John Brophy, he outlined the conditions on the ground. He wrote that 68 percent of tobacco workers at the four largest companies in Kentucky, North Carolina, and Virginia were Black. This included the behemoth R. J. Reynolds. Drawing on a survey of five tobacco plants, Davis found that the employers, like so many in the South, divided the work at their plants by race: white workers tended to work as foremen, chippers, and in other less dirty occupations, whereas Black workers worked as stemmers and pickers for the least pay, with average hourly wages of $0.25 to $0.30 and annual wages of $750. Next, Davis noted that the Southern Negro Youth Conference (SNYC), and in particular a talented young Black organizer named Columbus Alston, had laid the groundwork for a far-reaching union drive. By 1937, SNYC had already staged the first sit-down strike ever held in Virginia. As a result, 350 Black workers at the Carrington and Michaux tobacco factory won a 33 percent wage increase. SNYC organized a second strike that yielded a 20 percent wage increase for 468 workers, this time at I. N. Vaughan and Company. The speed and reach of the campaign, Davis stressed, were now outstripping SNYC's capacity to keep up. Membership in both unionized plants was at 100 percent; in just four short weeks, NNC youth organizers had formed four locals and signed up 1,154 workers for an average of over 250 members a week, all with an entirely volunteer staff. "On the basis of these developments," Davis wrote, "we wish to propose to the Committee for Industrial Organization the formation of a national tobacco workers organizing committee similar to those already installed in steel, textile, rubber and other industries." Crucially, he insisted that the tobacco campaign must be Black-led: "We believe that such a committee ought to be begun under Negro leadership both because of the absolute predominance of Negro labor in this industry and because of the tremendous prestige which such a move would give the CIO among the million and a half Negro industrial workers throughout the country." He added that Black workers and staff "would utilize large numbers of white workers and organizers in bringing in the minority of white workers employed in the industry."[38]

Davis's insistence on Black leadership was not mere posturing: it reflected the fact that Black people were leading the struggle on the ground. It was in fact a Black woman who first yelled "Strike!" at the Carrington and Michaux factory on the morning of April 17, 1937, and prompted other workers to stop working. Moreover, when the striking workers went to the white-led AFL and the newly founded Congress of Industrial Organizations (CIO) to ask for help, CIO staff said they did not have a tobacco union in place to organize them, while the AFL's racist Tobacco Workers International Union (TWIU) refused to let the Black tobacco workers affiliate. The workers thus founded their own independent union: the Tobacco Stemmers and Laborers Union (TSLU). It was only after the strike at Carrington and Michaux spread to the Vaughan factory that the big labor federations responded. John Suttle of the CIO took on James Jackson and Columbus Alston as volunteer organizers. Because he did not offer to pay them as the CIO had paid other organizers in the steel drive, Jackson and Alston were forced to work other jobs to make ends meet. The AFL's TWIU, too, rushed to claim the members of the TSLU, but the workers and organizers refused. Davis was to say, "You should have seen how the A.F. of L. rushed over to us with open arms after all the fighting was done . . . but we said no." From that point forward, the AFL attempted to sink the new union through a vicious combination of race- and red-baiting. Undaunted, the TSLU would go on to organize and strike two more plants in Richmond from 1937 to 1938. On June 30, 1937, two thousand TSLU members marched through the former capital of the Confederacy in support of a third campaign, this time at the Tobacco By-Product and Chemical Plant in Richmond's Fulton neighborhood. The struggle lasted into July, when the 160 strikers, who fought to be reclassified as skilled workers, were able to get wage increases but based on the old job classifications. Organizing then spread to the Export Leaf Tobacco Company, where 200 workers signed a contract on August 31, 1938, covering pay increases, vacation time, and a checkoff system for collecting union dues.[39]

Apart from the fact that Black people were in the vanguard of the tobacco struggle, two other facets of the campaign were distinctive. The first was that Black women—especially Mildred Hansley, a Carrington and Michaux employee—were the core leadership in tobacco. At a "Richmond Negro Forum" hosted by SNYC and led by Augusta Jackson in February 1938, renowned Black activist Louise Thompson gave a speech titled "The Place of Women in a Changing World," in which she reminded the audience that the majority of tobacco workers were Black women. Augusta Jackson would later recall, "The ones who talk to the press and take bows very often are men," but, she added, "women and black women have borne the great part of the heroism." Further, the struggle in Richmond provided the blueprint for a later upsurge in interracial organizing that spawned legendary Local 22 of the Food, Tobacco, and Agricultural workers union (FTA) in the 1940s. For example, Theodosia Simpson, who helped to organize R. J. Reynolds in North Carolina, had also been a SNYC organizer in her spare time. FTA and the CIO would go on to organize eight thousand workers in Virginia and twenty thousand workers in North Carolina.[40]

Black workers also led the fight to organize Chicago's giant meatpacking industry. Inspired by the steel campaign, a group of packinghouse workers asked SWOC to charter a similar organization called the Packinghouse Workers Organizing Committee (PWOC). In the spring of 1937, SWOC paid their organizer Hank Johnson to work on the campaign based on the earlier agreement with Davis and the NNC. The campaign began in Back of the Yards, the neighborhood just west of Bronzeville, with Black workers on the "killing floors" of several small meatpacking plants. Johnson organized regular mass meetings outside the hiring hall of Armour and Company. These smaller meetings built to a mass demonstration of several thousand Black workers at Du Sable High School in 1938. Randolph, who spoke at the meeting, was so optimistic about the campaign's prospects that he said, "The opportunity for the service of the Congress in the liberation movement of the Negro people is greater now than ever before." The campaign only grew from there. At another large rally held in July 1939, CIO president John L. Lewis himself spoke alongside Hank Johnson, who was by then PWOC assistant director. In all, PWOC and the NNC organized a total of fourteen local unions in a matter of two short years. Black workers were presidents of nine.[41]

. . .

From the beginning, Randolph had been convinced that the success of the NNC would depend on maintaining the strategy of a united front. No one organization should control the congress, he warned, for Black civil society would only unify around the broadest possible program. For example, at the 1937 NNC meeting in Philadelphia, he reminded the audience,

> the Congress is not Communist or Republican, Democratic or Socialist. It is not Methodist, Baptist or Christian Scientist. It avoids control by any single religion or political party. It shuns the Scylla and Charybdis of the extreme left and the extreme right. But, in the true spirit of the united front, and in the pattern and purpose of integration and coordination, for mass strength, embraces all sections of opinion among the Negro people.

Randolph never wavered from this position, and in fact defended the congress from repeated charges that it was a front for other organizations. Accordingly, when he arrived at the 1940 congress in Washington to find it in thrall to the Communist Party and the CIO, Randolph felt blindsided.[42]

The backdrop to this moment was the Second World War. In 1939, Josef Stalin and Adolf Hitler signed the Nazi-Soviet Nonaggression Pact, agreeing not to fight each other in the ever-widening European theater. After years of antifascist organizing, the Communist Party in the United States performed a shocking about-face. They rallied around the slogan, "The Yanks are not coming," and criticized the Roosevelt administration for preparing the American public to go to war. Meanwhile, Labor's Non-Partisan League (LNPL), which had been the New Deal's electoral machine inside the white-led labor movement, was also aligning with the Communists, though for their own reasons. CIO president John L. Lewis had by that point turned the LNPL into an advocacy group for his own ideological convictions. Lewis, unlike other LNPL leaders such as ILGWU president Sidney Hillman, was a lifelong Republican. In line with his party, Lewis favored isolationism in foreign affairs and thus opposed America's entrance into the war. Due to their roots in the Harlem Left and their success in organizing industrial workers, the overwhelming majority of delegates to the 1940 National Negro Congress were CIO and CP members, and it showed.

The meeting took place at the US Department of Labor in Washington, the very heart of the New Deal apparatus, but it was overwhelmingly anti-Roosevelt. The NNC's honorary guest was John L. Lewis. Randolph found himself awkwardly attending Davis as he greeted the CIO and LNPL leader and gave him a plaque for his support of Black workers. When the congress opened, it was not Randolph or Davis, the NNC's leading officers, who welcomed the delegates, but Lewis. Ever the skillful orator, Lewis set the majority-Black audience against the White House. Noting that Roosevelt "frightened a hall full of elderly ladies with immoderate and fantastic stories of plots against our country by foreign powers," he advised the government instead to "use their influence and high office to enact Federal anti-lynching legislation, so long delayed by the cowardly tactics of those who would knife it behind the scenes." Widening the aperture to include the broader working class, he added, "it is easier to interest the rich and powerful in sending other people's sons to Borneo than it is to get them to concern themselves about providing jobs and education for other people's sons." "There are people in this country who want to get us into war," he said, and proclaimed with finality, "We must not go to war." The speech drew thunderous applause.[43]

Thus when Randolph, the leading Black trade unionist in America, took to the podium, speaking second at his own meeting behind a white man, he knew that there would be trouble. In his speech, titled "The World Crisis and the Negro People Today," Randolph confessed, "Personally, I would not be a member of the Negro Congress, or any other organization which was a Communist Front or Transmission Belt, not only because I reject the Communist program, but because I wouldn't be a part of any organization which hypocritically professed one thing and did another." The task of the delegates, therefore, was "to wipe out the stigma of the Communist Front charge and make the Negro Congress an organization which is genuinely, in fact and function, what the name expresses and implies, a Negro Congress of Negro organizations, committed primarily to the liberation of the Negro people, sustained by Negroes' resources, for Negroes themselves must pay the price in sacrifice and struggle for their own hope and future." In contrast, the Soviet Union was not committed to their cause. He said, "Since the Communist Party of America stems from Communist Russia, its policies and program, tactics and strategy are as fitful, changeful and unpredictable as the foreign policy and line of Moscow. The Communist Party is not primarily, or fundamentally, concerned about the Negro or labor in

America, but with . . . the consolidation of the foreign position of the Soviet Union in world politics."[44]

Howard University professor Ralph Bunche, who had organized the conference with Davis, would later recount that as Randolph spoke, the audience dwindled from 1,700 to around one-third that size. The exodus began with a contingent of white Communists and grew into a stampede of offended delegates. The Black author Ralph Ellison was to say that he found Randolph's arguments "strange in the mouth of one who was supposed to be their leader." He added, "I did not realize it, but I had witnessed a leader in the act of killing his leadership."[45]

Randolph's remarks were so incendiary, in fact, that Davis felt the need to respond. He stayed up all night rewriting the report he was meant to give the following evening. Just before midnight on Saturday, April 27, Davis climbed the platform and tied his antiwar position to the NNC's two biggest sponsors. With respect to the CIO, he said, "We shall do well to heed the thrice-repeated warning of John L. Lewis against 'ventures abroad,' while there is growing misery at home." And he framed any criticism of the CIO within the congress as a betrayal of the cause of Black liberation. "Long has the Negro worker waited the extended hand of organized labor," he said, asking, "Are there those who would have us turn our back upon the friendly offer made by John L. Lewis in the name of labor last night? If there be such we are doubtful of their loyalty to the cause of our people." Of the Communist Party, Davis said,

> I have visited the Soviet Union. I have talked to the Soviet people. . . . I know of their deep friendship and aid to all oppressed peoples. And on the basis of that experience and knowledge, which is shared by thousands of people, I firmly believe that the American Negro people will refuse to follow victims to anti-Soviet adventures, will refuse to join American or world imperialism in any attack against the Soviet people.

Davis thus articulated for the record what many others were saying informally on the floor of the congress, namely, that if the United States were to go to war against the Soviet Union, African Americans would not fight.[46]

The back-and-forth between the centrist and left factions of the NNC, a conflict that had been latent since its founding, culminated in the Resolutions Committee meeting on Sunday morning, April 28. The committee proposed a "Resolution on the Imperialist War" that stated, "BE IT RESOLVED that the National Negro Congress declares that the Negro people have everything to lose and nothing to gain by American involvement in the imperialist war and sharply condemns the administration for the steps it has taken and the partiality already shown." In response, Edgar Brown, a Black federal employee, rose to defend the Roosevelt administration's foreign policy and position on civil rights. When the audience interrupted Brown's objection with boos and hisses, Randolph, who was chairing the meeting, scolded the assembled crowd. Brown continued by praising Randolph for being the greatest Black union leader in the history of the United States, a remark that received only polite applause. John P. Davis then rose in support of the resolution, and the committee passed it by acclimation.[47]

The Resolutions Committee then turned to the question of endorsing the LNPL. The body proposed the following resolution: "RESOLVED that a Committee of five be appointed by the incoming Executive Committee to explore the possibilities by which this Congress can work together with Labor's Non-Partisan League." Randolph rose to oppose the resolution on familiar grounds. Referring to the League's antiwar position, he said, "I am in opposition to the resolution on the grounds that it is in violation of the minimum program of the Congress. . . . A minimum program is one on which all members can agree. By aligning the Congress with the League you are breaking up the Congress." When the congress adopted the report of the

Resolutions Committee over his objections, including the resolutions on the LNPL and the Imperialist War, Randolph made a decision that would shape the trajectory not only of the NNC, but also of Black labor in general.[48]

Speaking without prepared remarks, Randolph said that the NNC had reached a point in its development when it had departed from the strategy of articulating minimum demands upon which all of Black civil society could agree. He disclosed that he himself disagreed with some of the policies just adopted. Then he said, "For these reasons it is impossible for me to continue as President of the Congress," adding, "whenever the Congress is tied up too closely with any organization, it loses its mass character. . . . We have received donations from the Communist Party, and that is not a healthy condition. . . . The Congress will be responsible to the organization from which it gets its money. . . . For these reasons I have concluded that I can no longer serve."[49]

With that, almost as if the NNC had been preparing for this moment, the Presiding Committee of the Congress rushed to name the Communist Max Yergen the new president. Though his ideological commitments were with the Left of the NNC, Ralph Bunche recalled Randolph's resignation with deep regret. Four months after the third congress, he wrote,

I could not help but reflect while this transpired that the one Negro among all those present who had really worked and sacrificed in the labor movement among Negroes, and who was thoroughly steeped in Negro working-class lore, was being replaced by a rank neophyte, a former YMCA Secretary, who had long engaged in missionary work in South Africa, and who now can only parrot the slogans laid down in Party tracts. . . . In my estimation, the Negro Congress dug its own grave at this meeting. It will now be reduced to a Communist cell.

If anyone else agreed with Professor Bunche's private thoughts, an observer would not have known it. The audience greeted the presidential succession with a standing ovation, as if this were the finest news they had ever heard. Randolph retired from his position with grace. Before leaving, he handed the gavel over to Yergen and stepped off the stage.[50]

.   .   .

Randolph's next act was shaped as much by the Second World War as his previous one. For if his colleagues' antiwar position pushed him out of the NNC, then racial discrimination in the armed forces and the defense industry pulled him into a new project: the March on Washington Movement (MOWM). The NNC was founded in large part to make the promise of the New Deal accessible to Black workers during the Great Depression. By 1940, Black workers were facing a new crisis. The robust economic growth of the 1940s owed much to the manufacture of munitions, tanks, and airplanes for the war effort, yet the defense industry refused to hire Black people, and in fact had as their policy never to do so. The president of North American Aviation, for example, declared, "regardless of training, we will not employ Negroes in the North American plants. It is against company policy." Likewise, when the Urban League inquired about job opportunities for Black workers in Kansas City, the Standard Steel Corporation replied, "We have not had a Negro worker in twenty-five years, and do not plan to start now." Nor was this only a problem with employers, for white-led unions continued to systematically exclude Black people from their ranks. When Black workers in Seattle asked to be considered for employment at a Boeing Aircraft plant, an official of the International Association of Machinists said, "Labor has been asked to make many sacrifices in this war and has made them gladly, but this sacrifice . . . is too great." The result of the color line in the defense industry and labor movement was a crisis of underemployment in the Black community to rival that of the Depression. In June 1942, the Federal Security Agency reported that "Over 500,000 Negroes who should be utilized in war production are now idle because of the discriminatory hiring practices of war industries. Several million other Negroes engaged in unskilled occupations are prevented from making greater contributions."[51]

As the crisis unfolded, Randolph returned to his work with the Brotherhood of Sleeping Car Porters, who, like other members of the Black community, were offended by the rampant discrimination in the armed forces. At the Brotherhood's fifteenth anniversary convention in September 1940, the delegates passed a resolution calling upon government officials "to see to it that no discrimination is practiced against American citizens entering all departments of the Army, Navy and Air corps on account of race or color." It just so happened that someone who had the ear of President Roosevelt was at that convention: Eleanor Roosevelt. The First Lady was for all intents and purposes the President's ambassador to Black civil society, and upon receiving a request for a meeting with the cabinet on the armed forces question, she called the President's secretary, Stephen Early, to set it up.[52]

The meeting was a disaster. On the morning of September 27, 1940, Walter White of the NAACP, T. Arnold Hill of the National Urban League, and Randolph submitted a memorandum to the White House calling for the integration of all defense preparations and met in conference with the President and Joint Chiefs of Staff. Two weeks later, on October 9, Stephen Early called a press conference, in which he told reporters that the President had held a meeting with Black leaders and "As a result of that conference the War Department has drafted a statement of policy with regard to Negroes in national defense . . . not to intermingle colored and white enlisted personnel in the same regimental organizations." The impression Early gave was that the White House and the leadership of the African American community had agreed to keep the armed forces segregated. Black leaders—who were not privy to White, Hill, and Randolph's memorandum to the Administration—called their three representatives "sellouts." Neither the president nor Early issued a public apology or retraction to disabuse them of this interpretation.[53]

Still, the White House meeting was productive in the sense that its abject failure made Randolph rethink his strategy. Milton Webster, the longtime leader of the Brotherhood's Chicago local, recalled the precise moment when Randolph began to formulate a new approach. In December 1940, just as the two leaders embarked on a tour by rail of the union's southern locals, Randolph turned to Webster and said, "You know, Web, calling on the President and holding those conferences are not going to get us anywhere." Webster, who was a Republican, was pleased to hear a bad word said about Roosevelt, but his mood changed when Randolph continued, "We are going to have to do something about it. . . . I think we ought to get 10,000 Negroes to march on Washington in protest, march down Pennsylvania Avenue. What do you think of that?" When Webster asked, "Where are we going to get 10,000 Negroes?" Randolph replied simply, "I think we can get them."[54]

Things moved very quickly from there. On January 15, 1941, Randolph issued a statement that was printed in newspapers across the country. In it he wrote, "Negro America must bring its power and pressure to bear upon the agencies and representatives of the Federal Government to exact their rights in National Defense employment and the armed forces of the country. . . . I suggest that TEN THOUSAND Negroes march on Washington, D.C. . . . with the slogan: 'WE LOYAL NEGRO AMERICAN CITIZENS DEMAND THE RIGHT TO WORK AND FIGHT FOR OUR COUNTRY'" [emphasis in original]. Benjamin McLaurin, one of the Brotherhood's founders and now a union official, remembered that after Randolph's statement, "It got out of hand almost overnight. People began writing us, 'What can we do?' How could they go about getting groups together?"[55]

It was once again labor who called upon the other sectors of Black civil society to join the effort. Though the NAACP and Urban League were not at that point familiar with the rhetoric or tactics of mass mobilization, they agreed to participate, largely because of Randolph's stature in the community. Lester B. Granger of the Urban League was to say, "It was Randolph's immense prestige among all classes of Negroes that made this idea something more than a pretentious notion."[56]

Like the NNC before it, the March on Washington Movement attempted to be a genuine mass organization, anchored among real people in the grassroots. The organization had three levels. At the top was the March on Washington Committee, officered by Randolph, and a Sponsoring Committee consisting of labor and civil rights leaders with genuine ties to the rank and file. They included people like Walter White, Lester Granger, Frank Crosswaith of the Negro Labor Committee, Reverend Adam Clayton Powell, Jr., E. E. Williams of the Blasters and Drillers union, Noah Walters of the Laundry Workers Joint Board, and Layle Lane of the American Federation of Teachers. Regional Committees operated at the intermediate level in cities across the country with support from local unions of the Brotherhood. These committees, in turn, sent out volunteer organizers to mobilize the grassroots in beauty parlors, street corners, shops, and bars. Unions provided the bulk of the funding and staff on the ground. It was rank-and-file members who organized the marchers and arranged transport to Washington by bus and rail.[57]

In the course of organizing, Randolph hit on a sly tactical innovation. Knowing that the FBI was surveilling his every move and word, he began to up the ante. In the streets of Harlem he spoke not of 10,000, but of 100,000, marchers descending on the nation's capital on July 1, 1941. In May, he wrote, "When 100,000 Negroes march on

Washington, it will wake up Negro was well as white America. . . . I call upon Negroes everywhere . . . to gird for an epoch-making march and demonstration. . . . Let the Negro masses march! Let the Negro masses speak!"[58]

Sure enough, the Washington elite lost their minds. Eleanor Roosevelt wrote to Randolph, saying, "I feel very strongly that your group is making a very grave mistake at the present time to allow this march to take place. . . . It may engender so much bitterness that it will create in Congress even more solid opposition from certain groups than we have had in the past." Stephen Early, on instructions from the President, then moved to enlist Randolph's friend, New York Mayor Fiorello LaGuardia, to intercede. Roosevelt reportedly told National Youth Administration head Aubrey Williams to "Go to New York and try to talk Randolph and White out of this march. Get the missus and Fiorello and [presidential aide] Anna [Rosenberg] and get it stopped." Meanwhile, Wayne Coy of the Office of Emergency Management urged FDR to support a bill in Congress that would have established a committee to investigate discrimination in national defense. Former labor leader Sidney Hillman, now with the Office of Production Management, mailed a circular to defense plants encouraging them to hire Black workers. Roosevelt, it seemed, was throwing everything he had at Randolph, but none of it worked. When the First Lady appealed to Randolph at the meeting with LaGuardia, the labor leader apologized but stuck to his guns. He said, "the march would not be called off unless the President issued an executive order banning discrimination in the defense industry."[59]

So it was that Randolph and Walter White once again found themselves in a conference with the president. Also in attendance were Henry Stimson, Secretary of War; Robert Patterson, Undersecretary of War; Frank Knox, Secretary of the Navy; William Knudsen and Sidney Hillman, of the Office of Production Management; Anna Rosenberg, the president's aide; Aubrey Williams; and LaGuardia. The meeting began amiably enough, with Roosevelt saying, "Hello, Phil. Which class were you in at Harvard?" When Randolph reminded him that he never went to Harvard, the President recovered, saying, "Anyway, you and I share a kinship in our great interest in human and social justice." Randolph replied, "That's right, Mr. President."[60]

Roosevelt attempted to distract the group with a filibuster of charming anecdotes, but Randolph cut to the chase. He said, "Mr. President, time is running out. You are busy. We want specifically to talk to you about the problem of jobs for Negroes in defense industries. Our people are being turned away at factory gates because they are colored. They can't live with this thing. What are you going to do about it?" When the president asked, "What do you want me to do?" Randolph replied, "We want you to issue an executive order making it mandatory that Negroes be permitted to work in these plants." Roosevelt declined, citing the familiar logic of the "slippery slope" and implying that he would not negotiate with a gun to his head. He said, "Well, Phil, you know I can't do that. If I issue an executive order for you, then there'll be no end to other groups coming in here and asking me to issue executive orders for them, too. In any event, I couldn't do anything unless you called off this march of yours. Questions like this have sociological implications. They can't be gotten at with hammers and tongs. They can't be settled with marches." Randolph pointed out that that such questions could not be settled with good intentions either.[61]

It was at this point that the president cut to his own chase. The negotiation came down to just how much power Randolph had amassed to back up his threat. Did he have the numbers or was he bluffing? The president looked at Randolph, appearing to take the measure of the man. He asked, "How many people do you plan to bring?" Randolph said, "One hundred thousand, Mr. President." Roosevelt then turned to Walter White, as if to suggest that the more moderate NAACP would tell him the truth, if the truth be otherwise. "Walter, how many people will really march?" he asked. White looked the President dead in the eye and said, "One hundred thousand, Mr. President."[62]

The number having been confirmed by both the howling socialist and the mainstream civil rights advocate, the president became genuinely alarmed. He said, "You can't bring 100,000 Negroes to Washington! Somebody might get killed!" Randolph assured him that no one would get hurt so long as the president addressed the audience. When FDR, now clearly incensed, returned to his earlier objection that he would not be ruled with a gun to his head, Randolph simply replied, "Then, Mr. President, something will have to be done and done at once." Roosevelt dug in his heels, saying, "Something will be done, but there must be no public pressure on the White House." Then, raising his deep voice to Roosevelt, Randolph boomed, "Mr. President, something must be done now!"[63]

To avoid an impasse, Mayor LaGuardia stepped in at once and suggested that he, Randolph, and the president's aides retire to the Cabinet Room to formulate a solution. When the group attempted to foist on Randolph the plan of asking defense contractors to hire more Black workers, an offer that the labor leader had already declined, both Randolph and LaGuardia rejected it out of hand. Eventually it was decided that a committee of five people would draft an executive order for the president to consider. That job fell to a young attorney named Joseph L. Rauh, whose drafts Randolph rejected over and over again for not being strong enough. Frustrated, Rauh reportedly marched in to see his superiors and said, "Who the hell is this guy Randolph? What the hell has he got over the President of the United States?" As it turns out, Randolph liked Rauh's next draft and his aides sent the language to Roosevelt to sign.[64]

But at the last moment, the president refused to sign the order and let the document sit on his desk for several days. Randolph deftly responded to the inaction by inviting Eleanor Roosevelt to speak to the marchers at the Lincoln Memorial. The invitation went out on June 23, eight days before the scheduled march. Acting on instructions from the First Lady, Anna Rosenberg "bought a new hat, marched into the president's office, fished out the order, and said, 'Sign it, Mr. President—sign it.'" Randolph's last-minute tactical maneuver worked: a memo from Roosevelt to the executive clerk Rudolph Forster reads, "Fix up for me a sign and send to Attorney General for language. Quick." Attorney General Robert H. Jackson did so on June 25, and President Roosevelt signed and issued Executive Order 8802 that same day. The order, which was the first major act of government since Reconstruction to improve the social conditions of Black Americans, prohibited employment discrimination in the defense industry and established a Fair Employment Practice Commission (FEPC) to hear complaints from the Black community if defense contractors refused to comply. For the second time in his career, Randolph canceled a major national demonstration, but this time he got what he wanted when he wanted it.[65]

· · ·

The March on Washington Movement forced the entirety of Black civil society to choose whether to join or step aside, and in this the National Negro Congress was no exception. It was a difficult decision for the NNC as Randolph had broken publicly with them, yet in the span of just one year organized by far the most important mass movement in America. At an Administrative Committee meeting attended by National Secretary John P. Davis and Youth Congress head Edward Strong, the NNC leadership attempted to strike a balance of not condemning the March on the one hand, and on the other hand continuing a positive agenda of pushing for Black employment in key industries. In a letter to Edward Strong, dated May 27, 1941, about a month before the scheduled march, Davis explained,

Why did we take such a position? We took it because any other course would be bound to lead to our isolating ourselves from the masses of the people. A great many people have come to me recently to ask the question 'How can we head off, how can we counteract, how can we nullify and destroy the Randolph march'? Others have said how can we maneuver to 'capture the movement'? My own opinion has been that there is a danger in such remarks. . . . [T]he very fact that the Negro press and a large section of local Negro leadership in a number of communities is actively engaged in support of the idea of a mass march on Washington would make it dangerous for us to attempt to discredit the march. Indeed we have no desire to discredit militant action of any group of people sincerely seeking jobs for the Negro people.

The NNC leadership's biggest fear was of isolating itself from the Black masses. Black America, including the Black press, was aflame with organizing for the March. Indeed, Davis went on to write that the MOWM had penetrated all aspects of Black life such that, for example, the Alpha Kappa Alpha sorority and Mary McLeod Bethune had organized a Conference for Negro Women as a way to activate their membership in advance of the March.[66]

This is not to say that the NNC had stopped resenting Randolph. Far from it. Davis, who had been Randolph's friend in the early years of the congress, went so far as to confide to Strong that he thought Randolph's position was morally bankrupt. Davis was especially critical of Randolph's decision to exclude white marchers and support the war, all while criticizing the progressive CIO and joining "Negro-baiters like [AFL president] William Green." He also found problematic Randolph's "splitting tactics," which had "the definite purpose to split away from the campaign precisely those forces that would give it the greatest impetus, namely the Congress and progressive labor movement."[67]

Though the NNC sincerely thought to pursue their own agenda in the area of Black industrial employment, the MOWM ended up shaping the NNC's practices anyway. On the very same day that Davis wrote to Strong, he also wrote a form letter to all members of the US Congress saying, "Dear Congressman: The situation confronting Negro skilled workers seeking employment in defense industries has become extremely acute. . . . This letter comes to you to solicit your interest in this grave problem." The NNC held to the MOWM line, especially after Randolph secured Executive Order 8802. Davis in fact used his relationships with the CIO's left-led unions to institutionalize the order in their rules and practices. In August 1941, two months after President Roosevelt signed the executive order, Davis wrote to James Carey, president of the United Electrical workers (UE), informing him that the goal of the NNC's Philadelphia Council, "following the President's Executive Order on June 25th, is to call upon labor unions and employers to break down barriers to the employment of Negroes in defense industries." He added, "I am sure a public statement from you on this would be of tremendous importance in our fight to get skilled jobs for Negro Workers and would result in further cementing the ties between Negro people and trade unions." On September 9, Carey wrote back to Davis, reporting that he had discussed the matter with UE leaders at their convention in Camden, New Jersey and that "positive steps will be taken to bring about a proper application of the President's Executive Order and the policies of the UE."[68]

The NNC chalked up a few other high-profile victories in this regard. The congress worked with the CIO's regional office in Baltimore to pressure the Glenn L. Martin Aircraft Company into integrating their workforce. Davis wrote hopefully, "Hundreds of Negro workers who will go into the factory will recognize that it was the National Negro Congress which made their employment possible." The CIO's regional director Frank Bender acknowledged the NNC's "willingness to cooperate to bring these employees into the CIO-UAW" and promised, "As soon as employment of Negro workers begins, I shall be glad to have a conference with you on a unified procedure to this end."[69]

Though the NNC was able to secure the cooperation of the CIO on occasion, the latter's top leadership was cool to the NNC's broader vision of interracial solidarity. For Davis, the organization of steel was meant to be a two-step process: interracial union membership, followed by first-class citizenship in the labor movement. Davis revealed his hopes of the relationship with the steel workers' union: "Once Negro workers are in the union . . . it must be our task and theirs to see to it that there is a complete trade union democracy." The Steel Workers Organizing Committee's white leadership, however, had no interest in first-class citizenship for Black members or any other agenda beyond working "24 hours a day" organizing steel workers. SWOC leader Van Bittner said, "Forget Spain situation, auto situation, and other world problems. . . . We are dictating all policies of all lodges until steel is organized." Whereas SWOC was once willing to split the costs of hiring NNC organizers in the Midwest, Phil Murray eventually began rebuffing Davis's requests for more staff and pamphlets, including a critical appeal for a staff member to organize steel workers in the South.[70]

The change in SWOC's attitude tracks with the experience of NNC activists with other CIO affiliates. For example, Detroit NNC president C. LeBron Simmons, in a retrospective interview, reflected on the abrupt shift in the United Auto Workers' (UAW) posture toward the NNC after organizing the Ford Motor Company. He said,

They no longer needed you. . . . Yeah, because they'd become established. They had become established; they had become respected. So they began to take over . . . because, once that they had organized themselves, they had adopted some of the same things that the

establishment had adopted. . . . [T]hey did not give black folks positions in their organizations, so that when we continued to struggle
and to fight for them to democratize their organizations to the point
of where black folks would have a position in it commensurate with
their strength in the union, then we were the rebels.[71]

The UAW, like SWOC, threw the NNC overboard once they had suc-
cessfully organized the auto industry in the 1930s and early
1940s. Once established, the union "adopted the same things that
the establishment had adopted." When the NNC began pushing for
leadership positions for Black members, the union branded them
"rebels."

If this first about-face strained the relationship between the CIO
and NNC, another about-face from the congress's other institutional
partner would alienate John P. Davis. After Hitler invaded Russia in
1941, thus breaking his 1939 nonaggression pact with Stalin, the
Communist Party in the United States dropped its once critical
stance of the Roosevelt administration and abruptly turned the NNC
into a "win-the-war" agency. Although Davis had been a member of
the Communist Party from the mid-1930s to late 1941, he was dis-
mayed with the latest whipsaw in the party line and found himself
increasingly at odds with its local leaders. Davis worried that continuing in his role as National Secretary would not allow the congress to
reinvent itself as it moved out of the Great Depression and into the
war years. He resigned in 1942 and began work as an assistant to US
Congressman Vito Marcantonio. SNYC leader Edward Strong would
take Davis's place, and the headquarters of the congress moved from
Washington to New York, where Strong was then based.[72] However,
neither Strong, nor any other man for that matter, would lead the
NNC through the tricky terrain of war-era Black politics.

· · ·

Black women, led by Thelma Dale, kept the congress running as men were drafted into the armed forces; more than that, they would save the NNC from the brewing sectarianism of the period and refocus it on the task of mass mobilization. Thelma Dale was born eleven years after John P. Davis, in 1916, and like Davis, was raised in the nation's capital. Her family was working class: her father, John Henry Dale, was a postal worker, and her mother, Lucille Emma Patterson, was a homemaker, though she occasionally found employment outside the home. She was one of four children. Her political awakening came in high school when an all-white discussion group exposed her to interracial radical politics. Her political education continued at Howard University, where Dale, all of sixteen years of age, became involved in student activism. Her mentors were radical faculty members like Doxey Wilkerson and W. Alphaeus Hunton. Dale completed her undergraduate degree in 1936, but having no job opportunities upon graduation, she undertook a master's degree in social work and did research for legendary sociologist E. Franklin Frazier. She was active in both the Howard University Liberal Club and the American Youth Congress (AYC) and established a local chapter of the Negro Youth Congress. Though the Negro Youth Congress would come to define her work in the years to come, it was an AYC conference in Lake Geneva, Wisconsin, that was perhaps most formative. There, she bonded with Black and white students of different class backgrounds from across the country. It was an experience that she said changed her life.[73]

By 1939, Dale had built a reputation as a leading youth activist. She was a representative of the AYC, a founding member of SNYC, and a key leader in the Washington, DC, local of the NNC. She had also found work as a civil servant. As an employee of the Federal Securities Administration, she became an active rank-and-file member of the Social Service Employees Union. Her political activity put her on the radar of the red-baiting House Un-American Activities

Committee (HUAC), then known more popularly as the Dies Committee, after its founder, Texas Congressman Martin Dies, Jr. Faced with intensifying harassment for her political views, Dale was forced to leave her job. She moved to New York City in 1943, where she took a job at the NNC's new headquarters. Almost immediately, she became the congress's National Secretary when Strong, her comrade in SNYC, was drafted into the armed services that same year. Together with public utilities organizer Mayme Brown, Labor Secretary Dorothy Funn, Director of Organization Jessie Scott Campbell, office manager Jeanne Pastor, and NNC cultural and educational attachés Maude, Ruth, and Jenny Jett, Dale led the congress through a tumultuous period of new organizing, internal division, and rebirth.[74]

Under Dale's leadership, the NNC worked around the CIO's top red-baiting officials to collaborate directly with the latter's left-led unions, including the National Maritime Union, the United Federal Workers of America, and above all the United Electrical workers (UE), the third largest union in the CIO with a membership 600,000 strong. The congress did so in part by establishing a wartime arm called the Negro Labor Victory Committee (NLVC). By mid-1943, the NLVC claimed to have won 6,000 jobs for Black workers in the furrier, merchant marine, and warehouse industries. The UE in particular worked with the NLVC to organize large firms like Ford Instrument, Western Electric, and Sperry Gyroscope. Sperry Gyroscope alone hired 1,200 Black people in twenty-four different occupations, including semi-skilled jobs. Two dozen Black stewards rose through the ranks at Sperry to represent the new workforce. The NNC also worked with the United Federal Workers of America to organize 1,000 workers at the Brooklyn Naval Clothing Supply Depot.[75]

But even as Dale attempted to steer the congress toward a positive program of mass mobilization, the organization became embroiled once again in a life-threatening sectarian conflict. After Stalin met with Winston Churchill and Franklin Roosevelt in Teheran in the Fall of 1943, the General Secretary of the Communist Party USA (CPUSA), Earl Browder, asserted that cadres no longer needed to take up radical positions or participate in mass mobilization. The postwar order, he predicted, would make such activity unnecessary, and so Browder dissolved the CPUSA and devoted all its resources to the support of Roosevelt's 1944 re-election campaign. Within the NNC, perhaps the most stalwart advocate of the so-called "Teheran line" was former Scottsboro Boys attorney Ben Davis, who was then a member of the New York City Council and the congress. Davis and Max Yergen called for the "liquidation" of the NNC. At the January 1945 Executive Board meeting, Davis said,

> Years ago it was necessary for us to mobilize masses of people in the streets on every struggle that we had. . . . Today that is not necessary except in rare instances. Today it is not done—not because of a lack of militance but the kind of struggle being conducted today is an indication of new conditions and of progress. . . . [W]e are working with all forces that are for winning the war. That kind of struggle today would not help the Negroes but would endanger the war effort and harm Negroes.

Ben Davis thus translated the Teheran line in terms that directly challenged the bread and butter of the NNC's trade union work, which was to integrate the institutionalized labor movement. The directive from the CPUSA was to wind the congress down.[76]

Thelma Dale had other ideas. Together with her all-woman staff and young NNC activists from Detroit (including LeBron Simmons, Shelton Tappes, Vera Vandenberg, and Coleman Young) and the Northeast (such as Ernest Thompson and Ewart Guinier), Dale engaged in a quiet campaign to undermine the Teheran faction, beginning with a statement of policy that mirrored what Randolph might call a "minimum program" upon which all factions could unite, namely, "to help galvanize . . . Negro organizations, the labor movement, and other progressive forces toward speedy victory in the war and a just and durable peace." While communicating "full accord" with the policy, Simmons, the Detroit NNC president, expressed "the need to further strengthen NNC organization in areas such as Detroit where the Council had played an important role in developing unity of action on the part of the Negro people." To that end, he urged that the congress assign a national staff member to Detroit.[77]

Underneath the calm exterior, the anti-Teheran faction fumed. Doxey Wilkerson, a mentor to Thelma Dale at Howard University who was also NNC Executive Board Chairman and vice president of the CP's International Labor Defense, said that with the Teheran line the party was effectively "giving up socialism." NNC Labor Secretary Dorothy Funn complained that local CP chief James Ford "had no contact with the larger sections of the population." From the front lines of the war, Edward Strong wrote to Thelma Dale, saying, "You know better than anyone of course . . . how under the illusionary concepts of Ben Davis, the major emphasis of Negro progressive leadership has been on securing formal agreement among a handful of top Negro leaders at the expense of organizing the Negro masses and this obviously false and dangerous line has been pursued in the name of 'Negro unity.'" Nor was this point of view confined to the NNC. William Z. Foster and French Communist Jacques Duclos gave the congress some much-needed political cover with the left when they publicly criticized Browderism for lacking any application of Marxism-Leninism.[78]

Eventually, both the CP and the congress had had enough of Earl Browder. In the summer of 1945, William Z. Foster unseated Browder as leader of the CPUSA; Ben Davis and his allies in the congress apologized for their mistakes and fell into line. Meanwhile the NNC's mass faction moved out into the open to consolidate their power. Their first move was to install a new National Secretary, Revels Cayton, a Black trade unionist who had come into the NNC through the Communist Party in the 1930s, and also the grandson of Hiram Revels, the first Black US Senator during Reconstruction. He worked as an organizer on the docks in Seattle, eventually joining the CIO's antidiscrimination committee in California. With the congress now firmly in their grasp, the mass faction rebuilt the NNC around grassroots networks of Black workers and adopted the Detroit NNC's model of mass mobilization and local council building. Dale came out publicly with her critique of the party's misadventures in the October 1945 issue of the Communist magazine *Political Affairs*. In an article titled "Reconversion and the Negro People," Dale held that the future of the party depended on "maintaining the faith of the Negro masses." By December 1945, the NNC's newspaper, the *Congress View*, would report that Arthur Bowman, the newly-appointed Midwest Director of the congress, was working to establishing local organizations in Gary, Chicago, and Toledo. In Detroit, the NNC was working with the UAW in their strike at GM to demand a 30 percent wage increase, upgrading of Black workers in GM plants, and an end to discrimination by the company. In Washington, DC, the local NNC Council assisted in the Capital Transit Company workers' strike in order that Black operators and conductors would be able to work on streetcars and buses. In 1946, the newly ascendant mass faction made plans to move the congress away from New York, where the CP held the most sway, to Detroit where the rebels were setting up shop. In January 1947, the NNC and SNYC convened in the Motor City.[79]

But just as the revamped NNC was getting under way, the white-led labor movement and the state moved in to crush it. On November 26, 1946, the CIO's director of Industrial Union Councils, John Brophy, sent a memo to the Los Angeles Industrial Union Council saying that the CIO was disavowing the NNC. The National Office of the Congress scrambled to contain the fallout, saying that the so-called

"Brophy memo" applied only to local councils and not to the CIO as a whole and that the NNC's working relationship with the CIO had not changed. Though Brophy did not raise the issue of Communism in his memo, the implication was clear and the press speculated as much. In their plan for 1947, which appeared in the January issue of their new magazine *Action*, the congress made it a priority to "FLAY [THE] CURRENT RED-BAITING CAMPAIGN," explaining that "Red baiting is the increasingly popular instrument of reactionary and conservative elements to disunify labor and progressive forces fighting for a better society" [emphasis in original]. Two months later, the congress reported with alarm that US Secretary of Labor Lewis B. Schwellenback told the House Labor Committee that "the Communist Party in the United States should be outlawed," and that President Truman himself pledged that the United States would "halt the spread of Communism throughout the world."[80]

The final blow came from FBI informants inside the NNC itself. Labor Secretary Dorothy Funn pointed the finger at sixty-six Communists with whom she had worked as a lobbyist in Washington and as a teacher in New York City Public Schools. Former NNC president Max Yergen also turned informant (he later became an advocate of right-wing causes, including apartheid in South Africa). Even Ralph Bunche, who was then being nominated for a diplomatic post at the United Nations, came under scrutiny when the US Senate discovered his old ties to the NNC. John P. Davis incriminated himself as a Communist in order to protect his longtime friend and claimed that Bunche was never a member of the party. Amid the chaos and betrayal of the Red Scare, Thelma Dale would write, "There's a limit to human endurance. . . . I'm afraid I've reached that."[81]

In a special committee meeting held on the morning of July 7, 1947, the NNC board approved plans to wind down the congress and merge it with the Civil Rights Congress. Under the plan, a national headquarters in New York City and a skeleton crew of two staff people would be maintained to execute the transition by October. The Board accepted the resignations of Edward Strong and Revels Cayton with thanks, though the two would stay on for a few more weeks to work out a summer budget and any outstanding personnel issues. With those mundane bureaucratic details taken care of, the once mighty National Negro Congress exited the scene.[82]

. . .

The entwined stories of the National Negro Congress and the March on Washington Movement reveal patterns that originated with the twin Brotherhoods and persisted through the Great Depression and Second World War. The first is that white support for the cause was inconsistent. After welcoming him into the inner sanctum of the steel workers' organizing campaign, the CIO stonewalled John P. Davis as he began to push for first-class citizenship in the new labor federation. Detroit NNC leader LeBron Simmons recalled a similar dynamic in the United Auto Workers. With the Ford Motor Company organized, the UAW cast the congress as rebels for demanding greater Black representation in union leadership. In 1946, the CIO disavowed the NNC completely. Nor were white-led unions amenable to the less radical March on Washington Movement. Though A. Philip Randolph was the president of a well-known AFL affiliate, unions like the International Association of Machinists stubbornly opposed the integration of Black workers in the defense industry.

Even white activists who supported the cause of interracial solidarity occasionally did more harm than good. The Communist Party is a signal example. The CP disorganized the National Negro Congress not once but three times. In the first instance, the 1939 Nazi-Soviet nonaggression pact led the congress to adopt an antiwar posture, which in turn prompted Randolph's resignation as president. The second instance occurred in 1941 when the Nazis broke the nonaggression pact and invaded Russia. The NNC once again shifted policy, this time to a pro-war posture that led to John P. Davis's resignation in 1942. Finally, the factional conflict over the Teheran line pitted the Browder faction led by Ben Davis and Max Yergen, which sought to dismantle the NNC, against the mass faction of Thelma Dale, Revels Cayton, and LeBron Simmons, which sought to rebuild the NNC around grassroots networks of Black workers.

Second, and conversely, Black labor proved itself once again to be the vanguard of interracial solidarity. Despite the distracting on-again, off-again support of white trade unionists, Black labor activists faithfully led the push to dismantle the color bar in organized labor. The NNC's tobacco campaign is an important case in point. The AFL tobacco affiliate in Richmond was downright hostile to the campaign, while the CIO provided minimal support, offering only to bring Black organizers on as voluntary staff. It was Black workers themselves, and in particular Black women, who began and led the strikes that organized the tobacco industry in the former capital of the Confederacy. To varying degrees, a similar pattern manifested in the campaigns to organize Black steel workers, auto workers, and packinghouse workers.

But third, the ongoing tension between the left and centrist factions of Black labor at times stymied their efforts, and at other times propelled them. The willingness of the competing factions to unify in a broad coalition depended on the articulation of what Randolph called a "minimum program," upon which all Black civil society organizations could agree. When the NNC colored within the lines of this program, as they did when organizing Black industrial workers in the 1930s, the congress unified. When they introduced controversial issues upon which the factions could not agree, the congress fractured. Nevertheless, it was precisely those conflicts that led Black trade unionists to innovate in ways that broadened the tactical repertoire and overall strategy of Black labor organizations. For example, the factional strife of the 1940 NNC meeting in Washington may have led to Randolph's resignation, but it also led Randolph to invent the march as a tactic in service to the strategy of integrating the defense industry. The MOWM's victory, Executive Order 8802, became the framework that would define the work of Black labor through the war years.

Fourth, the state was a key institutional player in this period. The March on Washington Movement confronted Roosevelt's New Deal administration directly over the segregation of the armed forces and defense industries. The foreign policies of the United States, the Soviet Union, and Nazi Germany tracked with the twists and turns of NNC policy. And finally, agents of the FBI exposed the plans they had been laying during the 1910s and 1920s in Harlem. By turning Dorothy Funn and Max Yergen into informants, the Bureau arrested the momentum of the NNC just as it was recovering from years of internal strife.

A fifth pattern is the rise of Black women. In 1937, Eleanor Rye led the effort to organize Black steel workers in Chicago and Gary; Black women were also the prime movers of the Richmond tobacco workers campaign. Toward the end of the war, Thelma Dale and her all-woman staff took over the day-to-day operation of the NNC. Nor were they simply minding the store while Black men were drafted into the armed forces: it was Dale's leadership that helped the congress navigate the tricky sectarian terrain of the mid-1940s and reestablish the mass character of the organization, especially in the industrial Midwest. Although the leadership of Black women was more muted in the March on Washington Movement, Black women's organizations like Alpha Kappa Alpha were important sites of on-the-ground organizing.

The mutual hostility between the centrist and left factions of Black labor would continue into the postwar period. The congress's conflict with the Communist Party and the persistent crisis of unemployment in the Black community would lead the mass faction of the NNC to establish a new independent Black labor organization, the National Negro Labor Council (NNLC). In fact, the youngest NNC cadres would become the NNLC's leading figures. These included Ewart Guinier, Coleman Young, Ernest Thompson, and Thelma Dale's close friend, Vicki Garvin. The centrist faction did not greet the new council's appearance with applause. Instead, the Negro Labor Committee-USA (NLC-USA), led by A. Philip Randolph and his associate Frank Crosswaith, maneuvered to kill the new organization in its cradle. The next chapter shows how the short but impactful career of the National Negro Labor Council was punctuated and eventually ended by successive assaults from the NLC-USA, the white-led labor federations, and the state.

FIGURE 1. A. Philip Randolph was President of the Brotherhood of Sleeping Car Porters, the National Negro Congress (1936–1940), the 1941 March on Washington, the 1963 March on Washington for Jobs and Freedom, and the Negro American Labor Council (1960–1965). Credit: Photographs and Prints Division, Schomburg Center for Research in Black Culture, The New York Public Library.

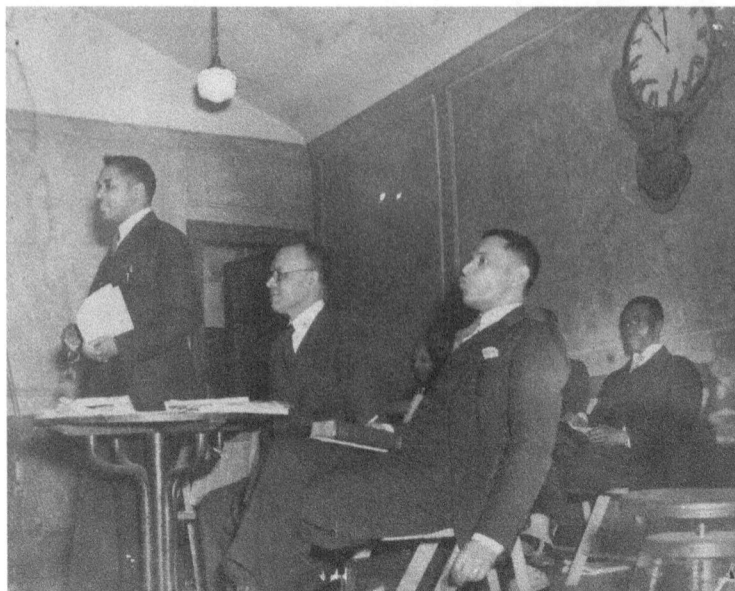

FIGURE 2. W.A. Domingo (standing), a Socialist, debates Richard B. Moore (seated in foreground), a Communist. Both were members of the African Blood Brotherhood for a time. Credit: Photographs and Prints Division, Schomburg Center for Research in Black Culture, The New York Public Library.

FIGURE 3. Grace Campbell was a comrade to Cyril V. Briggs and a leader of the African Blood Brotherhood. Credit: Photographs and Prints Division, Schomburg Center for Research in Black Culture, The New York Public Library.

FIGURE 4. Claude McKay worked with leaders of the African Blood Brother-
hood in the West Harlem Branch of the Workers Party. Credit: Photographs and
Prints Division, Schomburg Center for Research in Black Culture, The New York
Public Library.

FIGURE 5. Lucille Green Randolph, A. Philip Randolph's wife, owned a hair-straightening business and was the breadwinner of the family. She enabled her husband to edit the *Messenger* and organize the Brotherhood of Sleeping Car Porters. Credit: Photographs and Prints Division, Schomburg Center for Research in Black Culture, The New York Public Library.

FIGURE 6. John P. Davis was National Secretary of the National Negro Congress from its founding in 1936 to his resignation in 1942. Credit: Photographs and Prints Division, Schomburg Center for Research in Black Culture, The New York Public Library.

FIGURE 7. Thelma Dale was National Secretary of the National Negro Congress during the Second World War. Credit: Photographs and Prints Division, Schomburg Center for Research in Black Culture, The New York Public Library.

FIGURE 8. Negro Freedom Rally, organized by the National Negro Congress, Madison Square Garden, New York City, June 26, 1944 (floor view). Credit: Photographs and Prints Division, Schomburg Center for Research in Black Culture, The New York Public Library.

FIGURE 9. Negro Freedom Rally, organized by the National Negro Congress, Madison Square Garden, New York City, June 25, 1945 (aerial view). Credit: Photographs and Prints Division, Schomburg Center for Research in Black Culture, The New York Public Library.

FIGURE 10. Ewart Guinier was a founding member of the National Negro Labor Council. Credit: Photographs and Prints Division, Schomburg Center for Research in Black Culture, The New York Public Library.

FIGURE 11. Frank R. Crosswaith, head of the Negro Labor Committee–USA, led Black labor's Centrist faction in the 1950s. Photograph by Hansel Mieth. © Center for Creative Photography, The University of Arizona Foundation.

FIGURE 12. Vicki Garvin was a leading figure in the National Negro Labor Council. It was mainly due to her efforts that the NNLC emphasized the inclusion and upgrading of Black women. Courtesy of Lincoln Bergman and Miranda Bergman.

FIGURE 13. Bayard Rustin was Deputy Director of the 1963 March on Washington for Jobs and Freedom and later President of the A. Philip Randolph Institute. Credit: Photographs and Prints Division, Schomburg Center for Research in Black Culture, The New York Public Library.

4 The Council and the Committee

Ernest "Big Train" Thompson was born in 1906 on Maryland's Chesapeake Bay. He was the middle child of five. His parents, Joshua and Jennie Thompson, were farmers. Life was tough for Black folk on Chesapeake Bay, and Thompson's parents often had to leave the farm to earn extra money: his father cooked on ships, and his mother worked for wealthy families in Baltimore. Like the parents of Cyril V. Briggs, A. Philip Randolph, and John P. Davis, Thompson's insisted that he go to school even as his friends took five to six months off a year to work. Joshua Thompson was strict on this point. His rule was, "When you leave school, you leave here." When Thompson asked why, his father said, "You have to go to school so you can *be* something. . . . You got to learn to read and write just like the white man's boy, and then there's nothing they can hide from you. You can find it yourself."[1]

Thompson did learn to read and write. His favorite books were by or about his people: *Uncle Tom's Cabin*, *The Negro Soldier in World War I*, and the African American poets Paul Laurence Dunbar and Phillis Wheatley. The first beneficiary of his hard-earned education was Joshua's father, Philip Henry Thompson. He read the Bible to his grandfather, and in return Philip Henry told him stories about the days of slavery. One memorable story was of a Black man who lived in the master's house and ingratiated himself to white folks by telling tall tales about the other Black people on the plantation. Not appreciating this, they cut the house servant's big toe off to teach him a lesson. Thompson never forgot that story, because he saw that man limp by him every day.[2]

Thompson had another thing in common with his elders in the Black labor movement: he outgrew his hometown, decamped to the North, and there learned to organize. He got his first taste of the movement in Jersey City, where he lived with his aunt. Thompson had promised his mother that he would finish his education, so he attended night school while working at a bowling alley during the day. Upset about the low pay and long hours, he led his coworkers in a march on the boss, demanding a change in their conditions. The boss fired him for his insolence.[3]

His next brush with the movement was at the American Radiator plant in Bayonne, New Jersey. Like so many large factories, management divided the workers by race, with Anglos working in mechanical and warehouse jobs, Italians and Poles in middling occupations, and Blacks and Latinos in the foundry with the dirtiest jobs. The Black workers, led by Thompson, began organizing in 1934. They started by recruiting their Spanish-speaking neighbors in the foundry and then, having organized themselves into a tight militant unit, earned the respect of the Anglos and ethnic whites in other departments. Though they would lose their first strike, Thompson learned a valuable lesson: white workers would accept Black leadership provided that the latter were willing to fight and find common ground across the membership. In 1940, the workers elected Thompson president of the union and followed him in their struggle to affiliate with one of the CIO's left-led organizations, the United Electrical, Radio and Machine Workers of America (UE). He eventually left his elected post to become the UE's first Black staff organizer.[4]

Though the UE was one of the most racially progressive unions in America, Thompson had to overcome stereotypes about himself and the racially divided workforce he represented. On one occasion, a white UE leader asked for volunteers to help leaflet a nearby non-union plant. He told Thompson, "You can't come. It's mostly white workers and you can't organize white workers." Thompson replied, "We don't come together because we're Black and white; we come together because we're workers. You try to keep me from white workers because I'm Black, you'll undermine that unity." When Thompson and another Black volunteer leafleted the plant the following day, not one worker refused a copy. Gradually, he built a reputation for himself as a principled leader and brilliant tactician, so that when his union at the American Radiator plant formed an amalgamated local, Thompson again became an elected leader. The majority-white membership in fact re-elected him several times over.[5]

It was around this time that the postwar Red Scare began to wreak havoc on the labor movement. While the anti-Communist dragnet caused officials of the National Negro Congress to become FBI informants, in the UE the crisis manifested in a series of organizational splits. The CIO by this point had become an active agent of the Red Scare. Its top leaders established rival conservative unions to steal current and prospective members from their more radical counterparts. For example, the CIO founded the International Union of Electrical, Radio, and Machine Workers of America (IUE) to undercut the influence of the UE, its third-largest affiliate. In time, the UE would not stand the red-baiting for any longer. They left the CIO in 1946 and became an independent union.[6]

In addition to political persecution, Black trade unionists confronted other postwar realities. When white soldiers returned to their jobs from the front, they had more seniority than their Black coworkers. The fact that Black people were "last hired" and "first fired" convinced Thompson and his allies that they were on the brink of another crisis of Black unemployment. Moreover, despite the NNC's best efforts to convince the CIO to organize the South on an interracial basis, the situation had produced problematic results. In an internal memo to the leadership of the United Public Workers-CIO, Black board member Irvin S. Daniel and field representative Bill Stafford appraised the CIO's "Operation Dixie": "The CIO Drive staff and leadership have from the first compromised fundamentally and fatally on the essential issue of Negro-white unity. Where they have not set up Jim Crow locals, they have relegated Negro members to a back seat in union affairs." The effect was that instead of building momentum, the CIO's Southern drive weakened with each passing year, organizing 61,000 Southern workers in their first year (1946–1947), 32,000 in their second year, and 21,000 in their third. Frustrated with mounting political persecution, rising Black unemployment, and a stalled Southern organizing drive, Black labor activists began discussing the need for a new Black working-class organization.[7]

Accordingly, in April 1949, the old cadres of the NNC's Negro Labor Victory Committee (NLVC) reconvened to form the Harlem Trade Union Council (HTUC), the first Black labor council founded in the postwar era. They included Ewart Guinier, former NLVC secretary; Ferdinand Smith, former NLVC chairman and NNC board member; and Vicki Garvin, former National Research Director of the United Office and Professional Workers of America (UOPWA). Apart from their history with the NNC, each had other leftist bona fides. Guinier was a leader of the State, County, and Municipal Workers Union; John P. Davis came to his aid when he was suspended from his civil service job for radical political activity and "moral turpitude" (he was living with a white woman). Ferdinand Smith was once secretary of the left-led National Maritime Union (NMU) until an anti-Communist faction purged him from the organization. Vicki Garvin's union, like the NMU, had been another left-led CIO affiliate, well-known for its progressive racial policies. HTUC joined forces with Black activists in the UE, including Ernest Thompson, who himself had sat on the board of the NNC in 1945.[8]

Looking forward from that moment, it seemed as though Black labor's left faction was getting the band back together again. In May 1949, HTUC provided support to a Black local of the International Longshoremen's Association (ILA). White dock workers in New York had restricted Black members' access to work with the tacit approval of the white ILA leadership. In response, Black workers took over the ILA offices and demanded a pier of their own to unload cargo. When mounted police and white ILA members arrived to break up the occupation, HTUC threw up a picket line. Additionally, within the first eight months of HTUC's existence, the council placed 250 Black women and men in industrial jobs, some of them highly skilled positions in the technical field of the radio industry. HTUC also sponsored cultural events in the community, including a Paul Robeson concert at the Golden Gate Ballroom that attracted an audience of four thousand people. The combination of direct action, job placements, and community support to challenge the color line in organized labor was reminiscent of the old days. Soon Thompson, Garvin, Guinier, and Smith would call for a National Trade Union Conference for Negro Rights to be held in Chicago in June 1950.[9]

With all the heightened activity, Thompson and company did not perceive a lurking threat to their plans. Frank Crosswaith, a staunch ally of A. Philip Randolph, was watching the former NNC cadres with great interest. Crosswaith was head of an alternative Black labor organization that was closely aligned with the AFL leadership. He did not like what he was seeing. And so, just as Big Train Thompson and his old comrades began to gain traction, the centrists moved in to stop them in their tracks.

· ● ·

Frank Crosswaith was a fixture in Harlem politics. A West Indian immigrant like Cyril V. Briggs, he had worked as a Pullman porter before he assumed his position as Randolph's right-hand man. He was quite literally at Randolph's side in the secret meeting that founded the Brotherhood of Sleeping Car Porters in August 1925. On Sunday mornings, when he was still editing the *Messenger*, Randolph would invite his coeditor Chandler Owen, Crosswaith, and the contributors to the magazine to his apartment on West 142nd Street for political discussions. It was there that they formed the Friends of Negro Freedom to eliminate discrimination against Black people in the theater, athletics, and social clubs. When the Harlem Socialist Party split into left and right factions, with the left defecting to the Communists, Crosswaith remained with Randolph and Owen in the Socialist Party. J. G. Tucker, a spy for the federal government, called Crosswaith "one of the most active Socialists in Harlem," and noted that his party nominated him as their candidate for Congress.[10]

Though he was already ideologically at odds with the Communists, he did not come out publicly against the CP until 1930. Crosswaith published a series of articles in May of that year in Marcus Garvey's newspaper, *Negro World*, titled "The Negro and Communism," criticizing the Soviet Union for being intolerant of political dissent. He was then an organizer for the International Ladies Garment Workers Union (ILGWU) and head of the short-lived Trade Union Committee for Organizing Negro Workers. The editor of the *Negro World* said that he published the series because "the Communist movement represented to the Negro in particular and the working class generally a menace."[11]

This is not to say that Crosswaith refused to work with the party. In fact, he collaborated with the Communists on numerous occasions as the circumstances dictated or when Randolph himself expressed a willingness to work with them. On March 19, 1935, after the W. H. Kress store on 125th street refused to hire Black clerks and, in turn, touched off a riot, Crosswaith joined an Emergency Citizens Committee, which included James Ford of the CP, to highlight the underlying causes of the unrest. The committee wrote that the riot was due to "basic economic maladjustments . . . primarily segregation and discrimination against the Negro both private and public as well as in the administration of relief." In addition, when the *Amsterdam News* fired seventeen editorial employees in 1935 for joining the American Newspaper Guild, Crosswaith organized a boycott of the newspaper together with the Urban League, the NAACP, and the Socialist and Communist parties.[12]

Privately, however, Crosswaith was skeptical of the Communists' attempts to ingratiate themselves with Harlem civil society. In a letter to the white socialist leader Norman Thomas he wrote, "The Communists, having at last discovered that they cannot make headway in Harlem by their usual chauvinistic racial and irresponsible appeal and conduct, have been busy forming innocent organizations through which they hope to contact unguarded and misguided people." He added, "I have steered clear of their net, for I am convinced . . . that they are not to be trusted with the socio-economic problems of the Negro or the workers as a whole."[13]

His suspicion of the party was inconsistent with Randolph's position at the time, which was to work in a united front against fascism and racist unions. This was a somewhat tricky needle to thread, but he appeared to settle on a course of action. In his own union organizing work, Crosswaith took a hard line. For instance, in the aftermath of the Sleeping Car Porters' victory in the Spring of 1935, he pulled together a Negro Labor Committee of 110 trade unionists who claimed to represent 350,000 workers. On instructions from the Socialist Party, the committee vowed to work only with the AFL on ending the color bar in organized labor. At their founding conference, they refused to seat Arnold P. Johnson of the left-wing Emergency Home Relief Bureau Employees Association, except as a nonvoting delegate. One year later, when the Communist-aligned Harlem Labor Union was organizing to place unemployed Black workers in Harlem retail stores, Crosswaith worked to ban their activities. And as chair of the Harlem Labor Center, he advised the Amalgamated Clothing Workers Union and the ILGWU not to endorse the National Negro Congress. Outside of his trade union work, however, Crosswaith remained quiet for most of the period when Randolph was president of the NNC, from 1936 to the signing of the Nazi-Soviet nonaggression pact in 1939.[14]

In the year of the pact, the gloves came off. As the American Labor Party's nominee for Congress, Crosswaith issued a statement calling on civil rights leaders to purge Communists from positions of influence in Black life. With Layle Lane, the first Black woman vice president of the American Federation of Teachers, he wrote that Stalin's alliance with Hitler revealed the Soviet regime's true essence as an evil that must be crushed. They defined communism as a totalitarian movement similar to fascism and incompatible with a democratic society. By the fall of 1940, after Randolph's break with the NNC, Crosswaith, Lane, and Randolph himself were calling the CP a "Fifth Column" and went so far as to endorse the expulsion of Communists from trade unions.[15]

In Randolph's next act as a public figure, Crosswaith was once again by his side. For example, the March on Washington Movement's committee in Harlem consisted of Crosswaith, Lane, Walter White of the NAACP, Henry Craft of the YMCA, and Lester Granger of the Urban League. Fresh off MOWM's victory in 1941, New York Mayor Fiorello LaGuardia, who was pivotal to pressuring Roosevelt to issue Executive Order 8802, moved to appoint Randolph to the New York City Housing Authority. Randolph declined the appointment but recommended Crosswaith in his stead.[16]

Accordingly, when Harlem was hearing whispers of a new nameless threat, headed no less by the sometime cadres of the NNC, the centrist faction attacked. On January 31, 1950, Crosswaith and Randolph sent a letter to AFL and CIO affiliates urging them to support "The Negro Labor Committee, USA" (NLC-USA). The coauthors were explicit about their objective, which was to "offset" the efforts of subversives in recruiting Black workers. They hoped to do so, first, by organizing an alternative gathering called the "Negro Labor Conference." Their rationale was plain: "The reactionary forces of both extremes are busy trying to use the Negro trade-unionist in the Community and within the labor movement to gain their objectives." They reasoned, "If this tragedy is to be avoided then we in the labor movement must get busy and organize a constructive program to offset the scheming of all subversive and reactionary elements."[17]

Having made their opening salvo, the NLC-USA began lining up endorsements from the heaviest hitters in the institutionalized labor movement. On April 25, 1950, the committee sent a letter to Philip Murray, who was now president of the CIO. From this letter we can infer that Crosswaith and Randolph were scrambling to come up with an institutional response to the left's Trade Union Conference for Negro Rights. They disclosed to Murray that they had not yet decided on a time and place for their alternate assembly, and they noted ruefully that the centrist faction of Black labor had not been as active as their subversive counterparts, saying, "Our common enemies have gotten as far as they have mainly because of our silence." They remained clear on mission, however. "The purpose of the Conference," they wrote, "is to offset some of the destructive activities and influences which subversive groups are conducting among American Negro trade Unionists," adding, "The Conference will mark an historical chance in our struggle toward negating Communist influence in our midst and advance the cause of a united labor movement."[18]

Though Murray's reply is lost to history, we do have the reply of William Green, who was still president of the American Federation of Labor and appears to have received a similar letter. In a response addressed to Crosswaith and Randolph, Green wrote, "I am glad to extend to you my personal and official endorsement of the plan you report in your letter dated April 20, 1950, to hold a Negro Labor Conference sometime within the near future." Referring to the anti-Communist rationale for the conference, the AFL president continued, "The reason for such action as set forth in your letter are, in my opinion, sound and convincing."[19]

· · ·

Unaware of these machinations, Black labor's left faction hosted the National Trade Union Conference for Negro Rights (NTUC) on June 10–11, 1950. The conference was as large as any of the National Negro Congress's meetings at its height. Nearly nine hundred delegates, both Black and white, gathered in Chicago. They represented unions from the AFL, CIO, the railroad brotherhoods, and unaffiliated international unions. Among the radical white trade unionists present were Harry Bridges of the International Longshore and Warehouse Union and Maurice Travis of the Mine, Mill and Smelter Workers. Ewart Guinier was to say that it was the last time the big white union leaders came out for Black workers' rights. The goal was to develop a program to meet what William R. Hood, recording secretary of UAW Local 600, called "the outstanding unresolved challenge confronting Labor today—the question of Negro rights in the Trade Union Movement." Hood framed the challenge not as a problem of Black people alone, but rather of "making a substantial reality of Negro-White unity as an absolute pre-requisite to the achievement of working class solidarity." "History has taught us," he emphasized, "that without this solidarity in the ranks, no union movement can long survive."[20]

The delegates outlined their analysis in a Bill of Particulars. As in the Depression and war years, the urgent issue was a crisis of unemployment in the Black community. "The delegates were told that as you looked throughout the land you could see Negro men and women standing in long lines before the gates of the industrial plants," Hood recalled, "only to be told no help was wanted—while at the same time white workers were hired." This new crisis pointed up two additional aspects of Black joblessness: that "Negro women are denied the right to work in the basic sections of American industry" and that "those who were hired into industry in World War II have for the most part been systematically driven out—often in violation of union contracts."[21]

The keynote address, by the artist Paul Robeson, theorized the role of Black workers in this moment as well as the supporting role of white labor. Similar to the leaders of the NNC, Robeson suggested that Black labor had to lead the fight for the liberation of the entire race. He said, "The Negro trade unionists must increasingly exert their influence in every aspect of the life of the Negro community. . . . You are called upon to provide the spirit, the determination, the organizational skill, the firm steel of unyielding militancy to the age-old strivings of the Negro people for equality and freedom." He also pressed white labor into action. Robeson said, "And to the white trade unionists present—a special challenge. You must fight in the ranks of labor for the full equality of your Negro brothers and sisters."[22]

Accordingly, the NTUC action plan centered on the adoption—by unions, employers, and all levels of government—of a "Model FEPC Clause." Recall that President Roosevelt's Executive Order 8802, in addition to prohibiting racial discrimination in defense hiring, also established a Fair Employment Practice Commission (FEPC) as a body of redress should Black workers find that employers defied the order. Though historic, the order suffered from several problems, chief among these being the challenges of enforcement and presidential succession. Because executive orders are not legal statutes, the Black community had to push for a new executive order with each presidential administration. NTUC organizers aspired to apply the

FEPC beyond the defense industry and force such widespread adoption, including statutory legislation, that the prohibition against employment discrimination would become common sense. The NTUC resolved to make "every effort . . . to get the above Model Clause endorsed by trade union conventions" and to call "on all unions who succeed in getting such a Model Clause incorporated in their contracts to immediately organize the shops to guarantee that the bosses live up to its provisions."[23]

Before they adjourned, Ewart Guinier summarized the findings of the conference and explained what must be done. The action plan centered on rebuilding a mass organization, not unlike the local chapters of the National Negro Congress in the late 1930s. Guinier said, "We must set up anti-discrimination committees in our local unions, in the plants. We try to get these anti-discrimination committees to form Negro Labor Councils." The envisioned organization would not be a national-level lobbying group, then, but a network of interracial councils that operated in unions and workplaces at the grassroots. Guinier clarified this point when he said, "They must be mixed committees. It is no good doing it elsewhere if you are not fighting it in your own shop. It strengthens bonds to keep them together in these programs they work out in their own localities." Finally, Guinier evinced frustration with having to secure the rights of Black workers one executive order at a time and proposed that the body push for one omnibus bill that would address the conditions of Black America holistically. He concluded, "Let us put it all in one so that we won't have to be fighting separately . . . for FEPC, for more houses, more schools. Let's put it all in one for a federal jobs program." He said if NTUC did that, then "this conference will go down in history as the conference of the American people that stopped the fascism in this country."[24]

The proof that NTUC organizers were unaware of their centrist counterparts' scheming is in their attempt to garner endorsements from organized labor immediately after the conference. William R. Hood guilelessly wrote to UAW president Walter Reuther seeking a financial contribution: "It is because of this particular interest by the international union in the overall fight for Negro Rights, as well as a long established record on your part to support progressive causes, that I now call upon you for a substantial financial contribution in order to enable us to put our program into action." Hood noted that an undertaking of national scope entailed "considerable expense" and that NTUC had to "rely almost exclusively for its support upon advanced and militant organizations such as the international union."[25]

But even as the leaders of the fledgling organization encountered radio silence from institutionalized labor, their "Model FEPC Clause" spurred several local and national unions to intensify the fight for fair employment. The UE, for instance, made gains along these lines in their contract with General Electric. The furriers' union was able to place Black workers in highly skilled positions from which they had been historically excluded. The UAW amalgamated local in Chicago elected a Black woman, Octavia Hawkins, as unit president of a predominantly white section of that local. It was also in this moment that Vicki Garvin was elected International Vice President of UOPWA. Perhaps most importantly and likely a contributing factor to these foregoing victories, Black workers were establishing local councils across the country. With the new leadership going from strength to strength, they began to speak of a founding convention of something called the National Negro Labor Council, or NNLC.[26]

Vicki Garvin carried forward the demand for gender equity outlined in NTUC's Bill of Particulars, ensuring that the role of Black women would remain front and center. In addition to being UOPWA vice president, Garvin was the executive secretary of the New York City Negro Labor Council. Her biography bears special attention here, not only because she emerged as the most influential woman in Black Labor's left faction since her friend, Thelma Dale, led the

National Negro Congress, but also because the ensuing work of the NNLC would center on the hiring and promotion of Black women workers.

It is perhaps not surprising that Thelma Dale and Vicki Garvin were friends, for they were contemporaries in more ways than one. Like Dale, Victoria Holmes (Garvin) was born in 1916. Her parents were working-class people, also like Dale's: her father, Wallace Holmes, was a plasterer and a member of a Black trade union, while her mother was a domestic worker. In 1926, the Holmeses moved their daughter to New York City, joining millions of other African Americans in the Great Migration. During the Depression, it became increasingly impossible for Garvin's father to find work in his trade, while her mother bargained for wages in New York's infamous day laborers' market. The humiliation her parents endured was foundational to Garvin's analysis of labor and race. Her early political work began in the Abyssinian Baptist Church in Harlem; the church's youth program was run by future congressman Adam Clayton Powell, Jr. (she joined her first picket line for Powell's "Don't Buy Where You Can't Work" campaign). Though she did not attend a historically Black college, as Dale did, Garvin was also college-educated: she received her undergraduate degree in political science from Hunter College, where she served as president of the Black history club and had her first encounter with the Young Communist League. In 1936, after graduating, Garvin worked as a switchboard operator for an antifascist group called the American League for Peace and Democracy. It was at this point that she became an active member of the CIO's left-led UOPWA. Her commitment to radical politics deepened in 1940, when she moved to Northampton, Massachusetts, to study Marxist economics at Smith College under Professor Dorothy Douglass. Her thesis was titled, "The American Federation of Labor and Social Security Legislation," prefiguring her emerging interest in unions. She also served as one of Smith College's representatives to the 1941 Congress of Negro Youth in Washington, DC. During the war, she took a job with the National War Labor Board and while there helped to organize an in-house union of professional and clerical staff, in which she served as president. At the end of the war, she became UOPWA's national research director and co-chair of the union's Fair Employment Practice Committee. In 1947, a former coworker at the National War Labor Board recruited Garvin to the Communist Party. Though she also married Clinton Arthur Garvin, Jr., in the same year, she referred to joining the CP as the "key development" in her life, for, she said, it would shape "where my focus would be in terms of work . . . certainly something related to white workers and black workers or the general working class movement."[27]

Garvin and Dale became coworkers first at the NNC and then later at the leftist newspaper *Freedom*, which Garvin co-founded with Paul Robeson. Their political careers proceeded on parallel tracks. While Dale was acting National Secretary of the NNC, Garvin was executive secretary of the NNC's Manhattan Council. Like Dale, Garvin would come into conflict with the Harlem Communist Party over the strategic direction of the party. Their personal lives also became ever more entwined. Dale often stopped by Garvin's apartment after long nights working in Harlem. Garvin witnessed Dale's marriage in 1954 to Larry Perkins, whom she met in the offices of *Freedom* (thereafter Dale became known as Thelma Dale Perkins). Their friendship was a lasting one: it began when they were young adults and endured the red-baiting of the mid-twentieth century. They supported one another in navigating that frightening time, developing strategies for finding employment while being politically harassed and persecuted. Nevertheless, Garvin refused to give up or be ashamed of her politics. At the 1949 CIO convention, when the leadership sought to purge Communist-affiliated unions, Garvin gave a six-page speech, critiquing the CIO's failed Southern organizing drive and the move away from the "militant struggle for the rights of

Negro workers." Garvin would eventually lose her job at the UOPWA for lodging similar complaints against her union.[28]

The plight of Black women would become central to her political work in the years following. In a speech given in November 1950, Garvin said, "It is the responsibility of progressive trade unions and women's organizations to spearhead a militant and far-reaching program that will: Maintain Negro women in industry ... Eliminate wage differentials ... [and] Promote Negro women leadership at all levels of trade union activity." She ended the speech by suggesting the Black women were prepared to take part in the fights ahead. "Negro working women with their long tradition of militancy," she declared, "stand ready to be an integral part of the struggle for progress."[29]

William R. Hood, too, emerged as a leader of the NNLC. A native of Whitesville, Georgia, he moved to Detroit in 1942 in his thirties. Not long after, he was hired at Ford's River Rouge plant, whose workers belonged to Local 600 UAW-CIO. The Rouge was once the largest factory in the world, with 80,000 workers all told. Local 600 was correspondingly the largest local union in the world and had a long-standing reputation as one of the most radical and militant organizations in the country, unafraid to push for racial equity in collective bargaining and union leadership. Hood was elected recording secretary of the local in 1947 and was re-elected for four consecutive terms. He was the highest-ranking Black union official in the country after A. Philip Randolph. A fierce opponent of the 1940 Smith Act, which made advocacy of the violent overthrow of the American government a criminal offense, Hood also defended victims of political repression after World War II. He became president of the NNLC in 1951.[30]

Coleman Young was perhaps the most famous member of the NNLC leadership. Before becoming the first Black mayor of Detroit in 1974, he was a union organizer. Referred to affectionately as "Big Red," he was born in Tuscaloosa, Alabama but spent most of his life in the Motor City. He was an officer in the Army Air Corps during World War II and was reportedly thrown in the stockade for drinking coffee in the all-white officers' club. After working in various organizing jobs, he became organizing director for the Wayne County CIO. Prior to his time as mayor, he was state director of the Progressive Party and ran for State Senate. Young was Executive Secretary of the NNLC.[31]

Finally, Ernest Thompson was NNLC organizing director. His comrades nicknamed him "Big Train," because he was said to deliver the goods. Colleagues also described him as the "motor" of the organization and its leading "theoretician." He traveled extensively in his role as director of organization, taking the message, strategy, and tactics of the NNLC to local councils across the country.[32]

Coleman Young explained that strategy as one intimately tied to their overlapping identities "as Negroes and Black people, and as trade unionists." Accordingly, the NNLC saw itself in a dual role: "bringing democracy to a trade-union movement . . . and using that trade union base to move the trade-union movement and our white allies within it into the liberation struggle for Black people, with a primary concentration on economic issues as the key."[33] This posed a potential contradiction as a Black-led organization working in coalition with white workers, but as NNLC activist Jack Burch explained, "We saw no contradiction at all. On the one hand, we recognized the need of Black people in Black organizations—not separate unions—but organized into groupings to plan and discuss their interests and to plan tactics of how to further them." At the same time, they recognized that "oppression in the plant against Negro workers applies also to white workers and therefore you had a kind of natural alliance, if you could develop it."[34]

NNLC organizers had therefore done just about everything they could do to set the board for their founding convention. They had an analysis of the crisis at hand, a strategy that turned on Black working-class leadership, and a trade union base to push organized labor into the Black liberation struggle. Their core tactic was to campaign for the adoption of the Model FEPC clause in industry, unions, and all levels of government. And, thanks to the National Trade Union Conference, they had a coalition of Black and white trade unionists to execute the strategy and implement their tactic. The organizers secured endorsements and funding from a "founders' list" that included left-led unions like the UE, ILWU, Mine Mill, and the United Packinghouse Workers. In all, they mailed 15,000 copies of the convention call. Eleven hundred delegates were scheduled to arrive on October 27–28, 1951, in Cincinnati. Now all they had to do was find the delegates a place to stay.[35]

. • .

We know very little about the activities of the Negro Labor Committee-USA just prior to the convention, but we have a sense of their hand in the ensuing chaos based on Vicki Garvin's account of arranging accommodations in Cincinnati. Garvin opened up the convention at noon on October 27 after the singing of the "Star Spangled Banner" and the Black national anthem, "Lift Every Voice and Sing." In her speech, she said, "Rarely has any organization at its initial stage been confronted with such fierce opposition. The mere issuance of our Convention Call brought upon our heads the most powerful combination of forces." She identified these as big business, government agencies like the FBI and the Cincinnati City Council (which passed a resolution condemning the convention), and "top trade union officials such as Philip Murray, Walter Reuther and James Carey who dared try to intimidate and to instruct their Negro members to boycott our convention."[36]

The clandestine activities of organized labor were intensified by the fact that Cincinnati, Ohio, was then a Jim Crow town. This meant that white-owned hotels refused them accommodation, while Black-owned establishments that were not scared away by the vicious red-baiting were too small to fit the sheer number of delegates. Garvin had to resort to a complex system of billeting in the private homes of Cincinnati's African American community. She expressed gratitude to those community members who put delegates up, saying, "I am especially proud of the hundreds of Negro families in Cincinnati who rejected the red-baiting and opened their homes and hearts to all of us when the white hotels refused us accommodations." She explained, "These working men and women responded immediately to a mere postcard or telephone call when we told them of our plight. My people would not see us on the streets."[37]

Ernie Thompson spoke next and moved the conversation beyond the machinations of organized labor. It was his job to introduce NNLC president Bill Hood. Introducing a labor leader is a genre unto itself, typically consisting of a brief resume, a joke or two, and kind words that denote a familiarity between the speaker and the leader. Thompson's speech was more poetic than the usual fare, but it was precisely its strangeness that galvanized the crowd. He began, "We say something new is happening. It gets to your bones; it's on the breezes; it's everywhere. . . . It's a new wind of freedom blowing from the Seven Seas and touching the hearts of men and women." "This new wind," he continued, "has brought on the scene a New Negro, the sons and daughters of labor." Then, as if to suggest that his own words were not adequate to the moment, he quoted his favorite childhood poet, Paul Laurence Dunbar, in a mashup with the words of W. E. B. Du Bois. He said,

> Out of the darkness and out of the night
> The Black man crawls to the dawn of light
> Beaten by lashes and bound by chains
> Searching, seeking for the Freedom Train.

In that moment, Joe Johnson, a burly dockworker from the West Coast, jumped up and shouted, "Great God Almighty!" The crowd swayed, and behind Thompson, Bill Hood whispered, "Get me ready, Daddy, get me ready!"[38]

Thompson continued with Sterling Brown's poem "Strong Men." He recited from memory,

> They bought off some of your leaders
> You stumbled as blind men will . . .
> They coaxed you, unwontedly soft-voiced . . .
> You followed a way.
> Then laughed as usual.
> They heard the laugh and wondered;
> Uncomfortable;
> Unadmitting a deep terror . . .
> One thing they cannot prohibit . . .
> The strong men . . . coming on
> The strong men gittin' stronger.
> Strong men . . .
> Stronger . . .

The poem struck a note that would be repeated throughout the conference. The old Black leadership had misled their people, Thompson implied, and now a new leadership was "coming on"—a group of strong men, gittin' stronger. If there was any doubt that this was what he meant, Thompson then introduced Bill Hood as "the symbol of this New Negro, this symbol and fighter for freedom, for unity, a leader of our Council and a leader of the largest local union in America."[39]

Hood began his speech by reminding the audience of their identity as workers and of the significance of Cincinnati as a terminal on the Underground Railroad. He said, "On this day we, the delegated representatives of thousands of workers, black and white, dedicate ourselves to the search for a new North Star, the same star that Sojourner Truth, Nat Turner and John Brown saw rise over the city of Cincinnati over a century ago." But, he noted, their historic meeting marked the inauguration of a new leadership and approach to the question of Black liberation. He spoke of "the new stage in the Negro people's surge toward freedom," and, as if to suggest that the old leadership's obsequiousness to the white elite was now over, he announced, "Uncle Tom is dead. 'Old Massa' lies in the cold, cold grave. Something new is cooking on the Freedom Train." President Hood then outlined the council's reason for gathering in Cincinnati, namely, to confront a "world crisis," in which "our liberties are disappearing in the face of a powerful war economy and grave economic problems face working men and women everywhere."[40]

There was to be no doubt, however, that the NNLC would be Black-led and be part of the freedom struggle. "The proud black sons and daughters of labor," he said, would lead the response to the crisis, in coalition with "our democratic white brothers and sisters." He continued, "We, the Negro working sons and daughters, have come here to Cincinnati to keep faith with our forefathers and mothers who landed right here from the banks of the Ohio River in their dash for freedom from chattel slavery through the underground railroad. We come here to pledge ourselves that the fight for economic, political and social freedom which they began, shall not have been in vain." Hood was clear that while white workers were to be part of the council, Black people would not take direction from them. He explained,

> We wish to say further that the day has ended when white trade union leaders or white leaders in any organization may presume to tell Negroes on what basis they shall come together to fight for their rights. Three hundred years has been enough of that. We ask for your cooperation—but we do not ask your permission![41]

Though this statement was meant to clarify the relationship between the NNLC leadership and their radical white allies, it was also a direct challenge to the white leaders of the AFL and CIO and their collaborators in Black civil society who were actively working to purge the left from Black life. Hood took special aim at those who accused the NNLC of being "subversives," a word taken straight out of the NLC-USA's entreaties to organized labor in 1950. Hood said, "We know them for what they are—the common oppressors of both people, Negro and white. We charge that their false cry of 'subversive' is calculated to maintain and extend that condition of common oppression." To the Black leadership specifically, "all of whom attacked our Council at the beck and call of the Big white folks," he thundered, "You have spent your lives growing fat on Jim Crow while our brothers and sisters cannot find jobs. . . . You may yell when the big white folks tell you to, in order to keep us down, but the day of the white-haired 'Uncle Toms' and the sleek 'Uncle Thomases' is at an end."[42]

White union activists, for their part, signaled that they got the message loud and clear. M. E. Travis, Secretary-Treasurer of the International Union of Mine, Mill and Smelter Workers (Mine Mill), had lost an eye in a shoot-out with the Ku Klux Klan while defending Black and white members in Alabama. He began his address to the NNLC by acknowledging that the conference "was called by—and is devoted to—Negro workers, who came here to discuss the crucial issues which grow out of their life-and-death struggle against the white man's justice." He continued, "I didn't come here to tell the Negro workers of America, or their leaders what to do," but to speak to "white trade unionists—rank-and-file white workers and their leaders." Travis traced the failure of interracial solidarity in the labor movement to white people's paternalistic approach, which he described in this way: "The big white brothers, holding out a generous, fatherly hand, to lift up Negroes." "And of course," Travis observed, "as long as that approach was used, the Negroes somehow never got lifted up." Because "the Negro workers are not waiting," he said if "the temper and position of the Negro people has changed . . . I say to the white trade unionists—we had better change, too."[43]

From the marquee convention speeches, we can infer at least three themes in common. The first is that Black labor leaders understood themselves to be the successors to the Underground Railroad. The NNLC was the "Freedom Train," the new vanguard of the liberation struggle. The middle-class Black leadership, by contrast, were "Uncle Toms," and their efforts would be to no avail since "Old Massa" now lay in the cold, cold grave. The second entailed the new vanguard's attitude toward white labor. Not only were the latter meant to take direction from the Black leadership; they were also meant to mobilize the institutional resources of the labor movement on behalf of Black liberation. The third theme centered on the enemies seeking to undermine the Black vanguard. Vicki Garvin, Bill Hood, and M. E. Travis each referred to Black and white actors whose objective was to keep the NNLC from gaining any traction, whether by frustrating the council's ability to arrange accommodation for their delegates or by stigmatizing the organization as subversive.

The NNLC's resolutions anchored the foregoing themes to a set of benchmarks. The first was to place Black workers in 100,000 jobs by May 15, 1952. The second was to collect one million signatures in support of a new FEPC executive order. Once again, the council announced its intention to push organized labor into the struggle to end employment discrimination. A key precondition for the campaign was "that all unions, whether AFL, CIO, Independent, or Railroad, as a matter of policy be urged to adopt the model no-discrimination clause." The NNLC then sought to enroll their base in organized labor in the campaign to achieve their benchmarks. The delegates called upon "affiliated Councils, white allies, trade unions, and all fighters of freedom to support this campaign for 100,000 jobs" and "to deliver these million signatures around May 1, 1952, as part of a national March on Washington." So that Black labor would no longer be dependent on successive administrations to pass executive orders, the NNLC called upon local councils "to launch immediate campaigns for state and local FEPC laws."[44]

Finally, the NNLC passed a remarkable statement in support of Black women. The council recognized the first and second shifts that Black women worked in order to fulfill their roles both in industry and in the social reproduction of the household. "Negro women are employed in the lowest-paying jobs, are unable to support themselves adequately and certainly are unable to support a family," the council reported, pointing out that "a large number of Negro women are themselves heads of families, supporting their children and other dependents." They recognized the toll of these pressures on Black women. In terms of health, the council asked, "Is there any wonder that the life span of a Negro woman is nine years less than that of her white sister, that her maternity death rate is three times greater?" These and other stressors underlined the multiple oppressions that Black women endured, not only on account of their gender, but also due to "white supremacy and economic oppression in its crassest form." Their rationale for focusing their attention on Black women is also notable. Prefiguring the Combahee River Collective's insistence that the liberation of all is only possible when the most marginalized are free, the NNLC proclaimed, "The progress of the American workers and the Negro people can be measured by the status of Negro women." Accordingly, "to win freedom and equality for all workers," the council challenged the delegates to "win job opportunities for Negro women throughout industry," including job training and skills upgrading, and "support the organization of domestic workers, both in the North and South." The council also demanded inclusiveness in leadership. Black women of the council said, "We have demonstrated our ability and willingness to give leadership to our families and other struggles. We demand the right to play a comparable role in government, industry, and the unions."[45]

The NNLC articulated a commitment to independent organization that other Black-led labor groups held in common. As Vicki Garvin was to write in the newspaper *Freedom*, "As Negro workers who are subject to problems and pressures not borne by others, we assert and accept our responsibility to give leadership to develop programs for our freedom and equality." This was not to exclude white freedom fighters, but rather to suggest that white labor activists could not be counted on to carry Black liberation to fruition. Garvin wrote, "While the trade union movement can and must make a powerful contribution to these struggles, it cannot be a substitute for the independent movement of Negro workers. . . . The Council is a necessary and vital organization to the trade union movement, and vice versa."[46]

In all, 1,052 people registered for the NNLC's inaugural convention. Of these, 898 were delegates, 154 official observers, and roughly 200 other participants. Representatives of fifteen international unions attended, including the UE, UAW, ILWU, United Public Workers (UPW), Distributive, Processing, and Office Workers Union (DPOWA), United Steel Workers, and United Rubber Workers. Members of both the AFL and CIO were present. They hailed from twenty-two states, nine of them Southern. One-third of the delegates were women and four-fifths were Black. Twenty-three local Negro Labor Councils were organized.[47]

The convention energized all who witnessed it, both lay people and members. Ernest Thompson would call it "the most exciting of his life," while Ewart Guinier would say it was "the most hopeful." A resident of Cincinnati wanted to see what a subversive meeting looked like, only to find himself inspired. He said, "I thought from what I read in the paper this was to be a subversive meeting. I did not expect it to be like this. I'll say now that if nobody else tries to build a Negro Labor Council in Cincinnati, I am going to build one here myself." Reporters who had been predisposed to regard the gathering with suspicion found themselves clapping and cheering by the end. When the leadership presented its resolutions, the press table reportedly shouted "Aye" in support. The *Cincinnati Enquirer*, the city's paper of record and no friend of the council, would write, "Before our eyes in Cincinnati, we witnessed the transformation of the Underground Railroad into the Freedom Train."[48]

. . .

It was perhaps because of the Freedom Train's momentum that the Negro Labor Committee-USA stepped up its campaign to slow it down. By the winter of 1951–1952, just a few months after the council's inaugural convention, the CIO was warning its local affiliates against joining the NNLC. Because there seemed to be confusion about the two organizations, James B. Carey, the CIO's white secretary-treasurer and chairman of the CIO's Committee to Abolish Discrimination, clarified in an executive committee meeting that he was "working with the Negro Labor Committee, USA." The latter's leadership, he explained, consisted of "officers of AFL and CIO Unions" like Philip Murray and Walter Reuther, while the co-chairman of the NLC-USA was "Philip Randolph of the American Federation of Labor." By contrast, "the National Negro Labor Council adopted its name as a result of its meeting in April of this year under the auspices of UE, the Mine, Mill and Smelter Workers, and other organizations expelled by the CIO." Carey promised that the Committee to Abolish Discrimination would send a letter to "affiliated organizations" and also "publish the information in the CIO News," explaining that of the two Black labor federations, the NNLC was "the communist controlled organization."[49]

Similarly, in an internal memo, the UAW international leadership warned all affiliates against participating in the NNLC and further directed that they should preempt the NNLC from gaining a foothold by creating their own local FEPC campaigns:

> This memorandum is prepared to acquaint you with the newly organized Communist front organization which is called 'The National Negro Labor Council' which held its founding convention in Cincinnati, Ohio, October 27 and 28, 1951. This so-called National Negro Labor Council was convened by individuals [whose] political and social philosophy has been rejected by National CIO, the UAW-CIO, the NAACP, the Urban League, and a host of other organizations interested in civil rights throughout the nation.

The memo also reported that the International Executive Board of the UAW-CIO at its meeting in early October 1951 called the NNLC a "vehicle for Communist propaganda" and affirmed that "the UAW-CIO does not support, in any way, the National Negro Labor Council or any of its local labor councils."[50]

In the meantime, the NLC-USA itself was organizing its first convention, scheduled for March 1, 1952 in New York City. Having drawn organized labor's attention to the putative threat of the NNLC, Randolph's group now set about lining up endorsements and financial support for the meeting. A memo to Jim Carey states, "As you know the reconstitution of this group has been urged by our New York CIO people and others to provide an offset to the Commie National Negro Labor Council on which the Party is concentrating much of its efforts these days in Harlem as well as in other parts of the country." The constitution and by-laws of the NLC-USA formally affirmed its anti-Communist position and its corresponding loyalty to the nation's white-led labor federations. The founding document refers to itself as "an affiliate body of trade-union organizations in good standing with the American Federation of Labor, the Congress of Industrial Organizations and other bona fide trade unions with the exception of Communist or Communist dominated trade unions and all other anti-democratic groups."[51]

The minutes of the March 1 gathering suggest that the NLC-USA was attempting to set up a parallel anti-Communist network of local "committees" (as opposed to "councils") devoted to precisely the same goals to which the NNLC had committed. The NLC-USA called for a "civil rights program" consisting of "FEPC legislation" as well as the "Establishment of a National Negro Labor Committee with branches in any city where requests come from . . . trade union leaders." The committee also urged community activity to "aid Negro workers in getting apprenticeship training, and in organizing Southern Negro workers." The final plank of their action plan read simply, "Combat 'communism' and the National Negro Labor Council." The meeting was taped for broadcast on the Voice of America, a state news network.[52]

Ten days after the NLC-USA convention, the local council of the NNLC in New York held its own convention and there extended an olive branch to Randolph in hopes of working together in a coalition. Vicki Garvin, in her capacity as Executive Secretary of the local council, said, "Our Council is willing to join any genuine campaign around the issue of jobs for Negro workers. We made this clear in our letter to this organization last Saturday." However, she also took the NLC-USA to task for its attack on her organization. She continued, "We further call upon Negro trade unionists such as A. Philip Randolph [and] Frank Crosswaith . . . to reject splitting tactics, to dissociate themselves from those who would smash our Council or smear its purpose."[53]

Garvin's appeal fell on deaf ears. The NLC-USA moved full-steam ahead with building an organizational alternative to the NNLC down to the grassroots. The minutes of their first executive board meeting, held in Chicago on July 19, 1952, summarized this activity. Their work included the reorganization of the New York branch, the integration of Black workers in the beer industry, the resolution of racial problems in the AFL's longshoremen's union, and the establishment of an employment service as well as "machinery in Boston, Pittsburgh and Philadelphia."[54]

At the same time that Randolph and Crosswaith were establishing a competing network of local committees, the House Un-American Activities Committee began to take an interest in the NNLC. HUAC subpoenaed Bill Hood and Coleman Young, along with three other Black leaders: the Reverend Charles A. Hill, Arthur McPhail of the Civil Rights Congress (CRC), and former NNC leader LeBron Simmons. The NNLC subpoenas were part of a broader attack that also targeted the CRC and Hood's union, UAW Local 600.[55]

HUAC arrived in Detroit in February 1952 to take testimony. Instead of the usual fare of red-baiting vitriol and flustered witnesses, HUAC and the public were treated to a determined fight back, one that NNLC biographer Mindy Thompson credits with eventually bringing down HUAC in the years following. The NNLC leadership, while certainly aware of what the federal government could do to them, planned from the beginning to take an aggressive approach. Prior to the hearings, Hood said, "I dare them to put me on the witness stand." Noting that HUAC's chairman John Stephens Wood was from Georgia, Hood said, "I am from Georgia. . . . I will tell him what I suffered in Georgia—what I saw when I was a young man and which still exists there." A high point of the hearings was the exchange between HUAC lawyer Frank S. Tavenner, Jr., and Coleman Young. Against his lawyer's advice to "take the Fifth" and not answer any of Tavenner's questions, Young told Tavenner "where to go." When Tavenner began, "You told us you were the executive secretary of the National Negro Congress—" Young cut in and said, "That word is 'Negro,' not 'Nigra.'" Tavenner responded that he did say "Negro" and that the witness was mistaken. Young replied, "I hope I am. Speak more clearly." When it was Congressman Donald L. Jackson's turn to ask questions, he said to Young, "If you think of the lot of the Negro who have in eighty-some-odd years come forward to a much better position—" Young cut in again, saying, "Mr. Jackson, we are not going to wait 80 more years, I will tell you that." To this Jackson insinuated, "Neither are the Communists." Young replied, "I am speaking for the Negro people and for myself. Are you speaking for the Communist Party?" Young ended his testimony by reminding the Congressmen that he was a veteran of the late war and that he was now engaged in a struggle to fulfill the war's promise:

> I fought in the last war and I would unhesitatingly take up arms against anybody that attacks this country. . . . I am now in the process of fighting against discrimination against my people. I am fighting against un-American activities such as lynchings and denial of the vote. I am dedicated to that fight, and I don't think I have to apologize or explain it to anybody.

In their testimony, Bill Hood and Reverend Hill followed suit: they attacked HUAC but answered no questions. The hearings were broadcast over the radio, and the Black community reportedly cheered their leaders on. HUAC left Detroit in a shambles.[56]

.   .   .

In spite of the attacks from both the state and the labor movement, the NNLC managed to execute their plan to place Black people in 100,000 industrial jobs. The NNLC met at their second annual convention in Cleveland, Ohio, on November 21-23, 1952. There Black trade unionists reaffirmed their commitment to lead the liberation struggle. William R. Hood, still NNLC president, reminded the assembled delegates, "We represent the Negro people's greatest striking power. . . . Let us keep in mind that if in the struggle to win security, job equality, for ownership of the land, we workers and farmers fail, then the doctor, the lawyer, the shopkeeper, and the church, all of whom depend on us, will be in bad shape." Once again, it was not the Black middle class who, on Hood's reckoning, would realize the freedom dreams of the race, but Black workers. Coleman Young re-used the metaphor of the "Freedom Train" to cast the NNLC as the vanguard of the struggle. He said, "Our Freedom Train is rolling, brothers and sisters. Let us go among the people, the workers, Negro and white, singing, 'Get on board little children, there's room for many more.'"[57]

The second annual convention was also an opportunity for each of the local councils to report the result of their efforts. Many of these were part of a drive to win sales and clerical positions for Black women at the retail giant the Sears Roebuck Company. In 1952, Sears adhered to a strict policy of not hiring Black people above the position of janitor. It became the NNLC's first major national campaign. The hometown council in Cleveland won their first victory in September of that year by cracking Jim Crow hiring at their local Sears department store. The Cleveland NNLC worked with the Baptist Ministers' Conference, the Urban League, and the Community Relations Board, which then administered the city's Fair Employment Practice Commission. Together the coalition achieved in a few months what the Urban League had failed to do over the course of eight years. The NNLC in San Francisco broke down the color bar at Sears, too. After a three-week campaign, the local store hired fourteen Black woman as clerks and cashiers for the first time in the store's history.[58]

The St. Louis council's experience with targeting Sears's clerical and sales departments illustrates how the NNLC structured these first campaigns. The local council reported first approaching the

store manager in May 1952, and then holding several more conferences with him and the district manager. With the help of the Central
Business College and private individuals, the local council found fifteen qualified Black workers to apply. When Sears hired none of
them, the St. Louis activists threatened to post a picket line around
the store, at which point the district manager promised to interview
applicants and hire any that were qualified. Again he hired no one.
On October 4, the council threw up a picket line around Sears as
promised and maintained it every Saturday afternoon and on Monday, Thursday, and Friday evenings. St. Louis council members distributed some five thousand leaflets and mobilized support from local churches, unions, and other organizations.[59]

Following the early breakthrough in San Francisco, the NNLC
saw an opportunity to end Sears's Jim Crow hiring policy for good,
company-wide. The Newark, Philadelphia, Cleveland, and Detroit
councils immediately joined the fray. Picket lines popped up across
the country. By the end of 1953, Sears had surrendered to the NNLC
in nearly all department stores in the northern United States, with
the exception of Chicago.[60]

Conversely, the Chicago council had succeeded in integrating
every other department store chain in the Windy City. In addition to
this monumental achievement, the Chicago group also won campaigns in finance and meatpacking. Chicago activists reported that
their proudest early success was in integrating the Drexel Bank.
Alongside that, NNLC activists worked with Armour Local 347 of the
meatpacking union to "break down the lily-white Slice Bacon and
Pharmaceutical departments." Given the National Negro Congress's
overlap in personnel with the United Packinghouse Workers and the
NNLC, the stewards and officers of the UPW local were all members
of the Chicago council.[61]

The Greater Detroit Negro Labor Council (GDNLC) reported
success in grocery, auto, and the metal and printing trades, much of

it centered on the hiring of Black women. The council weakened the color bar at Big Bear Markets and Sams, Inc., leading to the hiring of Black women as cashiers and the upgrading of existing Black women employees to the sales department, respectively. Likewise, the Michigan Scrap Metal Company already had a substantial workforce of Black men but had refused to hire Black women as switchboard operators until the local council brought pressure upon them to do so. The Ford Motor Company gave in to council demands that they hire Black women for their front offices. In addition, the GDNLC scored a major victory in passing a local FEPC ordinance. In the town of River Rouge, the council's Downriver chapter organized a majority-white interracial coalition of primarily steel and leather workers to approve a town FEPC ballot measure by a vote of 4,180 to 3,175.[62]

In Los Angeles, the local NNLC chapter reported that "many trade unions in this area have adopted our model FEPC clause, and some have set up FEP committees within their locals." In accordance with the council's focus on Black women, the LANLC made strides both symbolically and in terms of job placement. They sponsored a contest for "Labor's Negro Woman of the Year" and invited Viola Brown, a Black woman and leader of the North Carolina tobacco workers, to keynote their convention. The local council was able to place Black women in industrial and clerical jobs, including at the RCA Recording Company.[63]

The Greater New York Council, where Ewart Guinier and Vicki Garner were based, scored major victories in a variety of industries, totaling at least 450 job placements. The Brooklyn Union Gas Company succumbed to council pressure and hired Black meter readers for the first time in its hundred-year history. The F & M Schaefer Brewing Company, which had refused to hire Black workers for 110 years, agreed at last to hire forty Black helpers, truck drivers, production workers, and sales personnel. The New York council also launched a major campaign to break down the color bar in the hotel industry, beginning with an open hearing that showed that Black workers were excluded from bartending, skilled maintenance, office work, and supervisory positions. Finally, in a few short months the GNYNLC was able to collect 50,000 signatures in support of a new FEPC executive order, one-twentieth of the one-million-signature benchmark, all on its own.[64]

Another dimension of the NNLC's activity in 1952 was their organizing in the transportation industry. Both the Philadelphia and East Bay (California) local councils focused their attention on mass transit. In Northern California, Key System Transit Lines had never hired a Black bus driver. During the Second World War, a number of organizations, including the NAACP, the Elks, Urban League, the Masons, and various churches, sent delegations to convince the company to change their hiring policy, but to no avail. The council stepped into the mix when the Key System argued that there was a labor shortage and sought approval from the public utilities commission to cut services to the community. In a pamphlet titled "Is the Key System joking?" the East Bay Council wrote that the labor shortage was a false claim as there were plenty of Black workers who could drive but whom the Company rejected out of hand on account of their race. Pointing out that cuts in service would harm low-income whites and Blacks, they urged the community to call, write, and visit the company's personnel manager to protest his Jim Crow policy. The community responded with enthusiasm, and at last, after withstanding years of pressure, Key System Transit Lines gave in. The council in Philly had similar success in taking on the Philadelphia Transportation Company. The employer in this case did not want to honor the seniority rights of existing Black employees and refused to hire Black women at the front of the house. With pressure from the council, seniority rights were upheld, and Miss Virginia Johnson became the first ever Black woman cashier in company history.[65]

Arguably the biggest national campaign in transportation was in the airline industry. In early 1952, the NNLC wrote to Vice President Richard Nixon, who then chaired the newly created Committee on Government Contracts. The council asked Nixon to accept jurisdiction over the airline industry, which had refused to hire Black workers. The rationale was in keeping with the NNLC's FEPC strategy: the airlines must adhere to the federal government's own fair employment practices if they were to hold government contracts. To bring awareness to the issue, the NNLC staged a mass picket of 1,500 people during their second annual convention in downtown Cleveland. The protest trained a spotlight on the airlines' racist hiring policies. When other organizations joined the campaign, the airline industry capitulated.[66]

The third year of the NNLC's existence began along similar lines, with local councils challenging hiring practices in a variety of industries, including hospitality, brewing, utilities, and manufacturing. The New York council took on Jim Crow hiring policies at area hotels. At their 1953 local convention, the delegates resolved to continue periodic picket lines to force the upgrading of Black women. The local council succeeded in pressuring the Park Sheraton hotel to upgrade a Black woman from maid to floor supervisor. They would go on to upgrade housekeepers and waiters at the Statler, Taft, Whitehall, and Waldorf Astoria. The Los Angeles Council placed fourteen Black women at the Bell Telephone Company in Santa Monica and began a pressure campaign to place Black engineers, firemen, brakemen, and conductors on the Southern Pacific, Union Pacific, and Santa Fe railroads.[67]

The proliferation of the NNLC's direct action campaigns seemed to be influencing other labor organizations. Though Reuther was no supporter of the NNLC, the United Auto Workers brought together four hundred delegates in Detroit for a Fair Employment Practice conference "to map out a drive to include a model anti-discrimination clause in all contracts." From October 30 to November 1, 1953, the United Packinghouse Workers convened a conference to eliminate the remnants of Jim Crow hiring in the huge meatpacking industry. The editors of *Freedom* gave the NNLC the credit for spreading these tactics. "Despite all efforts to defame and defile it," they wrote, "the Council has been a prod to the sluggards and a goad upon the conscience of the complacent."[68]

.   .   .

The council's local campaigns in the transportation industry crystallized into another nationwide campaign, this time on the railroads. At their third annual convention, held at the Pershing Hotel in Chicago, December 3–5, 1953, the NNLC leadership outlined the history of the industry and their rationale for targeting it. By way of setup, Coleman Young told the gathered delegates that legendary Black railroad worker John Henry "has turned over in his grave and is walking around at night with hammer in his hand" due to the lack of effort the National Negro Labor Council had put into organizing the industry. Though past NNLC meetings had called for a major national campaign on the railroads, Young admitted, "We have not done so." He then explained that for decades the industry had used Black workers as cheap labor. The proof of that fact came when the federal government claimed jurisdiction over railroad regulation during World War I and equalized the wages of white and Black workers. The industry, Young said, continued to pay Black workers two to three dollars less per day than white workers. Asked why they persisted in their course, management responded, "if we have to pay white man's wages, we might as well hire whites." And indeed, between 1910 and 1940, the number of Black firemen, trainmen, and brakemen was cut by more than half. The reason for raising the issue of railroad integration at the 1953 NNLC convention was that the balance of class forces had changed. Where once the railroad industry was once an impregnable fortress, it was now more vulnerable than it ever was. Young said, "The CIO, the left-progressive independent unions, and the whole world . . . now make victory in railroads possible, even if it were not possible then." If the convention took on this fight, he quipped, "Jim Crow's mother will never recognize his face."[69]

The NNLC called the ensuing campaign "Let Freedom Ride the Rails." In the campaign pamphlet by the same title, the council advanced a narrative of white and Black workers in the industry that mirrored the experience of African American workers in general. It began with their exclusion from white-led railroad unions. "Under the false illusion of protecting the jobs of their own members," it read, union leaders "yielded to white supremacy, and into the hands of railroad management." All four of the largest railroad brotherhoods had color bars in their constitutions that excluded Black people from membership outright, while the remaining unions (except Black-led unions) all had one restriction or another. Some had Jim Crow auxiliaries where Black members paid dues to the union but received no representation. Once again it was Black people, not their white counterparts, who consistently pled for unity. The pamphlet read, "In their age-old fight for first class citizenship, Negro workers have persistently fought for their place in every organization which seeks to promote the welfare and the progress of all—particularly in the unions." Black railroad workers were forced to do what they wished they did not have to, namely, form unions of their own. These included Randolph's Brotherhood of Sleeping Car Porters and the Railway Labor Executive Committee, which in turn consisted in the Association of Locomotive Firemen, Colored Trainmen of America, Dining Car & Food Workers Union, and the Southern Association of Colored Railway Trainmen & Firemen. Against all odds, these Black labor organizations won contracts, made gains over time, and in some cases organized with their white coworkers in victory.[70]

The NNLC made several demands for the year in prospect, 1954. They demanded first that companies commit to hiring, training, and promoting Black workers on all railroads. Knowing that unions excluded Black workers by restricting the industry's labor pipeline through apprenticeship programs and lily-white applicant pools, the council also called for the "unqualified admission of Negroes to railroad training schools" and the "encouragement of Negro applicants, both men and women, to apply for jobs on every railroad." The NNLC sought to democratize union executive boards and conventions by admitting Black workers as full and equal members. Finally, the council called for the reform of the Railway Labor Act to enforce the "duty of fair representation," which the US Supreme Court had affirmed as early as 1944. According to the court, the railroad brotherhoods—even those that retained white-male-only clauses— were obligated to represent fairly and equitably all workers in a bargaining unit irrespective of union membership, yet unions continued to deny fair representation to Black railroad workers who were excluded from the union.[71]

The "Let Freedom Ride the Rails" campaign was a two-pronged strategy. As the council itself noted, racial discrimination on the rails was technically prohibited. Though Black railroad workers had won monumental victories during World War I and in the 1930s with the Sleeping Car Porters, perhaps the most notable occurred on December 18, 1944, when the US Supreme Court ruled that all railroad contracts were invalid and illegal insofar as they discriminated against Black people. But as with so many prior rulings, the railroad bosses ignored the decision. The NNLC thus endeavored to do what the court could not, which was to enforce the ruling through mass action. The NNLC registered cracks in the fortress in both New York and Pennsylvania. In those states, the railroads hired Black people as firemen and trainmen, and the Brotherhoods even admitted those workers as members. In New York, the council achieved this in part by filing formal complaints with the State Committee Against Discrimination, the official state FEPC. Along with the ground game, the council pursued a parallel lobbying strategy. The NNLC wrote a letter to Vice President Nixon on February 24, 1954, on the railroad industry, similar to that which they used to lobby him on the airlines. After continual pressure, the Committee on Government Contract Compliance finally agreed to accept jurisdiction over the railroads.[72]

If the railroad campaign had been an unfulfilled promise of the NNLC in 1953, so, too, was the campaign to integrate the South, though the council had chapters in Winston-Salem, North Carolina; Louisville, Kentucky; and Bessemer, Alabama, among others. The clearest statement on the need for the campaign was a report called "Free Our Hand," by Viola Brown, Asbury Howard, and Sterling Neal, presented to the NNLC's third annual convention. Similar to the council's analysis of the railroad industry, the coauthors argued that big business had colonized the South to extract cheap labor. Southern employers kept wages low by pitting the white and Black fractions of the working class against one another. The solution was to preempt such division, and the report provided the example of the UE-affiliated United Farm Equipment Workers of America's (FE) campaign to organize International Harvester. After seven years of struggle, FE was able to build an interracial coalition around raising wages and eliminating the so-called "Southern differential" in labor standards that enticed large firms to start runaway shops in the region. In addition to boasting the highest industrial wages in the South, the FE collected five thousand signatures in support of a national FEPC law, the majority of which were from white members.[73]

Viola Brown and her coauthors had to do more than demonstrate that a campaign in the South was winnable—they had to show that the campaign was vital to Black liberation and the integration of organized labor. This was a straightforward task, for Southern wage differentials and unchecked white supremacy had historically depressed Black people's wages and left them bereft of labor organizations to reverse the crisis of Black unemployment. This they did in capital letters at the end of the report. They wrote, "THERE CAN BE NO FULL FREEDOM OF THE NEGRO PEOPLE IN OTHER SECTIONS OF THE COUNTRY UNLESS THE BLACK BELT OF THE SOUTH IS SET FREE! THERE CAN BE NO FREE TRADE UNION MOVEMENT IN AMERICA UNTIL THE SOUTH IS ORGANIZED ON A DEMOCRATIC BASIS!" What remained to be had, the coauthors wrote, were the resources to launch the campaign. They demanded, "Give us these tools. . . . All we ask is that you free our hand."[74]

Brown and her associates were not alone in their plea. Coleman Young noted in his keynote address to the third annual convention that "the shift in industry to the South is of particular concern to Negro Labor Councils, for big business seeks to exploit the lack of democracy and the lack of unionization in the South for lower wages and company unionism." Mary Robertson, a young white woman from Asheville, North Carolina, gave an electrifying speech, in which she promised, "The white workers of the South are not so bigoted that they can eat a 'white only' sign. We're hungry and we know that if Negro workers get their due, we will be able to eat, too." By the end of the convention, the sentiment in favor of a Southern campaign was strong. Apart from a resolution calling on the local councils to "Fight railroad Jim Crow," the delegates simultaneously passed a resolution to "Fight for jobs for Negroes on a mass industrial basis, singling out in the South the fight for Negro skilled jobs."[75]

Ground zero for the campaign was Louisville, Kentucky, the so-called "Gateway to the South." It was there that General Electric (GE) was building a massive runaway shop called "Appliance Park" with sixteen thousand new jobs. The Louisville council began laying the groundwork for the campaign by preempting the main objection to hiring Black workers: that they were not qualified. One of the local council's first projects was to get the Louisville Board of Education to start vocational training for Black workers so that they would be eligible for hiring when the time came. The council was insistent that the workforce at GE must match the demographics of the surrounding area. Because Louisville was approximately 16 percent Black, GE should be, too. When the plant opened in early 1953, however, it was clear that the company had other plans. Of the 1,000 initial employees, only 35 were Black. The only Black women hired were employed as "matrons," a glorified occupational category for toilet cleaners and scrubwomen.[76]

Though the Louisville council was game to challenge the apparent plans of the company, they could not do so alone. In April 1953, they wrote to IUE president James Carey, whose union represented the workers at Appliance Park; UAW president Walter Reuther who represented workers at the nearby Ford plant; AFL president George Meany; and UE president Albert Fitzgerald. Only UE expressed a willingness to help. The UAW was forced to enter the mix when Coleman Young and the Detroit NLC distributed leaflets about Louisville to the members of Local 600, which, to repeat, was the UAW's largest and most militant local. In the course of leafleting, the police arrested Young and two members of UAW Local 261. As the members fumed over the arrests, the Detroit Council stepped up its campaign and issued leaflets exposing the full extent of Ford's discriminatory hiring practices in Louisville, which were revealed to be even worse than those of GE's. Under pressure from Local 600 and the NNLC, the UAW had to investigate.[77]

Meanwhile, the NNLC, with the support of the UE and its own fundraising, printed 100,000 copies of a pamphlet called "Give us this day our daily bread" that instructed local councils and union members to send letters to GE in Louisville, demanding fair hiring practices and non-discriminatory treatment in upgrading and training. Again, the idea was to pressure the company to hire a proportion of Black workers no less than their percentage in the local population. Because Black women were shut out of production jobs and confined to the most menial work, the pamphlet also urged readers to demand that "women get equal pay for equal work and that they be included in all phases of G.E.'s training program." GE workers across the country responded to the NNLC. Some called upon their local management to protest GE's policies in Louisville, while others took direct action by sending protests and delegations to their respective GE plants. The New York council set up large pickets, four to five hundred members strong, in front of GE headquarters.[78]

Faced with nationwide pressure in the form of letter-writing, protests, picket lines, delegations, public relations nightmares, and appeals to the federal government, both GE and Ford backed down. GE at long last hired Black women to work on the production lines, while the Ford Louisville plant hired Black people to work in positions apart from janitor. It was the first time that either company had done so in any of its Southern locations.[79]

. . .

Just as the NNLC was going from strength to strength, warning signs appeared on the horizon. Recall that the House Un-American Activities Committee (HUAC) had subpoenaed Coleman Young and William R. Hood to a hearing in Detroit in 1952. Though HUAC receded into the background after their embarrassing tussle with Young, the US Attorney General officially designated the NNLC a subversive organization. In the midst of the Gateway to the South campaign, the council found itself once again embroiled in a back-and-forth with the state. In December 1954, the federal government published a pamphlet titled "The American Negro in the Communist Party." In typical Red Scare fashion, the state referred to mysterious sources that unmasked the NNLC as a "deceitful" Communist front, whose leaders did less for Black workers than they did for their nefarious political agenda. It read, "A study of the operation of the Council shows that, rather than helping the Negro worker, it has been a deterrent to him." As an example, the government claimed that the NNLC "has made charges of Negro discrimination against the United Auto Workers, CIO, which has done much to advance the cause of the Negro worker." According to the government, the NNLC had done nothing except "discredit the efforts of non-communist organizations." It "encouraged disunity," and thereby "performed a distinct disservice to the cause of the Negro worker." In response, the council wrote, "If the Attorney General considers the demand for full freedom—economic, political and social—now, not 80 years from now, as subversive, then he had better 'designate' the Negro people of America."[80]

It was also during the Gateway campaign that the AFL and CIO began to talk about a merger. NNLC leaders found it troubling that the two great labor federations were joining forces without ever having committed to fair employment practices or first-class citizenship for Black members, including the right to vie for elected leadership. Accordingly, Vicki Garvin, under the old auspices of the Negro Trade Union Conference, called for the merger to include language outlawing Jim Crow unions. In a pamphlet to the Black rank-and-file titled, "*NEGRO WORKERS—DANGER AHEAD*," the NTUC wrote, "Now is the time to convince the AFL and CIO before they merge on December 5th, that an important key to genuine labor unity is a clear-cut declaration of policy that Negro and minority workers everywhere are entitled to full, equal and unsegregated membership in every union" [emphasis in original]. In another pamphlet, distributed directly to the delegates of the inaugural AFL-CIO convention, NTUC wrote, "NOW IS THE TIME FOR ORGANIZED LABOR, THE FOREMOST LEADER FOR PROGRESS, TO CLEAN ITS OWN HOUSE OF REMAINING UNDEMOCRATIC, DIVISIVE,

DISCRIMINATORY POLICIES AND PRACTICES" [emphasis in original]. They proposed provisions in the merger calling for "the right of full participation in all unions for Negro and other minority workers," "Negro representation in the new merged Executive Board and on all other levels of union leadership," a campaign to organize the South, a strong FEPC committee, and "a definite time limit for all international unions and other subsidiary bodies to eliminate present policies of discrimination where they exist, with automatic expulsion the penalty for failure to comply." The newly inaugurated AFL-CIO adopted no such provisions.[81]

Elsewhere, pressure mounted on the left-led unions who had supplied much of the membership and financial support to the NNLC. As in the case of the UE in 1946, the major labor federations launched conservative and middle-of-the-road labor organizations to raid the members of progressive unions. For example, the Marine Cooks and Stewards and the ILWU, who had been the NNLC's base on the West Coast, were in a life-and-death struggle to survive. Even Bill Hood was forced out of his job as recording secretary of UAW Local 600 due to pressure from the International.[82]

And so, when the Subversive Activities Control Board (SACB) called the NNLC to a hearing set for April 30, 1956, the council decided to disband. They explained, "In surveying the situation, the leaders of the National Negro Labor Council came to the conclusion that we would not dissipate the energies of our members attempting to raise the tremendous sums of money required to go through the SACB hearing, and at the same time, jeopardizing their personal well-being when the freedom struggle is at its present height." Outwardly, they expressed their fury at US Attorney General Herbert Brownell. In a press release dripping with sarcasm, the council wrote, "Herbert Brownell . . . has at long last taken official action in regard to the much abused rights of Negro Americans!" Instead of taking to task the Ku Klux Klan, the council clarified, "he has singled out for attack a Negro organization that has been among the foremost exponents of constitutionally declared full freedom and first-class citizenship for the Negro people." They also put on a brave face for their members. Upon disbanding, they declared, "The striking down of the National Negro Labor Council will not prevent nor curtail Negro workers from organizing and fighting for their freedom, equality and justice. History will record that Attorney General Brownell and other subverters of democracy were unable to stem the freedom tide." Privately, however, the inner circle of the council was overwhelmed with emotion. When the leadership met for the very last time on April 29, 1956, on John R. Street in Detroit, they wept openly.[83]

The indignities persisted for some time thereafter. The government called on Coleman Young, who was the designated administrator of the defunct council, to appear in Washington twice. It fell to Big Train Thompson once again to deliver the goods and put an end to the kangaroo trial. In a public statement to the government, Thompson accused Brownell of dancing on the grave of the dead and charged that the state knew full well that the NNLC was no longer in existence. "I therefore plead with you to halt these proceedings," he said, "and relieve the Justice Department attorneys of the non-existent task of forcing the former respondent, the National Negro Labor Council, to register with the Board as 'subversive.'" Though he also quipped that the Attorney General should instead investigate the Klan and White Citizens Councils, the government agreed to dismiss the charges.[84]

. . .

Looking back on that moment at an NNLC reunion some forty years later, Vicki Garvin recounted some of her most painful and triumphant memories. She began by singling out one council leader. She said, "Especially do I pay unqualified tribute to 'Big Train' Ernie

Thompson, our Director of Organization." She called him "the brilliant theoretician who guided our agenda and its implementation." "Homeboy," she said, "did not lead from the ivory tower, but by example, having acquired knowledge and experience from the bowels of the black working class." Vicki Garvin also recalled with bitterness the persecution the council endured at the hands of white unions, the state, and the Black community. She remembered "broadside attacks from every source, many of the major trade unions, A. Philip Randolph, Lester Granger (National Urban League), a couple of Cincinnati black politicians and the mainstream press, labelling us a communist front organization." They weren't, she insisted. Instead, the council was "an independent, advanced, dedicated and uncompromising organization of black workers to militantly struggle for our inherent right as first class citizens, with our focus on the employment front. Our objective was not to create dual unions, but to promote genuine democracy in the labor movement." Finally, Garvin reflected on the council's commitment to the cause of Black women. She said, "I am especially proud that from the 'git-go' the NNLC declared that our women were equal policy making partners in our organization." "Our common experience," she added, "confirmed that black women . . . were not only dependable rank-and-file soldiers, but also leaders."[85]

Garvin's reflections on the NNLC are poignant in that they speak to the patterns that underpin Black labor's struggle with the institutionalized labor movement. The first is that white trade unionists were inconsistent proponents of interracial solidarity. The council sought the support of both the conservative and progressive sectors of organized labor, yet only the latter responded. The NNLC reached out to Walter Reuther of the UAW immediately after the National Trade Union Conference on Negro Rights, and, in the Gateway to the South campaign of 1954–56, worked to enlist the support of Reuther, IUE president Jim Carey, and the presidents of both labor federations, to no avail. The council's base was confined to an embattled group of left-led unions like Mine Mill, whose secretary-treasurer M. E. Travis was on the NNLC board; the Marine Cooks and Stewards, whose leader Ferdinand Smith was an early leader of NTUC; the International Longshore and Warehouse Union; Garvin's UOPWA; Ewart Guinier's United Public Workers; and perhaps most importantly, Thompson's UE.

Second, Black labor was once again the vanguard of interracial solidarity in this period. As their many programmatic statements suggest, the council's Black working-class activists saw their role as pushing the white-led union movement into the struggle for Black liberation. In this, the NNLC's analysis of their failure is telling of organized labor's inconstancy. In the years after the council's demise, Coleman Young would say, "I think we overestimated the potential support of the trade-union movement and underestimated the necessity of rooting ourselves in the ghetto. . . . We were way out in front."[86] At the time, however, the NNLC saw themselves as the prime movers of the coalition for interracial solidarity. The necessity of that coalition came down fundamentally to the limited resources that Black labor's left faction could muster on its own. Young explained, "We understood then that coalition meant partnership, it meant coming together as equals. It meant putting into a common pot that which you had and taking out of the pot that which you were able to take out because of your strength."[87]

A third pattern is that the conflict between Black labor's left and centrist factions conditioned the activity of each. The swift organization of the Black left in the late 1940s transformed Frank Crosswaith's relatively parochial Negro Labor Council in Harlem to a would-be national organization. Randolph and Crosswaith quite explicitly stated that the NLC-USA was meant to "offset" the influence of what they viewed as the subversive NNLC. Conversely, the NLC-USA impacted the trajectory of the NNLC. The NLC-USA used their connections with the white-led labor movement to undermine the council's work from the very beginning. This took concrete form in the NNLC's inability to do something as basic as arranging accommodations for their founding convention. Moreover, the NLC-USA's antipathy ensured that the council had fewer resources than they might otherwise have had with the full support of all unions.

Fourthly, the state greatly impacted the development of the NNLC. Immediately following the inaugural convention in Cincinnati, HUAC subpoenaed Hood and Young to testify to their involvement in Communist activity. Though this seemingly worked to galvanize the council's base and embarrass HUAC, the state re-emerged again in the work of US Attorney General Brownell, whose control over the Subversive Activities Control Board ultimately led the council leadership to disband.

Fifth and finally, if Black women were a nascent force until the 1940s, then in the 1950s, they moved to the center of the struggle. Indeed, the NNLC was the first independent Black labor organization to mobilize systematically around the exclusion of Black women from unions and the labor market. Though the Sleeping Car Porters represented maids in the Pullman Company, and while the National Negro Congress organized Black women in the tobacco industry and was led in its later years by Black women like Thelma Dale, it was the NNLC that pushed Black women to the top of the agenda. The struggle for 100,000 jobs focused primarily on the placement and upgrading of Black women in industries such as hospitality, retail, and manufacturing. In this, the leadership of Vicki Garvin was pivotal.

Garvin's role is critical for at least one other reason, however, as we prepare for the next chapter. The fight to pressure the AFL and CIO into adopting anti-racist provisions as part of their merger (a fight that Garvin herself led) prefigures the struggle for interracial solidarity in the 1960s when Randolph would rejoin his foes on the Black left in a marriage of convenience. The newly merged federation, the

AFL-CIO, would prove as impervious to the appeal of Black labor in the 1960s as white labor had been in prior years. This meant that Black labor would attempt to apply pressure on white-led unions through still another organization called the Negro American Labor Council (NALC). It is perhaps poetic that the very last item in Vicki Garvin's private papers on the NNLC is a single, unassuming, membership card. It reads, "Founding Convention, Negro American Labor Council, Vickie Garvin [sic], DELEGATE, May 27–29, 1960, Detroit, Michigan."[88] Garvin's presence at that convention alongside her nemesis, A. Philip Randolph, suggests that while the NALC was one unified organization on the surface, the left and centrist factions would once again compete for control. That subterranean struggle led the NALC to adopt a tactic that had once been threatened but never tried: a march on Washington.

5　*The March Triumphant*

Vicki Garvin was not the only Black trade unionist who weighed in on the imminent merger of the AFL and CIO in 1955. The leader of Black labor's centrist faction, A. Philip Randolph, published his own assessment in the *Chicago Defender*. Unlike Garvin, who was suspicious of the new federation's commitment to racial justice, Randolph greeted the merger with the optimism of an insider. He wrote, "I believe sincerely that the merging of the AF of L and CIO will . . . accelerate the efforts of the American Negro to eliminate racial bias from the American scene." For him the draft constitution of the AFL-CIO, a constitution criticized by the NNLC, was strong enough on civil rights to earn his praise. It featured a non-discrimination clause and called for the creation of a department of civil rights which, federation president George Meany promised, would be a "major wheel in the new AFL-CIO machinery." "It would seem that this department," Randolph concluded, "could do much in the beginning by starting the new department off with the firm determination to tackle racial bias and to use the organization's resources . . . in eliminating racial discrimination."[1]

Though Randolph was to be a vice president in the new AFL-CIO and a member of its executive council, the terrain was not quite so hospitable as his position or optimism might suggest. His longtime friend William Green died in 1952, leaving the presidency of the AFL to Secretary-Treasurer George Meany, a former rank-and-file plumber turned union bureaucrat who famously boasted that he never walked a picket line in his life. Randolph and Meany would eventually come to respect one another, but their relationship in the early years of the AFL-CIO looked more like a feud than a friendship.[2]

That feud came out in the open at the 1959 AFL-CIO Convention in San Francisco, where they clashed repeatedly over the racist practices of AFL affiliates. The first such exchange occurred in the debate over whether to readmit the International Longshoremen's Association (ILA), which had been excommunicated from the AFL in 1953 for corruption. Randolph said that he favored the ILA's readmission but that the union was "guilty of some incredible and unspeakable discriminatory practices against Negro and Puerto Rican workers." He demanded that the ILA end these racist practices as a condition of readmission. To this, Meany said,

> Now in regard to Phil Randolph. . . . [H]e is a member of our Executive Council. We appointed a Committee of the Executive Council in February to investigate this thing. . . . Phil Randolph never came to me with any complaint. . . . And to come at this late date, where he has an audience . . . and come up with this material, I just don't think that is playing the game. I don't think that is playing on the team.

Meany then implied that Randolph's detachment from the day-to-day operations of the federation was due to his involvement in independent Black labor organizations. He said, "I would like Brother Randolph to stay a little closer to the trade union movement and pay a little less attention to outside organizations that render lip service rather than real service."[3]

Meany then made an effort to smooth things over by promising to investigate Randolph's charges against the ILA, but the following morning the Sleeping Car Porters' leadership, including C. L. Dellums, Randolph, and Milton P. Webster, drew the AFL-CIO's attention to two railroad brotherhoods whose constitutions still excluded Black workers from membership. They moved that the AFL-CIO expel the unions "unless they eliminate the color bar from their constitutions within six months." The Resolutions Committee revised the motion to state that the Executive Council would work with the brotherhoods to bring them into compliance with the civil rights requirements of the AFL-CIO "at the earliest possible date." Randolph rose to challenge the change on the grounds that it set no time limit for the elimination of the color bar. Though he did not question Meany's commitment to civil rights, he reminded the assembled delegates that "the Brotherhood of Sleeping Car Porters will never back up in their fight on racial discrimination in the affiliates of the AFL-CIO, regardless of opposition" and that "the responsibility of keeping this question alive in the labor movement is the responsibility of the Negro trade unionists." He ended by returning to the question of timing, saying, "Let me advise you that the unions have had the color bar in their constitutions for over 50 years. How much more time do they want?"[4] Once again, Meany responded directly to Randolph, but this time in more measured tones. While expressing admiration for Randolph, he insisted that imposing a timeline on the railroad brotherhoods was impractical. He said, "I admire Phil Randolph for striving for his goal. And while he has made progress . . . none of us is going to live long enough to reach the state of perfection where we say this matter has been entirely and completely eliminated from the social structure of our country. We just won't live that long, and we know it."[5]

The mounting tension at the convention came to a head hours after the tussle over the railroad unions. Randolph, Dellums, and Webster offered another resolution, this time insisting "that racially segregated local unions be liquidated and eliminated . . . regardless of contention that some members of racially segregated unions desire to maintain" those unions. In proposing this resolution, the Brotherhood of Sleeping Car Porters sought to short-circuit the oft-cited reason that the AFL-CIO could not undermine local autonomy or union democracy. Randolph suggested that the federation itself broke with the principle of local autonomy when it prohibited Communism and corruption. Accordingly, the resolution read, "It is just as unsound and indefensible for national and international unions . . . to tolerate . . . unions under Communist domination and corrupt influences, on the grounds that the members of the said unions wish and desire said unions." The Resolutions Committee indicated that they would support the resolution so long as the porters removed the word "liquidated," but Harry Bates, a delegate from the bricklayers' union, said that he would not support the resolution under any circumstances, ostensibly because Black workers were allowed to maintain segregated unions of their own. Although Black unions had formed because white unions excluded Blacks from membership, the ensuing debate unfolded as if Randolph were imposing a double standard on his white brothers. Why, they demanded, should white workers not be allowed to maintain all-white unions when Black workers had all-Black unions?[6]

Harry Bates by himself would not have prompted a reaction from the Sleeping Car Porters, but Meany lent credence to his objection when he promised that the federation "does not intend to force national unions, despite their constitutions, to expel from membership unions that have every legal right to membership." Randolph rose immediately to challenge the president. He said, "Now, either we are for or we are not for segregated unions. It isn't logical to permit an organization to carry on a given type of behavior merely because the members want it. If it is true, then a Communist-dominated union is perfectly legitimate if the members wanted it." Meany went on the offensive then, challenging Randolph's own logic. He responded, "As

I understand it, it is your position that you put the desire of the Negro members to maintain their union as it has been maintained over the years in the class with corruption and communism. Will you consider it a violation of this policy if the Bricklayers union did not attempt to eliminate these segregated unions that they have had for so many years because the members do not want them eliminated? Is this your idea of a democratic process, that you don't care what the Negro members think?" When Randolph simply answered, "Yes," Meany replied in a fury, "This is not my policy. I am for the democratic rights of the Negro members. Who appointed you as the guardian of the Negro members in America?" Randolph responded, "We don't have to get emotional about it. I don't believe that the members of a union have a right to maintain a Jim Crow local." When Meany said, "That is up to them," Randolph asked, "What about a group of members in a union who want to have a communist-dominated union?" Meany responded, "They can't have it and belong to this federation." Randolph then pointed out the contradiction, saying, "But then they ought not to have it as a Jim Crow local either." "That is where you and I part company, Phil," Meany said, adding, "I think these Negro members have some rights and have a right to think for themselves."[7]

Meany's intemperate question, "Who appointed you . . .?" triggered a blowback in the Black community. The editor of the *Baltimore Afro-American*, which had had an on-again, off-again relationship with Randolph, said that Meany's words were "shocking and distasteful." The NAACP telegraphed the AFL-CIO president to say that the association "fully supports Randolph's demand for positive action against discrimination." And the Trade Union Leadership Council (TULC), the UAW's Black caucus in Detroit, likewise wrote to Meany, "we unqualifiedly support the position of Brother Randolph and . . . we are at a complete loss to understand yours . . . We also want to clear you up on the matter that seemed so vexing to you, the question of Brother Randolph's 'appointment' as guardian of all

Negroes in the labor movement." They explained, "Brother Randolph was accorded this position by acclamation of the Negro people in recognition of his having devoted almost half a century of his life to freedom's cause."[8]

Though Randolph himself had a much milder reaction to Meany's tantrum, having endured decades of white stalling and temporizing, he was not one to dismiss a gauntlet so carelessly thrown down. He was a stubborn man and a veteran of four Black labor organizations that for many years existed outside the House of Labor. Looking forward from that moment, the odds were that a fifth was on the horizon.

. . .

In the aftermath of the 1959 AFL-CIO convention, a gathering that once again proved the white-led labor movement's inconsistency in the fight for racial justice, Randolph accepted the presidency of another organization. He spoke to the steering committee of a proposed "National Negro Labor Committee," which the group would later rename the "Negro American Labor Council" (NALC) to distinguish itself from the defunct NNLC. On November 14, 1959, at the Hotel Carnegie in Cleveland, Ohio, he articulated the need to confront institutional racism in the labor movement. He said, "racially segregated, or jim crow-unions, local or national or international, are a violation of the moral law and also the union law of the AFL-CIO and, perhaps, the civil law of government, as well as a violation of sound trade union morality which stems from the concept of the unity of all workers." A new organization was necessary, he added, "because the AFL-CIO, though committed to a national policy against discrimination and segregation based upon race or color, will not voluntarily move toward the implementation of this policy unless it is caused to move, and it cannot be caused to move except through an organization which is committed to the elimination of discrimination and segregation." In this, Randolph went out of his way to exculpate George Meany and the leadership of the federation itself, suggesting that "racial discrimination and segregation has reached the stage of institutionalization in the labor movement," where it is "taken for granted" and "viewed with utter complacency, apathy, unconcern, if not indifference." Such institutionalized discrimination, he said, manifested in numerous ways, including exclusion from membership and apprenticeship programs, the attendant categorization of "white" and "Black" jobs, and the lack of representation at all levels of leadership.[9]

Randolph was also clear that the proposed organization must take judicious political positions relative to the labor movement and the two-party system. He said, "A. It is not anti, but pro-AFL-CIO. B. It is pro AFL-CIO leadership. C. It is non-partisan, but not non-political. D. It is pro-Republicans that are pro–civil rights and pro-labor. E. It is pro-Democrats that are pro–civil rights and pro-labor. F. It is anti-Communist and anti-fascist." To Randolph, the new council could avoid being tracked into competing ideological camps if conceived of as an independent organization similar to those of Jewish and Catholic immigrants, who established their own ethnoreligious trades councils. However, he clarified that the proposed organization would not be a Black nationalist organization either. While sympathizing with Black nationalists, he insisted that the new council must dedicate itself to removing "the basis of Black Nationalism by working to the end of eliminating discrimination and segregation in the labor movement and the government."[10]

The nascent Negro American Labor Council appeared as though it would wholly reflect the politics of Black labor's centrist faction, but Randolph's vision would encounter opposition from the left and Black women. Nor were these two constituencies mutually exclusive, as former NNLC officer Vicki Garvin's position as a delegate suggests. The opening session of NALC's founding convention took place at the Statler Hilton Hotel in Detroit on the evening of May 27, 1960. The convention began smoothly enough with TULC co-founder Horace Sheffield welcoming the delegates. Other speakers included Dorothy I. Height of the National Council of Negro Women, Walter Reuther of the UAW, and James Cobb of the National Alliance of Postal Employees. Each spoke to the central theme of the convention and of NALC, namely, that "Black trade unionists must organize to fight discrimination and segregation in labor, industry and government."[11]

The following morning, Randolph gaveled the first substantive phase of the convention to order. After the Credentials Committee reported that there were 501 voting delegates and 146 official visitors in attendance (there were upward of 900 unofficial guests), Randolph opened the proceedings with a major speech. As with the founding of past Black labor organizations, he described the broader context as a crisis of unemployment in the African American community. He said that if they did not erase the color line in organized labor, "Negroes may wind up, not only as unskilled and unemployed, if not unemployable, but as the forgotten slum proletariat in the black ghettos of the great metropolitan centers of the country." He then turned to the potential of the civil rights revolution to transform the labor movement. "This revolution against discrimination and segregation based upon race in the House of Labor," he declared, "is just as authentic as the revolution which involved an organizational conflict between craft unionism and industrialism in the 1930s, and which brought about a split in the labor movement lasting for two decades." The NALC, Randolph argued, could harness and direct the civil rights revolution into the ongoing struggle over racism in organized labor. He said, "It can give Negro trade unionists a sense of unity, both among themselves and with their white brothers. It can also provide them with a sense of purpose, direction and mission and dedication to the philosophy of trade unionism and the program for equality of Negro trade unionists in the labor movement." "Its major historical mission," Randolph added, "is to help complete an incompleted [sic] social and moral revolution."[12]

But as the delegates turned to the adoption of a constitution, the convention threatened to go sideways. At issue was Article III, Section 6, which read that one of the NALC's objectives was "To design programs to fight racism, communism, corruption and racketeering in the trade union movement." At this point, several delegates jumped to their feet to say that the NALC should concern itself with fighting racism and discrimination and not communism. Randolph then rose to proclaim that "the Negro American Labor Council is unalterably committed to fighting communism and racism and corruption equally, because no trade union can survive unless we have a democratic society." The exchange failed to generate alternative language, so the delegates referred Article III back to committee for revision, setting up a potential showdown the following day. Several delegates expressed dissatisfaction that they had not had enough time to study the draft constitution. Randolph agreed to adjourn the session and urged the delegates to read the document overnight.[13]

Randolph reopened the convention at 10:15 a.m. on Sunday, May 29, with remarks that were hardly conciliatory to NALC's left-wing delegates. He said, "history demonstrates that free trade unionism cannot exist except within the framework of our democratic order [for] free trade unionism is unknown in totalitarian countries." Randolph then called on Milton Webster, his chief lieutenant in the Brotherhood of Sleeping Car Porters. Webster, who was chair of the NALC Resolutions Committee, reported that the objection of some was the notion that NALC would design its programs to *fight* communism. The organization, they said, "could not afford to go on record as attempting to develop a program which would involve expenditures and time and effort" in this area. "Fighting communism" implied that the NALC would become a full-time agency of the Red Scare and allow itself to be distracted from the main objective of eradicating the color line in unions. Moreover, the delegates pointed out the state was using the pretext of communism to disrupt the activities of legitimate civil rights organizations, even though the Communist Party no longer courted a mass following. Randolph himself had recently signed a petition circulated by Dr. Martin Luther King, Jr., who charged, "if the Un-American Activities Committee is to have the power to subpoena everyone they will misuse the power to stand in the way of integration." Knowing Randolph had softened his stance on communism and seeking to avoid further conflict, Webster recommended that the term "fight" be stricken. Also, instead of excluding communists completely, the revised draft constitution stipulated that no local chapters could be "officered, controlled, or dominated by communists, fascists or other totalitarians." With that, the delegates agreed to pass the remainder of the constitution.[14]

Having approved the governing document of the organization, the body turned to electing its officers. Once again, the initial phase of the process went off without a hitch. Randolph asked Thomas Starks of the United Mine Workers to assume the chair for the election of NALC president. Horace Sheffield nominated Randolph, while Harlem labor organizer and New York NAACP president Joe Overton seconded. The delegates voted unanimously in favor. The convention then turned to the election of sixteen vice presidents. At least three of the vice-presidential nominees had progressive bona fides. Horace Sheffield and Buddy Battle, though not Communists, were elected officers of UAW Local 600, and Cleveland Robinson of New York was a former NNLC activist and vice president of District 65 of the Distributive, Processing and Office Workers Union. With this slate, the Negro American Labor Council was beginning to assemble Black trade unionists from across the political spectrum. The problem was that they were all men.[15]

When the delegates moved to unanimously adopt the all-male slate, UAW activist L. Joy Jennings rose in opposition. She said, "I am getting a little tired of our organization consistently giving us slates of men. We have a lot of women around here. You are saying . . . us rank and filers are going to have a chance to nominate people from local areas. That isn't enough, because according to this Constitution the vice presidents have a hell of a lot of power." She continued, "Some of the women have gotten together and have brought up some names. I think we should listen to them. I think we should be fair. We are fighting discrimination here. I am tired of being discriminated against as a Negro, but I am getting sick and tired of you men discriminating against me as a woman." Another delegate, Jeanette Strong of the United Steel Workers, then grabbed the microphone and spoke over Randolph while he tried in vain to regain the floor. Describing her as "a stocky woman in a brown sweater," the *New York Times* reported that "she became the center of a milling throng of angry male and female delegates." As arms swung and bodies crashed into one another, the *Times* continued, Randolph's "gavel thundered and through it all, Mrs. Strong kept talking." Eventually the chair recognized another woman delegate (unnamed in the official proceedings), who pointed out that the National Steering Committee was composed of two women representatives. She said, "If these women were capable and able to assist the National Steering Committee in helping to set up this Convention that we are so proud of here today, then I feel that if we are going to do this on a permanent basis, women should not be deleted." "We are fighting discrimination as far as the Negro in labor is concerned," she said. "Let us not here today discriminate against the women in this organization. . . . I can finish this up in one sentence. We are willing to pay for freedom."[16]

Had the NALC's all-male leadership conceded the point on the spot, the conflict likely would have ended and the convention adjourned, but Randolph ignored the revolt and proceeded with the vote on his original proposal anyway. The official convention proceedings politely called what happened next a "vociferous demonstration," but in fact the women delegates booed and jeered their president. They demanded that women be nominated to be national vice presidents and refused to adjourn without the question settled. The *Chicago Defender* reported, "For once Randolph was at a loss." At this point, Daisy Bates of the NAACP, who had addressed the convention the night before, suggested that Randolph allow seventy-five female delegates to nominate candidates for two more national leadership positions. At last, the president relented and offered to entertain a motion to amend the constitution. The amendment provided for two additional vice presidents on the executive board. Because the assembly was divided on the question and Randolph was unsure of the outcome, he called for a standing vote so that the yeas and nays could be counted. The motion carried. The women of the NALC then caucused and nominated Agnes Willis, a member of the left-led UE in New York, and Lola Belle Holmes, a garment workers union activist from Chicago, to be their representatives. Randolph read the new slate aloud with Willis and Holmes included, and the delegates approved the slate, again by a standing vote. With this last conflict resolved, Randolph said, "Let me say the time is now ready for adjournment."[17]

. . .

Though the NALC convention was raucous, it had accomplished something that had not been done since 1936 and the founding of the National Negro Congress: it united the left and centrist factions of the Black labor movement. Having come in behind their new organization, they set about building a mass organization. At their first executive board meeting on May 30, 1960, the leadership laid plans to found more local councils and hire a full-time national director and stenographer for the national office. Because they had exhausted the funds of participating organizations with the founding convention, the council launched a national fundraising drive through the sale of golden founding membership cards worth $25.00 apiece. In July, the board prioritized a membership drive. The national vice presidents agreed to assist their existing twenty-three locals with grassroots recruitment. Conversation also turned to a legislative program. The Executive Board voted unanimously to maintain a non-partisan position in their advocacy of civil rights so as to garner the maximum support of pro–civil rights members in both parties. As an adjunct to their legislative strategy, they sought the public endorsement of prominent civil rights leaders, especially NAACP Executive Secretary Roy Wilkins and Dr. King of the Southern Christian Leadership Conference. Finally, to further galvanize support for the new organization, Randolph proposed that the NALC sponsor a Workshop and Institute on Racial Bias in the Trade Union Movement. The purpose was to be three-fold: "to bring about a solution of the problems dealing with racial restrictions in local unions, a correction of trade union practices adversely affecting Negro employment opportunities, and also problems of racial discrimination in apprenticeship programs."[18]

George Meany was not pleased. He had in fact declined an invitation from Randolph to speak at the NALC's founding convention, but what Meany heard afterward about the gathering fueled his displeasure. The more progressive activists, as we have seen, put their differences aside to unify behind the NALC program. Meany, however, picked up on the conflict at the convention between younger militants who wanted the NALC to be an outside Black pressure group, and others who sought to maintain the council's relationship with the federation. Randolph downplayed the tension and assured the AFL-CIO president that the new organization wanted to increase the prestige of the labor movement in the Black community and hold the federation to its constitutional pledges against racism. Nevertheless, Meany issued another intemperate attack. Convinced that the NALC was a seething mass of Black separatists and nationalists and that Randolph was now beholden to them, he had this advice for the council: "Keep out of our business and attend to their own."[19]

Having earned the undeserved hostility of organized labor, NALC ratcheted up the pressure by hosting the slightly renamed Workshop and Institute on Race Bias in Trade Unions, Industry and Government on February 17, 1961, in Washington, DC. The council ran the workshop much like a Fair Employment Practice Commission, hearing testimony from a variety of witnesses and experts. Cleveland Robinson chaired the workshop, while law professors from Howard University and Yale presided. Among the speakers were Dr. King, Roy Wilkins, Congressman Adam Clayton Powell of New York, and President Kennedy's labor secretary, Arthur Goldberg. JFK himself sent a telegraph to the workshop that read, "I fully share your deep concern over the grave issue of unemployment and over the added burdens carried by those who suffer from the racial bias that still unhappily remains in our midst." Clearly, Kennedy had anticipated the NALC's message, for the workshop hit on precisely these social problems. Its "Time for Action" resolution read, "We are in a period of economic crisis. Many millions of working Americans are jobless, without food and shelter." But whereas unemployment among white workers was estimated at 7 percent, "it is more than 15 percent among Negro workers." The disparity, the participants argued, was "due to the long standing policy of racial discrimination levelled against the Negro people by Industry, Labor, Government and Education." And it was the Black worker's responsibility to overturn this policy. The workshop resolved, "The Negro workers through the Negro American Labor Council must lead the struggle for complete equality in the Labor Movement." The gathering also advanced proposals to address discriminatory practices against Black women such as sexist wage differentials and unequal job opportunities, including in industries where women had historically been excluded. Additionally, they proposed to host a series of workshops on Black women's grievances and appoint Black women to all NALC committees.[20]

The workshop had numerous positive effects from the point of view of the council. So energizing was the event that delegates from Connecticut, San Francisco, Philadelphia, Milwaukee, Detroit, and New York were inspired to host similar events to recruit new members and raise public awareness of the effect of trade union racial bias on Black unemployment. In New York, the local council hosted an Unemployment Action Conference in June 1961. In September, they convened an Emergency Committee for Unity on Social and Economic Problems, at which NALC invited none other than Malcolm X of the Nation of Islam to join the council's efforts. NALC's first big victory also came after the workshop. On March 6, 1961, President Kennedy issued an executive order requiring government agencies and federal contractors to take "affirmative action" to ensure that workers were treated "without regard to their race, creed, color or national origin." Meanwhile, Black women activists established women's departments in the local councils of Chicago and New York City. They also ascended to elected leadership in Jersey City, Philadelphia, and Oakland. Riding their momentum, NALC vice president Lola Belle Holmes asked Randolph for a committee at the second NALC convention to be devoted exclusively to the challenges of Black women. Rather than invite another fiasco, Randolph agreed. He wrote to Holmes, "May I say that I am in accord with your ideas. . . . [W]e do not want our Negro sisters to feel that we are separating them from the brothers of the Negro American Labor Council."[21]

From Meany's point of view, however, the effects of the workshop were pernicious, though these were largely due to his own stubbornness. Despite NALC's calls for the integration of apprenticeship programs, union leadership, and AFL-CIO staff, Meany refused to engage. Quite the contrary, when he discovered that Theodore Brown, assistant director of the AFL-CIO's Civil Rights Department, was listed on the NALC's letterhead, Meany became incensed. On April 30, 1961, he fired Brown on the bureaucratic pretext that he had charged the federation for travel to civil rights meetings. NALC's response to Meany's decision did not exactly ingratiate the council to the federation either. Council vice president Joe Overton announced that the NALC leadership would be meeting on May 7 to plan a work stoppage at AFL-CIO headquarters in Washington, DC. Cleveland Robinson opened that meeting by calling Meany a racist. Some recommended that the council sue the federation. Randolph worried that these counter-maneuvers would embolden conservatives to escalate their attacks on the labor movement. After a back and forth, Overton said, "Let's march on Washington." The suggestion hung in the air and was not dismissed, for after all the inventor of the March on Washington Movement was in the room. It was Horace Sheffield who recommended that the council delay such a march until Randolph had a chance to talk to Meany at the AFL-CIO executive council in June. In November, the delegates to the NALC's second annual convention would vote in favor of Sheffield's approach. They resolved to work through their local unions and elect delegates to the December 1961 AFL-CIO convention who would push the civil rights agenda.[22]

As it turns out, the June executive council meeting went about as badly as the 1959 AFL-CIO convention. Randolph showed up with a new memorandum, calling for stronger civil rights policies in the face of a widening gulf between the labor movement and the Black community. He also presented reports that affiliated unions in the port of New York City were discriminating against Black workers and that the Virginia AFL-CIO had agreed to desegregate its annual convention when the NALC threatened to boycott the event. This last victory prompted Randolph to announce a national campaign to ensure that "all AFL-CIO State Federation Conventions are completely desegregated." Meany responded by blaming Randolph for "the gap that has developed between organized labor and the Negro community." To make matters worse, at Meany's suggestion, the white members of the executive council voted to censure Randolph for making "incredible assertions, false and gratuitous statements, and unfair and untrue allegations." Countering Randolph's persistent call to expel segregated unions, the president of the conservative Brotherhood of Railway Clerks prepared a motion in advance of the AFL-CIO annual convention to expel Randolph from the executive council.[23]

The censure report took issue with the notion that segregated unions should be expelled on the grounds that expulsion would stall the civil rights agenda in organized labor. "Put outside the ranks of the federation," the report read, "the offending organization is left free to carry on its discriminatory practices—probably more stubbornly than ever." These unions, it said, would be "no longer accessible to corrective influences from the parent body through education and persuasion." When a New York Times reporter asked why this logic did not apply to the Teamsters who had been expelled for corruption, Meany rejected the premise of the comparison, insisting that their decision applied neither to the Teamsters nor to the Communists. He said, "I do not equate the problem of racial discrimination with the problem of corruption any more than I equate Hungary with Little Rock." He added further that Randolph was wrong to push his agenda through a hostile outside organization. "We can only get moving on civil rights," Meany said, "if he comes over to our side and stops throwing bricks at us."[24]

Black civil society and a handful of white-led unions panned the censure. NALC vice president Richard Parrish wondered why the so-called proponents of civil rights in the executive council did not rush to Randolph's defense. He asked, "Where was Walter Reuther, where was [National Maritime Union president] Joe Curran, where was [IUE president] Jim Carey? Where were all these liberals when the vote was taken?" NAACP leader Roy Wilkins said that the censure reflected the AFL-CIO's "moral bankruptcy," while Dr. King called the censure "shocking and deplorable." Even Jimmy Hoffa of the disgraced Teamsters piled on. He called the decision "a gross injustice to a labor leader who has done more than anyone in the labor movement to maintain its integrity and unity in the fight for the complete integration of Negro and white workers in the house of labor."[25]

The day after the censure, October 13, 1961, the US Commission on Civil Rights published a 246-page report, essentially confirming all of Randolph's charges. While the commission praised the unions in meatpacking, auto, and the needle trades for taking "forceful steps" to integrate the movement, they observed that "most international unions," especially in the building trades, "have failed to exhibit any profound concern over civil rights problems." The report further distinguished between the upper echelons of organized labor and the rank and file. "Within the labor movement itself civil rights goals are celebrated at the higher levels," but "internal barriers tend to preserve discrimination at the workingman's level." They therefore recommended that the federal government take active steps to prohibit discrimination among government agencies, federal contractors, and unions and deny collective bargaining protections to unions that denied membership to any individual on the basis of race, color, creed or national origin.[26]

In contrast, Randolph himself expressed calm determination in the face of a possible censure. At the December 1961 AFL-CIO executive council meeting in Bal Harbor, Florida, where the federation was holding its annual convention, Randolph said that while his colleagues had publicly denounced him, he was "willing to go through the fires in order to abolish second-class status for black people in this country." He warned, "It must be done, and it must be done now—not tomorrow. We cannot wait for tomorrow. In a nuclear age, tomorrow may never come." Randolph's stubborn resolve seemed to have an effect. By the time the convention adjourned, the AFL-CIO had voted down the motion to expel Randolph and passed a civil rights resolution to "intensify its drive to make fully secure equal rights for all Americans in every field of life and to assure all workers, without regard to race, color, creed, national origin or ancestry the full benefits of union membership." It was the first time that the institutionalized labor movement had adopted a civil rights resolution since Randolph began working with the AFL in 1929.[27]

. . .

But even as Randolph seemed to have some success in pushing the AFL-CIO toward a détente with the NALC, he faced conflicts with both the International Ladies Garment Workers Union (ILGWU) and the militants in the Council itself. The NALC's Greater New York chapter is a case in point. In a newsletter article titled, "Steel Workers Sold Out," local NALC activists excoriated the mainstream labor movement for bargaining what they deemed a sub-par contract in a time of widening inequality and mounting unemployment. The article read, "With millions of workers on the unemployment rolls; with the cost of living increasingly on the rise . . . with the income gap between the workers and the Power Elite rapidly opening into a gulf . . . the leadership of the United Steelworkers of America 'negotiated' (and we use this word very loosely) a sell-out contract." On May 28, 1962, Randolph scolded the New York chapter for their injudicious opinion piece. Though he disagreed with their analysis of the contract, his main concern was with maintaining the council's relations with organized labor. He wrote, "such reckless attacks can only win the implacable opposition of the Steelworkers Union to NALC and thereby cause both Negro and white members of the union to turn against our movement." In the same newsletter, the New York militants also charged the AFL-CIO with sabotaging the founding convention of the continental African trade union federation by organizing against "the domination of the Soviet Union's World Federation of Trade Unions." Here, too, Randolph warned the New York chapter of the article's political impact in the labor movement. He wrote, "The AFL-CIO and the [African federation] ICTFU can only interpret this attack, allegedly by the Negro American Labor Council, as evidence of its opposition to the philosophy of free, democratic trade unionism and its interest in fostering the progress and power of the totalitarian type trade union."[28]

In August, the New York chapter embroiled Randolph in the ongoing feud between Herbert Hill, labor secretary of the NAACP, and David Dubinsky, president of the ILGWU. Hill had charged Dubinsky with relegating his Black and Puerto Rican members to the lowest-paid and most menial jobs. The accusation against a union with civil rights bona fides caused such a sensation that Adam Clayton Powell held hearings in the House of Representatives to investigate the matter. The most controversial aspect of Hill's and the NAACP's challenge was the idea of using the Landrum-Griffin Act of 1959 as a tool to desegregate organized labor. Originally sponsored by anti-union legislators from Michigan and Georgia, the Act was framed as a way to protect union members from the corruption of so-called "union bosses." Though some unions were certainly corrupt, trade unionists both Black and white were concerned that anti-union government officials might use the Act (and the pretext of corruption) to destroy the labor movement. Herbert Hill hoped to use Landrum-Griffin for a purpose other than that for which it was intended, namely, to decertify unions that discriminated against Black and other minoritized workers. Decertification was what one might call the nuclear option, for it nullified the legal right of a union to represent their members in collective bargaining.[29]

Nevertheless, some NALC leaders, like Horace Sheffield of Detroit, and several in NALC's New York chapter, like Joe Overton, believed that the council should support the NAACP's Landrum-Griffin plan. Referencing Powell's congressional hearing, the New York chapter published a circular that read, "We of the Negro American Labor Council know that this investigation is long . . . overdue. We know how we suffered lower wages on account of race bias." Randolph intervened again to put out the fire. Three days after the circular was published, Randolph wrote to ILGWU president Dubinsky, "Permit me to say that this circular is unauthorized and does not reflect the position of the Negro American Labor Council on the long progressive history of the International Ladies' Garment Workers' Union, a notable symbol of social, free democratic trade unionism under your distinguished leadership." He informed Dubinsky that the chapter president Fred Hall had assured the NALC leadership that a group of rank-and-file ILGWU members would issue the circular in their own names. Dubinsky was unmoved. As if blaming Randolph for the actions of the NAACP, he wrote back saying, "Mr. Hill has circularized the members of the Senate and other distinguished citizens with a statement he describes as 'testimony' before [Powell's] Committee, despite the fact that the Committee refused to accept the statement." Dubinsky went on to write that with respect to minority representation in union leadership, no Black or Puerto Ricans were available to take on elected office. At this, Randolph became noticeably impatient and went so far as to affirm Hill's charges against the union, while—diplomatically—exonerating Dubinsky from any racial prejudice on his part. He wrote, "While I reaffirm my belief that you . . . and the ILGWU are not anti-Negro or anti-Puerto Rican, I don't mean by this that racial discrimination does not exist in the ILGWU." Incredulous of his "skepticism about the availability of competent material among the Negro and Puerto Rican workers for positions as business agents and vice presidents of the Union,"

Randolph continued, "May I suggest that your skepticism is hardly well founded, for I am quite certain that there are available workers among Negroes and Puerto Ricans who are capable of filling these posts."[30]

The foregoing developments—from the NAACP's feud with the ILGWU to Randolph's escalating conflict with the NALC's more militant activists—formed the backdrop of the NALC's third annual convention, which was held on November 10, 1962, in New York City. Randolph's repeated overtures to the white-led labor movement foreshadowed trouble with his critics in the council. Over the objection of several NALC activists, Randolph invited George Meany to address the convention and he accepted. Even David Dubinsky, who remained deeply unpopular with the Black community, was sufficiently appeased by Randolph's stern diplomacy that he sent a note of congratulations. In a telegraph, Dubinsky wrote, "The Negro American Labor Council is fortunate to have as its head one who has been tested and proven in the fight for . . . equal rights, and we congratulate you." Noting the palpable tension that this caused within the council, the *New York Times* observed that Randolph was engaged in "a two-front battle of enormous complexity." The nation's paper of record went on to encourage the AFL-CIO to have some sympathy for the longtime labor leader. "The Federation should be especially sensitive to the difficulty of Mr. Randolph's role," the *Times* wrote, "because it is caught in a similar squeeze between those who want more done against race bias and those who want nothing done." The council's militant members, meanwhile, were incredulous at Randolph's friendly posture toward what they viewed as their common enemy. James Haughton, who had served as Randolph's assistant since the NALC's inception, was to say that Randolph was "the greatest Uncle Tom in the American labor movement" and insisted, "It is impossible to fight discrimination from within the councils of organized labor."[31]

Given the emergent tensions, the NALC leadership tried to set the tone of the convention early. UAW president Walter Reuther gave a spirited address, targeting middle-of-the-road trade unionists who expressed support for civil rights while objecting to the speed with which Black people wanted those rights. He said, "You know I have no patience with these people who say, 'Well, I'm for civil rights. I'm for equal opportunity in employment, in education, in housing, but why aren't the Negroes a little patient?'" Reuther earned the applause of the largely Black audience by answering his own question. He declared, "I think that we will resolve this problem in America when white Americans quit criticizing the impatience of Negroes and become equally impatient so that we can get on with the job that has to be done." After Reuther spoke, Richard Parrish, a vice president of both the NALC and New York's powerful United Federation of Teachers, said, "Brother Randolph I'm sure speaks for everyone here when he just said to me the other minute, 'Dick, be sure to say that the Negro American Labor Council does not endorse slander against George Meany, or anybody else. Slander is not the method we use.'" Even the demands of Black women occasioned little controversy, a stark contrast to the fracas at the founding convention. NALC vice president Lola Belle Holmes said, "The Negro woman faces dual disadvantage—race and sex. We feel that Negro men have the responsibility to fight for equal pay for Negro women who supplement the family income to raise the standard of living for every Negro family." The convention adopted a resolution urging its local affiliates to "take whatever steps necessary to upgrade the Negro working woman, thereby putting the Negro woman in a position to meet head on the social, economic and education challenge in society in which we live." Despite their best efforts, however, the NALC leadership could not prevent what happened next.[32]

The trouble began when the leadership presented a report on the crisis of unemployment in the Black community that contained nothing about exerting mass pressure to resolve the crisis. A delegate named Jim Horton took the floor to say, "We can pass resolutions about what should be done, but if we don't have some statements of record from this convention that we will demonstrate around this question of the government and the labor unions and will not take direct action to solve this problem, I think that we should very clearly come out of this convention with an agreement on how we are going to implement our Negro program to deal with this question." At this point a delegate from New Haven named Charles Collins jumped to his feet to address Frank Evans, who was chairing the session on unemployment. He said, "Mr. Chairman, I've been very disappointed here this morning. This is my first experience at a convention. . . . Now it seems to me that we're losing something here at this convention, the spirit. Some of us came to see ourselves fighting for things which we represent. . . . I think we have waited too long until we have got into action." Referring to Parrish's remarks on slandering George Meany, Collins continued to applause, "We seem afraid to embarrass some top labor leaders, because we know there is jobs with discrimination, period. . . . [I]t's what we have found to be an acute fact. I think we have to use strong language to that effect." Frank Evans denied that the NALC was backing away from the program they set out in 1960. Winning some applause for the leadership, he said to Collins, "we're not worried about embarrassing anybody. . . . [I]f you don't think the language in this resolution is strong enough all you have to do is say so, but let's don't start out stating that somebody is afraid of hurting somebody else. The NALC is not afraid of anybody." At that, the contending delegates agreed among themselves to amend the report to include stronger language.[33]

Conflict seemed to be averted until NALC vice president Joseph Beavers presented the recommendations of the convention's workshop on discrimination. At issue was the language "that the NALC support the National Association for the Advancement of Colored

People in pursuance of promotion and equal job rights and opportunities for all minority workers." Once again, those advocating militant action clashed with those who seemed to advocate more polite support for the NAACP. Once Beavers finished, a speaker from the floor said, "I believe that our support of the NAACP does not go quite far enough." They suggested instead that any union found to be restraining the "promotion or placement of Negroes working within the union should be certified for deeper inspection." Another speaker referenced the recent controversy in the garment industry, saying, "I think that the question of discrimination has to be placed before the country from this NALC convention from the point of view that this is a no-holds-barred struggle." When Frank Evans, who was still chairing the session, said that a resolution on the garment industry was coming, the previous speaker took to the floor again and cut in. He said, "Brother Chairman, I wanted to bear with you but I am making a point that the significance of this resolution that's been presented here that must go out to the country [is] that we regard the struggle against discrimination in industry, government or the trade unions as a no-holds-barred struggle." Evans again attempted to say that they had a resolution prepared "on this specific question of what happened in New York in the garment industry." The delegate then clarified that he wanted the council to support militant action in all industries. He said, "We support the fighting and militant actions of other organizations and we think that it ill behooves people who have not made struggle such as are necessary say in the railroad industry. I'm speaking of those industries that bar Negroes."[34]

When a third speaker rose to speak, it became clear that this was a coordinated action. The new speaker said, "My point on this report is that we understand and we make clear, brother chairman, going from here that we intend to carry this struggle in a no-holds-barred fashion not in one single industry . . . and where all kinds of methods of struggle are necessary." A fourth speaker rose to say, "I'd like to make a motion to amend the report to reflect the sentiments of the brother here that this organization go on record of carrying out a no-holds-barred fight against discrimination in labor, industry and government." They then added another provision, which revealed that action on the floor was coming from those who supported Herbert Hill's Landrum-Griffin plan. The speaker continued, "And we go on record as being in favor of decertification of those unions that have discrimination against Negroes and other Minority groups." After some back and forth on what happened at the workshop, still another speaker took the floor. They said to applause, "Brother Chairman, listen, I paid to come to this convention and I'm going to say what I have to say and I'm not going to give this mike to anybody. Now, there's too much of this railroading going on and we're not going to have it. . . . [Y]ou're going to have to kill me to take this mike, but I'm going to have it."[35]

Randolph had held his fire throughout this and the previous floor fight, but at the charge of railroading, the NALC president himself took and held the floor. He said, "Now, brothers, here we are in a convention seeking to work out problems that are of eminent concern to the great masses of the Black people in this country. You can't do that in . . . a mob. We can't have a riot in this convention. I'm amazed at you. It's ridiculous. . . . We never had anything like this before at NALC." Randolph then reminded the assembly that the press was watching their deliberations. He continued, "We've got the press here that will go out to the country and point out that you've got a bunch of people—a bunch of clowns at this convention who have no common sense whatsoever." With the eyes of the world upon them, he declared, "We can afford to be opposed. We can afford to be denounced, but we can't afford to be laughed at." Randolph then sought to quiet the militants by insinuating that they were being undemocratic and seeking to overturn the result of the voting at the convention's workshop on discrimination. He pointed out, "Now the fact is we've got a group here that lost out in the election and that is the group that is creating the rumpus—the riot. Now that's a disgrace. I have absolutely no patience with it. . . . You are making a clown out of the working class of this country, we are not going to stand for it."[36]

If Randolph had hoped to scold the militants into line, it was not at all clear looking forward from that moment that he had succeeded. Having referred the question of the council's support of the NAACP back to the NALC Executive Board for consideration, Cleveland Robinson invited Secretary Clay Stout to read the new resolutions aloud. The proposed language, which Robinson himself crafted, signaled strong support of the NAACP without mentioning the Landrum-Griffin decertification tactic. The resolution registered the "full support of the labor program of the NAACP, which has worked for more than 20 years to eliminate the racist practices of many important trade unions through conciliation, negotiation, and persuasion with very limited progress having been achieved for Negro workers." It then endorsed "completely the NAACP's efforts to seek relief for Negro workers through the courts and develop a new body of labor law on the question" and further resolved "that this convention views any attack on the NAACP as ultimate attacks on all of us who support the NAACP Program."[37]

At this point, Horace Sheffield took to the floor to argue in favor of including explicit language on decertifying unions found guilty of racial discrimination. He said, "I obviously am in support of the resolution. The question is that I don't think it goes far enough." Disclosing the resolution that was defeated by a vote of 7 to 6 in the Executive Board, he said,

This section was left out. That is this: 'Be it further resolved that it is the judgment of this convention that unions which persist in discrimination against Negro workers, and other minorities, should be deprived of the protection of certification by the United States government, as the exclusive collective bargaining agent, and that we specifically endorse the NAACP's action in seeking the de-certification of trade unions that have been proven guilty in engaging and persisting in discriminatory practices. . . .' We also suggested that copies of the resolution—I notice that's been deleted—should be sent to George Meany, to all members of AFL-CIO Executive Council, NAACP Secretary Roy Wilkins and the press.

Sheffield ended by stating, "anything short of the inclusion of this is a backward step on the part of the NALC." He vowed to exert "what influence I can to militate" support for the NAACP.[38]

Richard Parrish of New York rose in opposition to Sheffield. He admitted that the voting was tight on the draft resolutions but supported the proposed language anyway because he did not believe the NAACP's legal tactics would succeed without developing "political and economic strength in the labor movement" as the NALC was doing. Parrish in fact speculated that organized labor "would be glad . . . if the NALC were to leave that task aside and join the NAACP because they know they have control of the courts." He added, "What they fear, is the power of Black men and women working in the labor movement, for democracy." Parrish then shared an example of the real work to be done. Randolph and the NALC, he reminded the audience, "desegregated the Virginia State AFL-CIO convention by their political force," and George Meany issued a corresponding edict applying to all state affiliates. He said, "I submit this is the reason we are in the Negro American Labor Council. . . . [W]e are not going to rely upon de-certification or any other legal tool even—and I say even—if it's in the hands of the NAACP." Parrish prevailed. After the amended resolution on the NAACP passed, Cleveland Robinson, a known leftist who was also a skeptic of the Landrum-Griffin Act, said with relief, "We were on the brink of disaster."[39]

As if the level of conflict were not enough already, a fight broke out about communist-controlled locals in the NALC. Over the course of the previous year, a number of NALC leaders charged that the CP had infiltrated their affiliates in Buffalo, Cleveland, and Chicago. Some denied the charges, while others admitted to them, but either way, no one knew how this so-called information had come to light. All became clear at the convention. NALC vice president Lola Belle Holmes told her fellow delegates that she had been working with the FBI to counter communist infiltration in the NALC, NAACP, and other Black organizations in Chicago. Informing on other NALC members, she insisted, was consistent with the council's anti-communist politics. L. Joy Jennings, who had helped to get Holmes elected to her leadership post at the founding convention, held a different opinion. She called Holmes's actions "disgraceful, shameful, and extremely damaging to the Negro people's movement as a whole and to the NALC in particular." On January 24, 1963, just two months after the NALC's third convention, Holmes testified against her comrades as promised, disclosing that the FBI had paid her to join the Communist Party in 1956 and inform on the NALC's Chicago local. Facing down an angry crowd as she left the hearing, Holmes said, "I expect to get more of this treatment, but it's worth it. It is the price of freedom." Randolph relieved Holmes of her leadership position in the NALC but sent council officials to investigate her allegations anyway. Timuel Black, a leader of the Chicago NALC, was outraged that the leadership was giving credence to the testimony of "an admitted communist and government spy," saying, "we certainly do not intend to stand idly by and watch honest persons vilified and slanderized." It was at this time that James Haughton resigned from his post as Randolph's assistant and blamed the council's apparent decline on "the present lack of militant leadership." He also accused Randolph and other NALC leaders of "serving as agents for a white, reactionary, labor leadership that is playing a vicious and unprincipled role in the struggle of all workers, black and white."[40]

Here, then, were two competing approaches to desegregating the labor movement. On the one hand, Horace Sheffield and the militant faction sought to use the full range of tactics at their disposal, a "no-holds-barred struggle" that included direct action and legal remedies like union decertification to kick organized labor in the backside. On the other hand, Randolph, Parrish, and even the leftist Cleveland Robinson hoped to mobilize the strength of Black workers to exert pressure on organized labor from within. This called for a more diplomatic approach of holding white labor leaders by the hand until they lived up to their stated commitment to racial equality. The mounting pressure generated by these competing forces—now under the same roof instead of two warring organizations—would lead Randolph to call for another March on Washington in 1963. Though he had been resistant to Joe Overton, who proposed the tactic in the heat of the conflict with George Meany, after the ugliness of the 1962 convention Randolph asked a trusted ally to plan the march: Bayard Rustin.

.   .   .

Bayard Rustin was born in 1917 in a West Chester, Pennsylvania, Quaker community. His maternal grandmother was a charter member of the NAACP, and Association leaders like James Weldon Johnson and W. E. B. Du Bois were regular guests in the Rustin home. Like so many of Black labor's legendary organizers, Rustin was an excellent student. He was class valedictorian at West Chester High School and went on to attend Wilberforce University in Ohio. In 1937, at the age of twenty-five, he dropped out of Wilberforce and traveled to Harlem, in part to explore his sexual attraction to men, which he did while working for a New Deal public works program and singing in

Greenwich Village cafés. Rustin joined the Young Communist League at this time but left when Stalin signed the Nazi-Soviet Non-aggression Pact. From that point on, he became part of a nucleus of anti-Stalinist radicals, who were generally socialist, democratic, and pacifist in their politics.[41]

Rustin's focus in those early years was the bellicose tenor of American foreign policy. The Cold War, he believed, was precluding any path toward peace and distracted the public's attention from basic social needs. In a pamphlet put out by the pacifist organization the Fellowship of Reconciliation, Rustin wrote, "The argument runs that getting tough with the Russians will bring them to their senses . . . when, actually, a rather substantial case can be made that our present discord with the Soviet Union may be in large part the result of our own past policies and unfriendly acts." Similarly, in a speech he delivered in 1948 at the Arch Street Meeting House in Philadelphia, Rustin said, "the struggle to provide men with bread, beauty and brotherhood, has been relegated to second place." "Our fears have brought about an armaments race," he reasoned, "and until we have broken the vicious circle of this race with the Soviet Union, there cannot be attention, energy and money given to the basic causes of war and injustice."[42]

Rustin was an activist of the highest order with bona fides stretching back to 1941, when he became a youth organizer for Randolph's original March on Washington (he in fact criticized the older organizer for canceling the march). He repeatedly put his body on the line for his beliefs. In 1942, police in Tennessee beat him savagely for refusing to give up his seat in the white section of a bus. That same year, Rustin not only co-founded the legendary civil rights organization the Congress of Racial Equality (CORE) with Paul Farmer, but also began a three-year prison sentence at Lewisburg Penitentiary for refusing to fight in World War II. In 1947, Rustin was arrested again, this time for conducting CORE's first "Freedom Ride" to desegregate the South (he served twenty-two days on a chain gang). After organizing overseas in India, Ghana, Nigeria, and England, he returned to the American South to help Dr. King with the 1955 Montgomery bus boycott and drafted the blueprint for the Southern Christian Leadership Conference. In the first three years of the NALC's existence, Rustin worked as executive secretary of the War Resisters League, which was led by Randolph's longtime friend, Fellowship of Reconciliation leader A. J. Muste.[43]

In December 1962, one month after the NALC's troubled convention, Rustin dropped by the Brotherhood of Sleeping Car Porters headquarters in Harlem to chat with Randolph, as he often did. Randolph, who was then seventy-three years old, and Rustin, who was fifty-two, were like two peas in a pod. They shared similar politics, each committed to an economic approach to the Black freedom struggle. They even looked the same. Both stood over six feet tall, with athletic physiques; the author Robert Penn Warren would write that Rustin's appearance was a "strange mixture of strength and sensitivity." On this particular visit, Randolph suggested that while Dr. King's demonstrations in the South were critical, the moment required a complementary mass protest that could push for civil rights and economic justice simultaneously. Randolph asked Rustin if he had any ideas. Rustin said he had none except possibly a march on the nation's capital, calling for jobs, a minimum wage, and guaranteed basic income. The elder statesman said that the march was an excellent idea and asked the younger organizer to draft a memorandum.[44]

Two months later, in January 1963, after conferring with Tom Kahn, a white socialist who was college friends with SNCC leader Stokely Carmichael, and Norman Hill, assistant program director for CORE, Rustin reconvened with Randolph to discuss the plans. The idea was to stage a mass demonstration "to draw attention to the economic crisis confronting the masses of unskilled and semiskilled Negro workers—a crisis which could be resolved only through a program of full employment for black and white workers." When Randolph pointed out that the demands were only economic in scope and recommended that they be broadened to include freedom more generally, Rustin said, "Fine. We'll call it a march for jobs and freedom."[45]

Having made the decision to move forward, Randolph and Rustin now had to mobilize the political will of Black civil society and organized labor. The first step in this process was to win the approval of the Negro American Labor Council, for it was the NALC, more than any other group, who would assume the primary operational command of the march. This they did on March 22-23, 1963, at the NALC's Executive Board meeting in New York City. The group approved a multi-pronged plan. To begin, the NALC resolved to be in the lead. In a letter to the NAACP's Roy Wilkins, Randolph wrote that the "Jobs Rights March . . . would be developed by the Negro American Labor Council with the cooperation of other organizations," including the NAACP, National Urban League, CORE, SCLC, and SNCC. Second, the board agreed to carry out a two-day event on June 13-14, 1963, including a march down Pennsylvania Avenue ending at the Lincoln Memorial, a lobby day with the members of the House and Senate, as well as a speech by, and a White House conference with, President John F. Kennedy.[46]

Though Rustin once said that Randolph's genius "was to use Dr. King as his left leverage"—that is, to gain King's approval first before asking the other leaders so they had no choice but to say yes—in fact, Randolph asked Wilkins first. This may have been done out of deference to the country's oldest Black civil rights organization and possibly because of its recent confrontation with the ILGWU and AFL-CIO. Be that as it may, Randolph approached Wilkins before anyone else. He made three requests: that the call for the march go out with Wilkins's signature; that letters be sent to all branches of the NAACP informing them of the march and urging their participation; and a cash contribution to get the organizing off the ground. To be fair, the very next person on Randolph's list was indeed Dr. King, followed by Dorothy Height of the National Council of Negro Women and Rosa Gragg of the National Association of Colored Women's Clubs. To them, Randolph sent a telegram that read, "Negro American Labor Council at Executive Board Meeting in New York March 23 went on record to develop a Negro emancipation march and mobilization on Washington for Jobs." It continued, "This effort must be massive in order to carry impact upon American conscience = We thus need support of major Negro leaders and organization. . . . We need the great moral weight of your name on the call. May I hear from you on this matter immediately." Similar communiqués would go out to James Farmer at CORE and Whitney Young of the Urban League.[47]

What is notable about this outreach is that the NALC had to cajole some organizations to support the march. This provides further evidence that Black labor was in the lead. Though some, like James Farmer of CORE, asked and promptly received approval from their respective boards, others required more persuasion. Whitney Young of the Urban League implied that he would be unwilling to join the coalition if it did not occupy equal status with the other groups. He wrote, "before affirmative answers can be given to the requests you have made of us, our Board wishes clarification around certain points." He explained, "we would prefer a relationship with your group and the others mentioned of a peer nature, which would suggest co-sponsorship rather than cooperation." Young also expressed concern over who might be at the head of the organization, likely because Rustin's reputation as a gay radical preceded him. "It would be necessary that a joint decision be reached, agreeable to all," he wrote, "as to the individual who coordinates this activity." Randolph worked to soothe Young's concerns. He wrote, "The Negro American Labor Council is in complete accord with the interest of the League to share in this project on a basis of equality with other organizations."

He further assured Young that, "Inasmuch as the Negro American Labor Council had to serve as the convening movement, some decision making and planning have already been done, but nothing too definitive which would exclude further discussion." But if Young had signaled an openness to co-sponsoring the march, then by April 13 he had withdrawn his support. The leader of the Urban League explained that the timing of the march (which by this point had been pushed back to October) and their nonprofit status prevented them from participating. But arguably the most important reason was that the League was worried about preserving their political relationships in the nation's capital. Young wrote that their reservations "centered around our present active working relationship with most of the departments and officials in Washington." He explained, "These would be quick to point out that their doors are completely open to us, and they would look with some suspicion, if not confusion, on our participation in the March."[48]

The April 10 planning meeting of the major Black organizations, which was both fractious and small, foreshadowed this disappointing result. The representatives of the Urban League wanted to have their cake and eat it, too: while declaring that "there would be some activities that the National Urban League could not participate in, such as the demonstrations," they said they "definitely want to be included." The NALC wanted the name of the demonstration to highlight the economic dimension of the struggle. Reminding the group that the NALC Board had suggested the "Emancipation March for Jobs for Negro Workers," Randolph suggested that they stick with "Emancipation March for Jobs." No one from the NAACP bothered to show up. Roy Wilkins said that he would send over John Horsell or Herbert Hill to represent the Association, but neither of the NAACP representatives was present.[49]

As late as April 23, four months and five days out from when the march would eventually take place, the coalition seemed to be in a shambles. At a meeting at march headquarters on West 130th Street in Harlem, Randolph informed the group that Roy Wilkins "has since found it impossible to participate in the march." He also reiterated that the Urban League remained fearful that "the march will interfere with its financial position as a tax-exempt organization." The one bright spot was that Dr. King had at last given his permission to use his name in connection to the march, albeit one month after Randolph asked him. The problem was that CORE, NALC, SNCC, and SCLC had no funds to offset the handicap of losing both the Urban League and the NAACP. Randolph revealed the shakiness of the coalition at this late date when he said to the group that he was "determined to go on if no one but NALC participated." It seemed more and more likely that Black labor would be alone in this fight.[50]

If the onus was on the NALC to unify Black civil society, then it was also on the council to mobilize the white-led labor movement. On two handwritten manuscript pages from the early days of the campaign, Rustin sketched out a six-part plan. The first move was to enroll the help of William Schnitzler, Secretary-Treasurer of the AFL-CIO and chairman of the federation's Civil Rights Committee. Rustin hoped that Schnitzler would be a co-chair of the march, pass a resolution urging all state federations, central labor councils, and affiliates to participate, and name August 28 the AFL-CIO's Jobs and Freedom Day. The second part of the plan was to schedule an interview with Walter Reuther, then the head of the AFL-CIO's Industrial Union Department. Rustin hoped to ask Reuther to be a march co-chair, too, and in that capacity to call upon all unions in his department to support the effort with cash and turnout. Next, Rustin sought to organize a meeting with Randolph and eight to ten sympathetic trade union leaders to raise funds, solicit organizers, drive turnout, and designate a labor council within the march administrative structure. It is worth noting that despite the supposedly civil relations between the council and the ILGWU, Rustin deleted the following from the plan: "Arrange a meeting with Gus Tyler to discuss ILGWU participation and support fundraising and community mobilization for March." The remaining parts of the labor plan consisted in asking all major unions to contribute marchers and funds and bring the unemployed to Washington.[51]

The plan worked well but not perfectly. On May 9, 1963, NALC Secretary Joe Overton sent letters advertising the march to all labor unions in New York City, all joint councils across the country, and the presidents of all international unions. Though Schnitzler never did become a co-chair of the march and the AFL-CIO did not issue an official endorsement, Meany was able to pass a compromise resolution at the AFL-CIO executive council in St. Louis that expressed support for its goals. The resolution read, "We are convinced that the AFL-CIO can make its major contribution to victory by continuing its all-out legislative activity on Capitol Hill and its efforts in cooperation with other like-minded groups to bring an end to segregation and inequality of opportunity in the local communities of America." On May 21, Overton sent copies of the Meany resolution to all board members, vice presidents, and secretaries in the NALC as well as to all labor affiliates in New York City and the nation.[52]

But true to the white-led labor movement's inconsistency on the question of interracial solidarity, George Meany became embroiled in a racial conflict that seemed to contradict the very resolution he helped to pass. In June 1963, several hundred union leaders in New York vowed to address the issue of racial discrimination, but as Vice President Lyndon Johnson soon discovered when he met with the city's building trades, articulating a civil rights program was different from executing one. After thirty-five hours of talks in late July, Johnson said, "Nobody can move these people. . . . They simply don't mean to do it." Perhaps the most famous case of white labor's continuing intransigence in this moment was Meany's very own Plumbers Local 2, the union that had launched his career in the federation.

The local struck the Bronx Terminal Market construction site when the contractor tried to hire one Black and three Puerto Rican workers. Meany said that the union struck because the four workers were scabs, but in fact the men had tried in vain to obtain union membership. The president of the NALC's New York local said that Meany's action "demonstrates that he is an outright prejudiced individual and cannot serve everyone in the American labor movement."[53]

NALC's appeal to Reuther went better. In late June, Randolph invited Reuther to attend a July planning meeting in New York. Days later, Randolph wrote again, notifying the UAW leader that clergy of the Catholic, Protestant, and Jewish faiths had joined with Black civil rights organizations in a coalition to stage the jobs march. He wrote, "All are agreed that organized labor should be a part of this great moral crusade," adding that the leaders of the march "asked me to urge you to join us as a co-chairman of our overall policy committee." Reuther telegrammed back simply, "Pleased to serve on Committee Re Washington Freedom March."[54]

Donations from organized labor soon began to flow. For example, on July 30, less than a month from the march, Alex Sirota, president of Local 140 of the Bedding, Curtain and Drapery Workers, wrote to James Farmer of CORE to say, "In accordance with the pledge made at our July 25th membership meeting, we are enclosing a check of $1000.00 as our contribution to the March on Washington Committee." Especially supportive were left-led unions with an established record of organizing minoritized industrial workers. Randolph wrote to Leon Davis, head of Local 1199, New York's health care workers' union, acknowledging receipt of their $1,000 contribution. He wrote, "It will always be a source of great pride to me personally and, this I am sure, to scores of other leaders of the Negro and Puerto Rican communities, that we were successful in mobilizing the full and active support of hundreds of thousands of minority group citizens behind the just struggle of your union in the 1959 and 1962 strikes." He continued, "Local 1199 is charting a road that all labor should emulate."[55]

Eventually, Black civil society came around, too. A turning point was the June 23 "Walk to Freedom" in Detroit, which Horace Sheffield and Robert Battle's Trade Union Leadership Council (TULC) organized together with Reverend C. L. Franklin. Both the NAACP and the Urban League opposed the Walk to Freedom, as they did the March on Washington, because they worried that militant action might jeopardize their relationships with the white power structure in the Motor City. Sheffield and Battle brokered the peace among the more cautious and militant elements by ensuring that the walk would bring together the struggles for fair employment and Southern civil rights. Over 125,000 people packed Woodward Avenue, a street the width of a multi-lane highway, and marched to a rally at Cobo Hall in downtown Detroit. It was the largest civil rights protest in US history up to that point. Dr. King, who spoke at the rally alongside the mayor of Detroit and Walter Reuther, said, "I have a dream this afternoon that one day, right here in Detroit, Negroes will be able to buy a house or rent a home anywhere that their money will carry them and that they will be able to get a job." Given the fact that Randolph and Rustin promised a march of 100,000, the Walk to Freedom proved that a mass demonstration of that magnitude could be peaceful and orderly.[56]

On July 2, Roy Wilkins of the NAACP and Whitney Young of the Urban League at last joined the leaders of the NALC, SNCC, SCLC, CORE, and the UAW in the leadership of the March on Washington for Jobs and Freedom. There they decided on both the final date of the action and the shape of the administrative team that would have operational control of the protest. The group moved up the date from October to August 28 in recognition of the eight-year anniversary of the murder of Emmett Till. Rustin then presented the draft demands, including a federal jobs program; a higher minimum wage; a Fair

Employment Practice law prohibiting racial discrimination in unions, industry, and government; and support for President Kennedy's civil rights bill. He estimated that the protest would cost $65,000 to pull off. Though the newest members of the leadership were broadly in agreement with this outline, they resurrected the issue of being associated with Bayard Rustin, a known Communist and conscientious objector, who had been arrested in California in the 1950s for engaging in homosexual activity. The atmosphere was tense, but in the end Randolph prevailed. The Chief agreed to be the director of the march, but in that role he would select Rustin as his deputy and national organizer. The group also elected the progressive Cleveland Robinson, leader of District 65 of the Distributive workers union, to head the march's Administrative Committee.[57] Once they had finally gathered all the principals under one umbrella in July, they had just under two months to organize what would become the largest public protest in US history up to that time.

· · ·

Though it has been said that the NALC was no mass organization, in fact, the structure the council put in place looked and acted like one. The march was a strict hierarchy. At the very top were the chairmen, consisting of leaders of the NAACP, NALC, CORE, SNCC, SCLC, UAW, and the Urban League. They were responsible for policy, the program, and expenditures, with payment handled by the treasurer of the march (the NALC) and the finance committee. The second level consisted of the vice-chairmen, who were national, civic, religious, labor, and fraternal leaders, both Black and white. The bulk of the operational work outside of paid staff members like Bayard Rustin and Rachelle Horowitz fell to the Administrative Committee, which was chaired by Cleveland Robinson and composed of one representative each from the main sponsoring organizations plus one woman and two representatives from the South. The Administrative Committee supervised the day-to-day implementation of policy as set by the chairmen but could also act fully for the chairmen in their absence. The director, A. Philip Randolph, set up the organization on a national scale in order to carry out the project, help raise funds to finance it, and assemble a staff and volunteers to see that the work got done, though in practice Rustin did the lion's share of these tasks. Next was a group of coordinators, one each from the main sponsoring organizations. The coordinators worked full-time out of the march's national office with the director; together they were responsible to the Administrative Committee. The only committee that was responsible for a special constituency was the Labor Committee, which was composed of an interracial group of trade union leaders, whose staff traveled nationally to enlist participation and financial assistance. Last, there were the local affiliates. Because the NALC understood that the local chapters of the sponsoring organizations were busy with their own work, they established separate march committees across the country, consisting of labor, civic, fraternal, church and youth members. The local committees were where the rubber met the road: they mobilized people to go to Washington, raised funds for transportation, educated people on the lobbying and activities that were to take place, and explained in their cities and on chartered transport the procedures to be followed in the nation's capital.[58]

The social connections of the leadership complemented the march's tight organization. Robinson's and Overton's extensive networks in the labor movement helped to establish strong local organizing committees, while Norm Hill, another Black trade unionist and NALC activist, crisscrossed the country in July and August to coordinate labor's efforts. Roy Wilkins did outreach to every NAACP branch, youth council, and state conference; NAACP labor secretary Herbert Hill worked with these local actors to build their organizing capacity. Anna Hedgeman, who was one of only two Black women in the leadership, organized religious groups, including white Christians from the South and the National Council of Churches. Meanwhile, Randolph and Reuther worked to bring along seventeen international unions, several state and municipal labor councils, and the AFL-CIO's Industrial Union Department. When it became clear that white and Black churches would not be able to fund transport from the South to the degree promised, it fell to Black trade unionists to make up the difference by requesting funds from their contacts in organized labor. On August 9, just eighteen days before the protest, Rustin wrote to Randolph saying, "The finance committee of the March on Washington for Jobs and Freedom urgently requests you to bring to the attention of the top labor leadership the necessity for their taking major responsibility for the transportation costs of bringing unemployed workers and freedom fighters from protest areas in the South to Washington on August 28th." NALC activist Corrine Smith organized a midnight benefit show at the Apollo Theater in Harlem, featuring Tony Bennett, Quincy Jones, and Stevie Wonder, that raised $30,000 to send unemployed workers to the march.[59]

Indeed, the "Freedom Train" took on a literal meaning as NALC pushed the white-led labor movement to supply the buses, trains, and planes necessary to transport marchers from across the land. Labor-organized transport came in at least three waves, according to the memos that Rachelle Horowitz sent to Rustin in August. An August 6 memo identified the early adopters: the Retail Wholesale and Department Store Union (RWDSU), NALC, ILGWU, and UAW. The ILGWU alone chartered a sixteen-car train and eight buses and hired doctors and nurses to help care for the marchers. By August 14, Horowitz reported that the IUE, International Brotherhood of Electrical Workers (IBEW), and the American Federation of State, County, and Municipal Employees (AFSCME) had joined the effort. The final list, dated August 22, reveals that organized labor added over two dozen more unions, including the Transport Workers Union

(TWU), Service Employees International Union (SEIU), American Federation of Teachers (AFT), Hotel Employees and Restaurant Employees Union (HERE), Amalgamated Clothing Workers (ACW), National Maritime Union (NMU), and United Steel Workers (USW).[60]

IUE's correspondence with their locals provides just one example of the discipline and union outreach that characterized the march. In one letter, Al Lowenthal, the union's human relations director, wrote, "A good job is being done, local by local, preparing transportation and food arrangements for volunteer delegations to participate in the Washington March on August 28th." He noted that members would be able to identify themselves with arm bands, sashes, hats, flags, signs, and local banners, but that the national office of the march would supply the placards. "No other slogans will be permitted," he warned. He added that IUE would have a reception area in the nation's capital and reminded local leaders to send their district office the size of their delegations no later than August 15th. Finally, Lowenthal advised that all buses would be boarded at 4:00 a.m. from New York City the day of the march and that each bus should have a captain.[61]

Transportation was not the only area in which Black labor convinced the wider union movement to provide support. Bayard Rustin persuaded the ILGWU and UAW to donate $20,000 for a high-powered sound system that could project speeches from the Lincoln Memorial to the Washington Monument, a distance of nearly one mile. Rustin also called upon the Guardian Association, a fraternal association of Black police officers, to provide security. Guardian president William H. Johnson recruited the help of similar associations to furnish a total of two thousand officers on the day of the march.[62]

Most Americans are familiar with the march's civil rights platform, and indeed, its purpose, as laid out in an internal memo, included "a call for effective civil rights legislation and a demonstration against any filibuster" in the US Senate that might derail President

Kennedy's civil rights bill. However, the crisis of unemployment and NALC's long-standing economic demands were the main focus. Lest we forget, though the civil rights bill famously prohibited racial discrimination in public accommodations, including the segregation of public schools, it also outlawed employment discrimination. The overarching goal of the march was in fact to foreground the demands of the unemployed, both Black and white, and to "raise dramatically and decisively the crisis of the economy." The rationale for a planned demonstration at the White House was to challenge the "failure of the administration to propose a program to meet the unemployment problem." "The Negro community realizes," the plans read, "that until there is a massive program for full employment the Negro struggle for jobs cannot be realized." NALC, like the independent Black labor organizations before it, understood that unemployment and labor market competition undercut interracial solidarity. A jobs program was vital, because "the failure to achieve a full employment program serves only to deepen the resistance of white workers to the struggle for economic freedom by minority groups."[63]

The march staff and leadership thus saw their demands as consisting in two parts. The second part articulated two demands centered on the civil rights struggle in the South, including the protest against a possible Senate filibuster. But the first part, which outlined four demands, was meant "to arouse the conscience of America to the economic plight of the Negro 100 years after emancipation." They called for a public works and training program, a federal Fair Employment Practice Act to bar job discrimination in government, government contractors, and trade unions, and a demand to broaden the Fair Labor Standards Acts to not only include those areas "where Negroes and other minorities work at slave wages," but also set up a minimum wage of no less than $1.50 per hour.[64]

The economic nature of the demands was reflected in the scenes of the march itself. At 9:30 a.m. on August 28, as forty thousand marchers gathered at the foot of the Washington Monument, Peter Ottley, a Black labor leader representing health workers in New York City, held a press conference with one hundred union members wearing yellow SEIU hats. Ottley was flanked by six boys carrying a union banner that read "Local 144." At 10:00 a.m., ushers directed the marchers, now ninety thousand strong, across Constitution Avenue to the Ellipse, and as they walked, they carried the official placards that displayed slogans like, "An End to Racial Bias," "Jobs for All," "Higher Minimum Wage Coverage for All Workers," "An FEPC Law NOW!" Union banners punctuated the procession. One read, "I.U.E. AFL-CIO for Full Employment."

When the marchers, who had swelled to two hundred thousand by the early afternoon, converged around the base of the Lincoln Memorial, they would have seen a veritable Who's Who of the American labor movement seated on the platform. Most conspicuous were the trade unionists who led the march: Randolph, Cleveland Robinson, Joe Overton, and Norman Hill, all from the NALC, and UAW president Walter Reuther. Among them also were William Bowe and Benjamin McLaurin of the Brotherhood of Sleeping Car Porters, IUE president James B. Carey, NMU president James Curran, Local 1199 president Leon Davis, ILGWU president David Dubinsky, UAW secretary-treasurer Emil Mazey, RWDSU president Max Greenberg, Packing House Workers union president Ralph Helstein, and USW president David McDonald.[65]

The program began just as the assembled crowd began to wither in the summer heat, with Red Cross volunteers handing out ice cubes and hauling away marchers overwhelmed by the temperature. Yet it was not Dr. King who greeted the marchers, but A. Philip Randolph, the president of the Negro American Labor Council and Brotherhood of Sleeping Car Porters. Randolph looked out at the largest civil rights demonstration in American history and rearticulated his vision of Black labor's leading role in the cause of interracial solidarity.

In booming Shakespearean tones that recalled his theatrical training as a young man, he opened the program by saying, "We are not a pressure group, we are not an organization or a group of organizations, we are not a mob. We are the advanced guard of a massive, moral revolution for jobs and freedom." "It falls to the Negro to reassert this proper priority of values," he explained, "because our ancestors were transformed from human personalities into private property. It falls to us to demand new forms of social planning, to create full employment, and to put automation at the service of human needs, not at the service of profits—for we are the worst victims of unemployment." A chief lesson of these years of struggle was that Black people could not count upon whites to fight this fight for them, because they were themselves constrained by racist institutions and ideologies. He said, "Negroes are in the forefront of today's movement for social and racial justice, because we know that we cannot expect the realization of our aspirations through the same old antidemocratic social institutions and philosophies that have all along frustrated our aspirations."[66]

In this moment, like so many other moments since he and other Black trade unionists inaugurated this struggle, Randolph understood that racial division intensified the general depravation of the working class. Randolph continued, "We have no future in a society in which 6 million black and white people are unemployed and millions more live in poverty." In this, civil rights legislation was not the end goal of the protest. "Yes, we want all public accommodation open to all citizens," Randolph said, "but those accommodations will mean little to those who cannot afford to use them. Yes, we want a Fair Employment Practice Act, but what good will it do if profit-geared automation destroys the jobs of millions of workers black and white."[67]

Randolph ended by explaining the need for the kind of militant direct action they were engaging in that day. It was only by taking to the streets, he said, that the people could extract any meaningful concession from the white power structure. Comparing this struggle to when "the labor movement took its struggle into the streets," he said, "the plain and simple fact is that until we went into the streets the federal government was indifferent to our demands. It was not until the streets and jails of Birmingham were filled that Congress began to think about civil rights legislation." Randolph then addressed those who in the last several weeks had decried the march in the name of gradualism, the go-it-slow approach to civil rights. In a stinging rebuke to these voices, he said, "Those who deplore our militance, who exhort patience in the name of a false peace, are in fact supporting segregation and exploitation. They would have social peace at the expense of social and racial justice." Nor would the civil rights revolution end with this historic protest. Randolph promised that "the months and years ahead will bring new evidence of masses in motion for freedom. The March on Washington is not the climax of our struggle, but a new beginning not only for the Negro but for all Americans who thirst for freedom and a better life." To waves of applause, he concluded, "When we leave, it will be to carry on the civil rights revolution home with us into every nook and cranny of the land, and we shall return again and again to Washington in ever-growing numbers until freedom is ours."[68]

· · ·

The March on Washington for Jobs and Freedom generated such immense pressure on the labor movement that the state affiliates of the AFL-CIO at long last began imposing civil rights discipline upon their white members. They did so by going on record as supporting civil rights legislation and by confronting the forces of white supremacy through direct action. At a special convention of the Alabama Labor Council on March 24, 1964, the delegates voted in favor of presidential electors pledged to Lyndon B. Johnson. Johnson, who was running on a pro-labor and pro-civil rights platform, became president after John F. Kennedy was assassinated in November. Alabama Governor George Wallace hoped to substitute the pledged electors with unpledged electors, all of whom were segregationist Dixiecrats. In a remarkable move, the Alabama state federation argued that the success of labor's legislative agenda depended upon defeating Wallace and the forces of white supremacy. Alabama Labor Council vice president E. C. Pippin said, "the unpledged slate is mainly composed of anti-labor Dixiecrats." As examples, he noted that Jim Allen, who headed the Dixiecrat ticket and campaigned for governor, ran on a right-to-work platform, which would have made it optional for workers to pay union dues. McDonald Gallion, he continued, "handed down the most unfavorable ruling against labor while Attorney General." Another Dixiecrat, Art Hayes, "headed Plant Security at Hayes Aircraft where they tried to break a strike by an AFL-CIO Union." Pippin concluded, "For the above reasons we oppose unequivocally this effort to take away the votes of the citizens of this State and recommend the election of the . . . pledged electors."[69]

The ensuing debate was lopsided, with most speakers rising in favor of Pippin's recommendation. After noting that he was in favor of the civil rights program stalled in Congress, a white delegate named Paul Hampton linked mounting unemployment not to Black labor competition, but to the structural inability of the economy to provide enough jobs. He said, "The most important issue before the working people of this state is how are they going to live. As I say at this point, 4500 men and women are losing their jobs every day. Two million boys and girls are coming on the labor market each year after school closes. What kind of program are these Dixiecrats going to do for these people?" Hampton explained, "When I was out of work two months ago there were two Negroes in a line of thirty some odd whites. The reason for that is there is not enough jobs for all of us.

The Democratic Party has a program for the working people and that is the reason as a member of organized labor that I am supporting that program." When Barney Weeks, president of the Alabama state federation, called for the vote, the convention adopted the recommendation.[70]

Similarly, the convention of the Mississippi AFL-CIO on May 25–27, 1964, was a pro-civil rights affair. State federation president Claude Ramsay put together a lineup of guest speakers that left no doubt as to the position of the House of Labor. Stanton Smith, president of the Tennessee AFL-CIO, spoke in favor of Black integration. Hazel Brannon Smith, a newspaper editor from St. Paul, Minnesota, said that whites needed to "take their foot off the neck" of Black people. But perhaps the clearest statement on Mississippi labor came from Ramsay himself.[71]

Like the Alabama state federation, he linked the fate of labor's legislative priorities with their support of pro-civil rights forces and their corresponding opposition to segregationists. He began by saying, "There has been some bad legislation enacted by this session of the legislature . . . all under the guise of segregation measures." "Each and every one of them," he explained, "can be used against our labor organizations." As an example, Ramsay pointed to several anti-picketing bills and said, "Building trades might as well get ready: they're going to use them on you. In 1960 when they passed legislation of this kind, you know where it was used first? In the City of Hattiesburg on a picket line that I was maintaining. . . . Frankly, I'll tell you right now, they're shooting at you with this issue." Ramsay went on to suggest that racist hate groups were anti-labor. After Medgar Evers enrolled at the University of Mississippi, white people in the City of Pascagoula organized a hate group called the Jackson County Emergency Union. Ramsay recalled, "We had a newspaper in that town, one of the few papers in this State that was friendly to our cause. This newspaper was the particular target of this group. They shot the windows out of the place, threatened the life of the editor, and what have you." Arguing that "this hate group was going to absolutely destroy the economic progress of Jackson County and our labor movement with it," he explained: "Practically every ship produced by this company is subsidized to some degree by federal funds. A racial disturbance can cause this company to lose future contracts. . . . We couldn't afford to see Ingalls Shipbuilding destroyed and result in the loss of a lot of jobs for our people." Although this was no ringing endorsement of the civil rights revolution, Ramsay and the Mississippi AFL-CIO maintained that engaging in racist behavior threatened to intensify the crisis of unemployment for their members. For the time being, the fate of civil rights and labor were linked in the minds of even white Southern trade unionists.[72]

The activity of Southern state federations complemented the ongoing work of the NALC. The AFL-CIO's affiliates in the former Confederacy lobbied in support of the late president's civil rights bill and opposed the efforts of Senate Dixiecrats to stall its progress through Congress. Meanwhile, the NALC refocused its attention on the jobs agenda. The theme of the council's fourth annual convention, which began in Cleveland on June 2, 1964, was "Fight for Freedom from Poverty Through Fair and Full Employment." The convention pointed out that the Black unemployment rate was twice that of whites' and that while Black people made up one-tenth of the population, they constituted one-quarter of all those living in poverty. Speaking in support of the jobs program, Randolph reiterated his commitment to direct action in order to achieve it: "We will continue our boycotts, sit-ins, and civil disobedience until our grievances are completely redressed." Five days later, the NALC called for a national one-day strike to be held on August 28, 1964, the one-year anniversary of the March on Washington, if the Senate blocked the measure. The threat seemed to have landed in the way intended. Later that month, the Senate voted in favor of closing off debate for the first time in the history of civil rights legislation. With the filibuster defeated, the Civil Rights Act became the law of the land.[73]

The world witnessed a high point of interracial solidarity when the South met the so-called "Negro-Labor Alliance" with violence and bloodshed. In Selma, Sheriff Jim Clark used tear gas, whips, and clubs to disperse demonstrators on a daily basis. Two people died in quick succession: in February law enforcement killed a Black civil rights worker, and a few weeks later, police clubbed to death a young white minister from Boston. Organized labor joined with the Black community in protest. The AFL-CIO and its state affiliates condemned the brutality in Selma. Leaders of labor and Black civil society marched in demonstrations in New York, Detroit, and Boston. UAW shop stewards raised funds to support the voter registration drive in Selma. When Dr. King called for a boycott of Alabama manufacturers, the longshore and warehouse union (ILWU) voted not to handle Alabama-made products. ILWU president Harry Bridges, a white Socialist, said, "It is time to quit talking, it's time for some action." Bridges's regional director William Chester drew applause at a protest when he said, "the Marines in Vietnam could be better used here at home to bring democracy to the deep South." When Viola Liuzzo, the wife of a Detroit Teamster, was killed during the march from Selma to Montgomery in March 1965, the entire labor movement turned out, including Cleveland Robinson of the NALC and Don Slaiman, director of the AFL-CIO's civil rights department. Eventually, the leaders of the March on Washington, including Walter Reuther, met to consider a second march to protect the rights of Black voters. The mass protests (and the threat of future action), combined with the draconian response of the state in Selma, pushed the federal government to action. In an address to a joint session of Congress, President Johnson said, "The real hero of this struggle is the American Negro. His actions and protests, his courage to risk safety and even to risk his life, have awakened the conscience of this nation." A second march proved unnecessary, for Congress swiftly passed the Voting Rights Act of 1965.[74]

. • .

The story of the Negro American Labor Council evinces many of the same patterns as previous independent Black labor organizations. The first is that the white-led labor movement showed itself to be an inconsistent advocate of interracial solidarity. The early years of the NALC were ones of hostility between A. Philip Randolph and AFL-CIO president George Meany. In 1960, Meany confronted Randolph's persistent protests against the color line in organized labor with the infamous question, "Who appointed you as the guardian of the Negro members in America?" In 1961, the feud threatened to escalate as the AFL-CIO Executive Committee censured Randolph and made plans to expel him from the leadership. As Black labor turned up the pressure, Meany began to relent, though the AFL-CIO stopped short of endorsing the March on Washington. It was only after the NALC broke off a substantial proportion of organized labor to mobilize for the march that the House of Labor finally embraced the cause of interracial solidarity. From that point forward, the AFL-CIO, including its state affiliates in the Deep South, lobbied and engaged in direct action in support of the Civil Rights Act of 1964 and the Voting Rights Act of 1965.

Conversely, the second pattern is that Black labor remained the vanguard of interracial solidarity. Time and again, it was Randolph and the NALC who continually pushed the AFL-CIO to take a hard line against the racism of state and local affiliates. The council built a national organization of local councils to advance their agenda at the grassroots level, and it was the council that inaugurated and organized the March on Washington. The leadership of Black labor applies as much to Black civil society as to white-led unions. Though some organizations like CORE responded immediately to the call to march, the NAACP and the Urban League did not come on board until July 1963, the month prior to the protest. They did so only because the Detroit Trade Union Labor Council (TULC), the UAW's Black caucus, had staged a successful mass protest of 125,000 people in June.

Third, the NALC's development tracked with the ongoing conflict and consensus between the centrist and left factions of Black labor, what I have called "Black Politics." Although the council was one unified organization, tension took hold over several questions: whether or not to engage in militant direct action, whether or not to support the NAACP's tactic of decertifying segregated unions, and whether or not to include Black women in leadership. Indeed, the historical record suggests that Randolph acceded to the call for the March on Washington because of the mounting conflict between the NALC's militants and those who sought to operate within the machinery of the AFL-CIO. Joe Overton proposed the idea of the march in the fall of 1961, but it was not until December 1962—after a contentious annual convention in November—that Randolph asked Rustin to develop a plan. Once the competing factions at last unified in the weeks prior to the march, they resuscitated an organizational form born in 1920s Harlem. The leaders of Black civil society put aside their ideological differences to unite in the cause of interracial labor solidarity.

But fourth, if Black labor was the Freedom Train—or in Randolph's words, "the advanced guard" of a social revolution—then the state affected the train's progress. State surveillance and repression persisted and threatened to derail the NALC when vice president Lola Belle Holmes was co-opted by the FBI to infiltrate the Communist Party and investigate its activity in the NALC. Additionally, the strife between liberals and Southern segregationists in the Democratic Party framed much of the strategy of the NALC and the March on Washington's leadership. Indeed, though most of the march's demands centered on economic concerns about joblessness and job discrimination, they also included a warning to Senate Dixiecrats not to filibuster civil rights legislation. In a related vein, President John F. Kennedy's civil rights bill was a touchstone during the mobilization for the march. Finally, state repression in Selma, Alabama, and Governor George Wallace's attempt to substitute presidential electors pledged to President Johnson with unpledged Dixiecrats were important contextual factors in the passage of civil rights legislation. The Alabama state AFL-CIO, for example, organized around seating Johnson's pledged delegates and made this campaign a centerpiece of their annual convention in March 1964.

Fifth and finally, though the demands of Black women were more muted in the NALC than they were in the NNLC, they were by no means absent. This was especially true at the founding convention of the NALC, when Black women delegates refused to let Randolph adjourn the meeting if the council did not include Black women in leadership. The NALC also featured the exclusion and working conditions of Black women at their Workshop and Institute on Race Bias in Trade Unions, Industry and Government in February 1961. It bears repeating, however, that this early militance and Randolph's acquiescence thereto eroded as the NALC pivoted to the March on Washington. This is reflected in the lack of representation not only on the march's administrative and executive committees, but also in the program of the march itself, in which Black women had no speaking roles.

The foregoing factors shaped the struggle for interracial solidarity, sometimes for the worse, but through it all Black labor remained the driving force behind the substantial gains of this period. In cajoling, persuading, organizing, and pressuring the institutional actors around them, Black labor inaugurated the multiracial labor movement we have today and forced the passage of the most sweeping civil rights legislation since Reconstruction.

This is not to say that the struggle for interracial solidarity was over. Although civil and voting rights were now the law of the land, unions continued to exclude Black workers from leadership and membership. Organized labor also clashed with communities of color, most famously in a wildcat strike by the United Federation of Teachers in Brooklyn's Ocean Hill-Brownsville neighborhood. Nor did the civil rights revolution chasten racist employers. The Negro-Labor Alliance engaged in two high-profile struggles against employment discrimination in the late 1960s: the Memphis sanitation workers' strike of 1968, during which Dr. King was assassinated, and the 1969 South Carolina hospital strike. As tensions heightened once more, the left and centrist factions of Black labor re-emerged after a period of relative quiet. The A. Philip Randolph Institute, whose executive director was none other than Bayard Rustin, was from the beginning a project of the AFL-CIO itself. The institute defended the AFL-CIO and its affiliates from charges of racial discrimination, even as it worked tirelessly to institutionalize the Negro-Labor Alliance within the federation. Though it, too, became an official constituency group in the AFL-CIO, the Coalition of Black Trade Unionists, led by William Lucy, emerged initially as an independent Black labor organization to tackle the enduring racism of organized labor. Lucy and Rustin clashed repeatedly throughout the post–civil rights period, to the point that on the occasion of Randolph's death, Black labor activists tried to end the feud with a merger. The merger failed.

6 Freedom Is a Constant Struggle

Despite their titanic victories, after the March on Washington independent Black labor organizations would continue to experience a series of euphoric highs and tragic lows. The Equal Employment Opportunity Commission (EEOC), which was created to enforce the employment provisions of the 1964 Civil Rights Act, sought in its early years to tackle segregated seniority rules in union contracts. The AFL-CIO seemed to revert to its old ways. Donald Slaiman, who was the head of the federation's civil rights department, went to Washington in May 1966 to urge the commission to rule against Black members. After the 1965 Watts Rebellion, the federal and state governments committed funds to rebuild affected neighborhoods in Los Angeles. The local African American community had proposed that unions admit Black workers into the building trades before breaking ground, but the construction unions rejected the plan. A *Los Angeles Times* article from September 10, 1965, read, "Unions Balk on Job Help for Watts Men." No wonder, then, that in July 1966, the NAACP once more found itself in a direct confrontation with organized labor. Its fifty-seventh annual convention observed that the labor movement "has failed to eliminate anti-Negro practices by affiliated unions in the North as well as in the South."[1]

In the context of this apparent backsliding, A. Philip Randolph and Bayard Rustin established the A. Philip Randolph Institute (APRI) in May 1965. Rustin became the Institute's executive director. In a series of letters with AFL-CIO president George Meany, Rustin asked for and received a one-year seed grant to fund the Institute to the tune of $2,000 per month. A paltry sum, it was nevertheless sufficient to set up headquarters at 217 West 125th Street in Harlem, an early meeting space of the March on Washington executive committee. Though Randolph and Rustin would fundraise to cover the rest of the operating budget, the AFL-CIO was the largest stakeholder. The Institute thus became a constituency group inside the House of Labor.[2]

Tactically speaking, APRI was a civil rights lobby or advocacy group, not the vanguard of a mass movement as the NALC once was. According to the *Industrial Bulletin*, the official magazine of the New York State Department of Labor, Rustin asserted "that the time had come for the American Negro to move from protest to politics." Said Rustin, "The Negro struggle must now give its attention to political and economic matters. . . . It must form alliances with labor, the best elements of the three major religious groups, with students, intellectuals, and other minorities . . . to form a political movement strong enough to create a will for the destruction of slums, the creation of jobs, and the reconstruction of our school system." Consistent with the call to politics, APRI's prospectus spoke to the need for coordination among individuals who were active in these separate policy spaces. Their talents were needed for "the preparation of far-reaching social and economic programs; serious school integration plans; briefs and studies of the mechanics of Congressional and political party functioning, the issuing of pamphlets and study guides on automation, nonviolent strategy, community organizing . . . the drafting of testimony for Congressional committees, the staffing of education conferences, workshops and institutes."[3]

There can be no question, then, as to APRI's role as an important node in civil rights and labor networks, but it was a support role, with special emphasis on policy and political education. In his regular reports to Meany from that period, Rustin summarized the Institute's achievements over the preceding months. They included Congressional testimony, orientations and trainings, speaking engagements, conferences, and pamphlets.[4]

More could be said about APRI's activities, but the main consequence for our purposes is that the sometime leaders of the Negro American Labor Council—Rustin and Randolph—no longer insisted upon maintaining an independent Black labor organization. APRI's staff and leadership set for themselves the unprecedented task of institutionalizing a Negro-Labor alliance that, paradoxically, had been achieved by pressuring the union movement from without. The role of outside pressure group thus passed from the Chief to Cleveland Robinson, a NALC stalwart and the former chairman of the March on Washington's Administrative Committee.[5]

Though he had too much respect for Randolph to contradict him in public, in fact Robinson was a different kind of leader, one whose radical politics more readily favored direct action and aligned more closely to Black Power. As the secretary-treasurer of New York's District 65, Robinson led a strike of 2,000 textile workers to open up jobs for Black and Puerto Rican applicants. In New York City, only the drug store and hospital workers union, Local 1199, mobilized this sector of the working class. Whereas Randolph was firm but conciliatory, Robinson was a firebrand. At the 1962 AFL-CIO convention, for example, he said, "We belong to the house of labor, but when the house becomes so rotten and dilapidated that the walls crumble and the roof leaks and the floor sags, then it's time to get out and build a new, clean house." Of President Johnson's War on Poverty, Cleveland Robinson said that the government was trying to treat "cancer in our society with aspirin tablets." And recalling the Black nationalism of the African Blood Brotherhood, Robinson embraced the discourse of Black Power. Under his leadership, he hoped that the NALC would become "the greatest manifestation of power ever to be realized by us. Power to demand—power to negotiate—power to decide. Power to make decisions, politically, economically, and socially."[6]

When Robinson became president of the NALC at its 1966 convention, he pledged to continue the struggle to integrate the AFL-CIO. In a speech that seemed to criticize Randolph's famous diplomacy, he said, "We reject compromise and tokenism, and we will tear away the mask and expose the hypocrisy that still exists in too many places." The NALC under his leadership would push not only for admission to membership, but also a top-to-bottom integration of the labor bureaucracy. They would fight "to insure widespread democratic reforms in the life and structure of the unions to the end that the Negroes will have a voice and a presence on bargaining committees as well as leadership councils where policy is determined." Such restructuring was necessary in order to invest in the organization of the most exploited sectors of the working class, especially Black people, Puerto Ricans, Mexicans and other minoritized groups.[7]

Perhaps most importantly, however, Robinson was among the first of his generation to insist that the labor movement must shift its focus from heavy manufacturing, where labor had gained a foothold and made significant gains, to the service industry. Noting that 50 million out of 70 million workers remained unorganized, Robinson said that "the unorganized are to be found, in the main, among the 70 percent of the nation's work force who are not industrial workers but in service industries." Accordingly, the NALC outlined a plan to organize service workers. Theodore Mitchell, who was vice president of Local 1199, wholeheartedly endorsed Robinson's analysis and encouraged the NALC to begin the service-sector campaign immediately. Mitchell said, "We are only a local union, and we cannot do this alone. The labor movement—and I accuse the AFL-CIO—is not doing anything about it. Yet this is where the majority of the Negro and Puerto Rican workers are."[8]

It was during this time that Dr. King began his much-discussed shift in focus from Southern civil rights to questions of poverty and economic justice across the country. Though he had spoken at the conventions of many labor unions in the early 1960s, his tone on economic issues after 1965 became more strident and aligned with the progressive sectors of the US labor movement. For example, at a meeting of Local 1199 in early 1968, Dr. King spoke of two Americas, one white and affluent, and the other Black and poor. He said, "Probably the most critical problem in the other America is the economic problem. By the millions, people in the other America find themselves perishing on a lonely island of poverty in the midst of a vast ocean of material prosperity." He clarified that the problem was not just unemployment, but *under*employment, namely, "people who work full-time jobs for part-time wages." "Most of the poor people in our country," he said, "are working every day." Nor was this due to a lack of resources. Referencing the immense treasure funding the Cold War, Dr. King echoed the importance that Rustin placed on the coordination of political will. He said, "the resources are here in America. The question is whether the will is here. . . . I am afraid that our government is more concerned about winning an unjust war in Vietnam than about winning the war against poverty right here at home." In a bid to rearrange the nation's priorities from Vietnam to the urban poor, Dr. King announced the "Poor People's Campaign," to be launched in the spring of 1968 with a new March on Washington.[9]

The uprisings of 1965–1968 formed the backdrop of Dr. King's words. The 1965 Watts Rebellion was only the first; in 1967, other rebellions, led largely by the Black poor and working class, broke out in Detroit, Newark, Cleveland, and several other smaller cities throughout the nation. The immediate reaction from organized labor was to denounce the so-called "riots." Horace Sheffield and Robert Battle, leaders of Detroit's Trade Union Leadership Council and once members of the NALC's militant faction, released a statement that called the rebels "hoodlums and hatemongers" and claimed that "one day of violence threatens to destroy years of effort to build a community Negroes and whites can be proud of." Black Detroiters were unmoved by this scolding and soon after the rebellion booed the popular Black US Congressman John Conyers, Jr. because his father had been a leader of the TULC. Such popular discontent prompted union leaders in Detroit to reassess their initial condemnation of the uprising and form a task force to address its underlying causes. Walter Reuther insisted, "Labor has got to get into this and do something meaningful for the jobless youth living in the ghetto. The key to the situation is Negro-white unity to change things." Teamsters vice president Robert Holmes echoed Reuther's remarks. He said, "Labor has to use its great powers of pressure, independent political action, to change the conditions which cause these upheavals. Labor has to cleanse itself of this stigma of discrimination, of refusing to see what's happening to these Negro youngsters who can't get jobs, to the older workers, the unemployed and the Negro workers generally who earn less, have less work, whom employers toss into the scrap heap when they don't need them." The AFL-CIO, despite having toed the civil rights line in the two years immediately following the March on Washington, was notably impervious to these appeals.[10]

While Dr. King was preparing for the second March on Washington, 1,300 Black city workers struck the Department of Public Works in Memphis, Tennessee. Two events led to the walkout. The first was the death of two Black sanitation workers. Because of the Byzantine rules of Southern segregation, it was imperative that Black and white employees work in separate spaces even on the same truck. The drivers, who sat in the cab, were white, while the haulers, who threw refuse into the compactor, were Black and hung off the back of the truck, exposed to the elements. During a particularly heavy rainstorm, two Black workers took shelter in a compactor that malfunctioned and crushed them to death. However tragic, the deaths by themselves did not precipitate the strike. The spark to the flame took place in the sewer department. There, twenty-two workers reported for their shift on January 31, 1968. Whereas management sent the Black workers home when it started raining, they kept the white workers at their posts. After the rain stopped, the white employees got to work and were paid a full day's wages. The city paid the Black workers for only two hours of work, so-called "call up pay." As soon as they received their paychecks in the mail, the members of all-Black Local 1733 of the American Federation of State, County, and Municipal Employees (AFSCME) called a strike, though they were in fact not a recognized union.[11]

Some had hoped that the new mayor-city council form of government, approved in January 1968, would make Memphis more responsive to the Black community, but those hopes evaporated with the walkout. Mayor Henry Loeb, who had been in office just four months before the strike began, said that the job action was illegal and that he would not under any circumstances negotiate with the union, let alone approve a dues checkoff system or recognize AFSCME as the workers' exclusive bargaining agent. The city council, in the early weeks of the struggle, seemed more pliable. On Thursday, February 22, the council's Committee on Public Works held a public hearing on the strike, with about one hundred people present, including union officers, ministers, and other supporters. Fred Davis, the chairman of the committee, seemed convinced that a group of outside agitators were responsible for the whole misunderstanding and expressed concern that "the men as individuals have not been able to bring out their views." The workers gave him what he asked for. Union officials called down to the Rubber Workers' Hall where the strikers rallied every day at noon, and in short order the audience at City Hall swelled to seven hundred people. At this point, Davis did not seem to want to hear directly from the workers anymore and declared that the committee had to adjourn because the assembly had exceeded the room's 407-person seating capacity. The workers defied Davis and occupied the room, singing spirituals and eating ham and bologna sandwiches while they waited for the city to capitulate. One of the Memphis newspapers observed, "The plush, red-carpeted council chamber was jammed with strikers who vaulted across the railing onto the dais reserved for city officials," lamenting, "The usually immaculate carpet for the chamber soon became spotted with bread crumbs." When the committee reconvened at 5:30 p.m. that day, they agreed to recommend that the city recognize the union and implement dues checkoff.[12]

The recommendation was supposed to be presented to the City Council at 2:30 p.m. the following day, but city officials pulled a dirty double-cross. In place of the original recommendation, the Committee on Public Works substituted a different recommendation that the mayor agree to all points *except* for union recognition and dues checkoff. Once the council members voted nine to four to approve the recommendation (with all four Black members voting no), Council Chairman Downing Pryor adjourned the meeting without public comment at 2:45 p.m., a mere fifteen minutes after gaveling the meeting to order. The underhanded maneuver electrified the audience. Local 1733 president T. O. Jones said, "We are ready to go to their damned jail." Dr. Vascoe A. Smith, Jr., a Memphis dentist and NAACP leader, said, "Don't let them hoodwink you. You live in a racist town. They don't give a damn about you." The strikers and their supporters improvised a march down Main Street, but no sooner had they started walking than the violence began. A police cruiser, presumably an escort, edged over the center line, bumping and nudging the marchers, and came to rest on a woman's foot. When the marchers tried to move the cruiser off the woman's body, the police moved in with billy clubs and mace. Jacques Wilmore, staff director of the regional office of the US Civil Rights Commission, said that he saw the police grab a man and pull him to the curb while "a third policeman came up and cracked the man across the head." When Wilmore approached the police to stand up for the man and present his identification, the police squirted him in the eyes with mace. The white *Memphis Press-Scimitar*, a local newspaper, blamed the strikers for the mêlée. They wrote, "leaders of the union have shown no respect for Tennessee law."[13]

The brutality of February 23 united the Black community in Memphis as never before. The following Sunday, ministers went to their pulpits to call for a wide-ranging boycott of all downtown stores, the city's two daily newspapers, and a chain of barbecue restaurants owned by Mayor Loeb's brother, William. Marches occurred daily from February 26 to March 2, but still management would not budge. Accordingly, the Memphis coalition of unions, clergy, and the NAACP invited Dr. King to address the strikers. Before he left Atlanta for Memphis, MLK wrote a letter to Cleveland Robinson that he hoped would be read to the delegates of the NALC's seventh annual convention. The NALC, Dr. King wrote, represented "the embodiment of two great traditions in our nation's history: the best tradition of the organized labor movement and the finest tradition of the Negro Freedom Movement." He urged Robinson to direct the NALC's resources to the "deteriorating economic and social condition of the Negro community . . . heavily burdened with both unemployment and under-employment, flagrant job discrimination, and the injustice of unequal educational opportunity."[14]

King would visit Memphis three times. On March 18, 1968, he addressed a rally of fifteen thousand people and called for all-out support for the strikers. On March 28, he led a parade of six thousand that turned bloody. A group of young militants disregarded King's insistence that the parade be nonviolent; they removed the placards from their picket signs and began smashing store windows. The police responded with characteristic ferocity, at one point shooting so much tear gas that the chemicals drifted into the Clayborn Temple where the paraders had taken refuge. Choking for air, some went back out into the street, where the police met them with clubs. Despite the disastrous events of March 28, King returned to Memphis on April 4 to lead a second parade. On that occasion, he spoke with AFSCME leader Jerry Wurf. He said, "What is going on here in Memphis is important to every poor working man, black and white, in the South." That night, King was assassinated.[15]

Black people across the country launched a fresh wave of rebellions out of grief for their fallen leader, and on April 8, forty thousand people gathered for the parade that Dr. King could no longer lead. His wife, Coretta Scott King, stood at the vanguard of the march, along with Reverend Ralph Abernathy (who would become head of the SCLC), Jerry Wurf, Walter Reuther, Donald Slaiman, and Local 1733 president T. O. Jones. Among the featured speakers of the day was Cleveland Robinson, who promised the strikers that he would devote the NALC to organizing Black service-sector workers like them. Though Mayor Loeb had the temerity to reject the workers' demands even after Dr. King's assassination, President Johnson sent Undersecretary of Labor James J. Reynolds to inform Loeb that the time for intransigence was over. On April 16, 1968, the sixty-five-day strike ended at last. The workers made progress on all of their demands, including an end to workplace discrimination, a promise of no reprisals for striking workers, a grievance procedure, voluntary dues checkoff, union recognition, and two raises, to take effect May 1 and September 1.[16]

Coretta Scott King and Reverend Abernathy would join forces with organized labor again less than a year later in the city of Charleston, South Carolina. When twelve hospital workers were fired on the spurious charge that they had left their patients unattended, four hundred workers from the State Medical College and one hundred workers from nearby Charleston County Hospital walked off the job in solidarity. All the workers were Black, and most were women. Isaiah Bennett, business agent for the Retail, Wholesale, and Department Store Workers Union, which represented tobacco workers in the city, called on Local 1199 to help with the strike. 1199 had recently scored a major victory in establishing a $100 per week minimum for hospital workers in New York City, and Bennett hoped that organizer Elliott Godoff and other 1199ers might have similar success in the South. Whereas the national minimum wage was $1.60 per hour, Charleston hospital workers earned only $1.30. Those who had been certified as practical nurses and thus were entitled to a higher wage had to work as nurses' aides because they were Black.[17]

Since public employees, like the Memphis sanitation workers, had been excluded from the 1935 National Labor Relations Act, and because the state made no provision for collective bargaining in South Carolina's public sector, the bosses felt no need to meet with the union. They responded with typical anti-union propaganda. The head of the State Medical College, Dr. William M. McCord, wrote in a staff memo, "I am sure that a majority of you would not want to get mixed up in an outfit such as this and I, of course, have no intention of meeting this tobacco workers' union." He added that the union had no interest in the workers themselves. "This union," he wrote, "is interested in only one thing and one thing only. That is money, your money." The memo was accompanied with two cartoons, one with an overweight union boss smoking a cigar while a young girl sat on his lap. In an interview with *Business Week*, McCord added a memorable note of contempt, one that the workers circulated widely. He said, "I am not about to hand over the administration of a 5 million dollar institution to people who never had a grammar school education."[18]

Though the state and city did not behave as violently as Memphis law enforcement, they did intimidate the workers through a series of other tactics; some of these backfired and intensified the pressure to settle the dispute. Charleston, like Memphis, looked like a war zone during the strike. The workers, decked out in their blue and white 1199 paper hats, marched under the watchful eye of National Guardsmen, who were armed to the teeth. Because the workers picketed at night, government officials instituted a curfew. No one could enter the city at night during the height of Charleston's tourist season. Downtown businesses suffered accordingly. Law enforcement also arrested waves of strikers, first jailing a group of five, and then a group of thirty-five. Far from recoiling in fear of the law, the workers dared the police to arrest even more of them. After a forty-five-minute meeting with Governor Robert E. McNair, union officials asked the workers how many of them were willing to go to jail, and dozens came forward to volunteer. 1199 organizer Elliott Godoff was to say, "It was one of the most dramatic things I ever saw." Mary A. Moultrie, the rank-and-file leader of the strike, said, "When one is involved in a struggle it is not a crime to go to jail without bail, it's a pleasure." So important was the tactic that the coalition made fundraising for bail a central part of the campaign, complete with a countrywide speaking tour by the workers.[19]

The struggle soon became nationalized. On April 29, 1969, the leading lights of Black civil society issued a joint statement of support. Among the signatories were the leaders of the March on Washington, including Roy Wilkins, A. Philip Randolph, Bayard Rustin, Whitney Young, and Dorothy Height. The statement read, "We view the struggle in Charleston as more than a fight for union rights. It is part of the larger fight in our nation against discrimination and exploitation—against all forms of degradation that result from poverty and human misery. It is a fight for human rights and human dignity." Noting its similarity "to the same issue that led to the tragedy in Memphis last year," the statement continued, "We, therefore, applaud the efforts of Local 1199B . . . for spearheading the campaign to win justice for the terribly exploited hospital workers."[20]

Like the Memphis debacle, the Charleston hospital workers' strike threatened to touch off a nationwide crisis. While President Richard Nixon and his henchman John Erlichmann worried about how federal intervention might undermine their popularity among white Southern voters, Labor Secretary George Schultz sent a mediator to Charleston, who ordered Dr. McCord to settle the strike. After over one hundred days of struggle, the workers won. The July 1969 issue of 1199's newspaper read, "1199 Union Power Plus SCLC Soul Power Equals Victory in Charleston." The workers won a $1.60 minimum wage along with raises of 30 to 70 cents an hour, a grievance procedure, a credit union, and the reinstatement of the original twelve workers who were fired. Though the union did not win recognition, it was thought that the grievance procedure and credit union were tantamount to recognition.[21]

. . .

As the post-March on Washington period unfolded, Bayard Rustin found himself increasingly at odds with the movement he had helped to build. His drift toward institutional politics was out of step with the rest of Black civil society, which was becoming more militant and hewing closer to Black nationalism. Rustin even found himself disagreeing with his old friend Martin Luther King, whose vocal opposition to the war in Vietnam he thought foolhardy. In a conversation recorded by the FBI, Rustin complained to King's lawyer, "That's the trouble with people who hear voices. . . . Every little tack they want to take becomes a religious crusade."[22]

The gap between Rustin and the Black community was on full display in the United Federation of Teachers' (UFT) two strikes in 1967 and 1968. The New York City public school system was then experimenting with decentralizing power to the many individual districts in the city. The residents of one district in Brooklyn, Ocean

Hill-Brownsville, had elected an all-Black school board who objected to a UFT contract provision that allowed teachers to remove "disruptive" children from the classroom. UFT president Albert Shanker maintained that their contract proposal asked only "in the case of continual behavior of such a type as to prevent teaching from taking place in the classroom, that a child have several opportunities to adjust within that same class. If this fails, the child should be given similar opportunities with a number of other teachers." But as the conflict escalated, the local school board fired over a dozen UFT members, most of them Jewish. Following a series of short-term walkouts, the UFT engaged in a reactionary wildcat (i.e., unauthorized) strike in 1968 that pitted white teachers against Black students and parents. The New York Association of Black School Supervisors and Administrators issued a press release on September 17, 1968, stating, "The racial and religious tensions accruing as the result of the action taken by the United Federation of Teachers and Council of Supervisory Associations in closing and, in some instances, padlocking the schools can only lead to deeper divisions in our city."[23]

Rustin supported the UFT in that conflict. In an "Appeal to the Community from Black Trade Unionists," which he wrote and published in the September 19, 1968, issue of the *New York Post*, Rustin called the racial story a "distortion." The real issue, he insisted, was due process. He wrote, "It is the right of every worker not to be transferred or fired at the whim of his employer. It is the right of every worker to be judged on his merits—not his color or creed. It is the right of every worker to job security." To undermine these rights by opposing the UFT's demand for due process would end badly for the Black community. He explained, "These are the rights that black workers have struggled and sacrificed to win for generations. They are not abstractions. They are the black workers' safeguards against being 'the last hired and the first fired.' We have a long way to go to make these rights a reality. But if they are weakened or disparaged—for whatever reason—in the society at large, we will ultimately be the worst victims." Tying these threads together, Rustin concluded, "These rights have been denied to teachers in the Ocean Hill-Brownsville district by the local governing board," and he urged "all our black brothers and sisters not to permit their justified frustrations to lead them into strategies and tactics that are self-defeating."[24]

Rustin's continuous support of the UFT, even in the 1968 wildcat strike, drew condemnation from both the Black community and white teachers who experienced first-hand the racial dynamics of community meetings. Edward Urquhart, a Black civil servant and union member, wrote, "To try to make Black people think the UFT teacher strike is not racial is a damn lie. It is part of that white power structure that has been keeping the Black community from self determination. If your group regard yourselves friends of the Black community then we don't need any enemies." Another writer, who pointed out that the only teacher who lost their job in the conflict was Black, wrote, "It is regrettable that you must spend the last and now lamentable years of your life parroting the filthy deceptions of zionist racism. May god have mercy on your traitorous soul."[25]

The UFT saga did not appear to chasten Rustin's opposition to the Black Power movement. A few months prior to the second UFT strike, he criticized Black Power leaders for having no policy solutions to the pressing social problems of the time. This, he suggested, made them worse than segregationists like the governor of Alabama. Rustin said,

Now, if the Black Power people believe this nation is vile and that the Negro can never get justice and freedom here, logically they cannot have a program. What does that extreme group have to say about medical help? Nothing! What is their program for jobs? None! What is their program for housing? None! What is their program for education? None! If they cannot believe in the society and they cannot have a program, then their energy will be directed against those Negroes who do believe in programs; thus they are much more dangerous to these people than George Wallace.

If the Black Power movement turned their critique inward to Black people like him, then the labor movement, he argued, redirected that critique upward to the powers that be and in doing so united all workers behind a positive legislative agenda. In an article titled "The Failure of Black Separatism," Rustin acknowledged that Jim Crow unionism had "given impetus to the separatist movements," but, he added, "Labor's legislative program for full employment, housing, urban reconstruction, tax reform, improved health care, and expanded educational opportunities is designed specifically to aid both whites and blacks in the lower- and lower-middle classes." This program Rustin credited to A. Philip Randolph, whose vision was one of "interracial alliances on the basis of class."[26]

Rustin's advocacy of a legislative agenda based on interracial class solidarity was clearly a response to Black labor's resurgent left faction, which drew political inspiration from both Marxism and revolutionary Black nationalism. Rustin's resistance to Dr. King's Poor People's Campaign, among other Black-led initiatives, did not ingratiate himself to these new elements. The *Inner City Voice*, a newspaper edited by the leaders of the League of Revolutionary Black Workers and the Dodge Revolutionary Union Movement (DRUM), people like John Watson, Mike Hamlin, and General Gordon Baker, spotlighted Bayard Rustin as their "Tom of the Month" in June 1968. The Kennedy administration, Watson wrote, had used Rustin "to cool the marchers out" and turn "the planned militant demonstration against brutal racist oppression" into "a casual stroll to the Lincoln Memorial." He continued, "The Johnson Administration is trying to pull the same thing on the Poor People's Campaign." Watson found it curious that "before the campaign got underway Uncle Rustin was set against it," but after Dr. King's death, "up pops Bayard Rustin the Tom Wonder, in the leadership of the campaign." As evidence of a conspiracy, Watson pointed out that Rustin had postponed the second March on Washington, substituted Dr. King's original demands with a "jibe-time sellout program" called the Economic Bill of Rights, and conceded before the battle could be joined that 'We recognize that this economic bill of rights cannot be adopted overnight.'"[27]

DRUM came into being with a wildcat strike in May 1968 at Chrysler's Dodge Main plant in Hamtramck, Michigan, a suburb of Detroit. The long-standing grievances against the company included unsafe working conditions, long hours, and constant harassment on the part of a racist white management. The precipitating cause was an assembly line speedup from forty-nine to fifty-six units per hour on May 2. The afternoon shift walked off the job at the lunch hour, locked arms across the factory gate, and refused to let their coworkers reenter the plant. The picket lines swelled as the day shift joined the strike. At this precise moment, the UAW was meeting in Atlantic City, New Jersey, where Walter Reuther was quoted as saying that he "would not give Afro-Americans command posts in the Union just because they were Black." Unable to get any help from the UAW, the strikers returned to work on May 6. Reprisals came swiftly. Though both white and Black workers struck Dodge Main, the company targeted Black workers in particular with firings and suspensions. As a consequence of both management's and the union's inaction, Black workers founded DRUM, which they described as "an organization of oppressed and exploited black workers . . . the victims of inhumane slavery at the expense of white racist plant managers." Noting that Black workers comprised 60 percent of the entire workforce at the Hamtramck plant, DRUM believed that they had "exclusive power." Rather than subjugate themselves to an ineffective and racist bureaucratic grievance procedure, DRUM resolved to cut out the middleman and win their demands through direct action. In this, DRUM spared no criticism of the union. "We have attempted to address our grievances to the UAW bureaucracy, but to no avail," the DRUM program read, charging, "The UAW bureaucracy is just as guilty, its hands are just as bloody as the white racist management of this corporation." DRUM thus saw itself as an independent Black labor organization, separate from the UAW, not an internal caucus. The program concluded, "We black workers feel that if skilled trades can negotiate directly and hold a separate contract, then black workers have more justification for moving independent of the UAW."[28]

In the immediate aftermath of the boss's reprisals, General Baker published an open letter to the Chrysler Corporation. In it, he thanked management for escalating the conflict: "By taking the course of disciplining the strikers you have opened that struggle to a new and higher level and for this I sincerely THANK YOU" [emphasis in original]. He explained, "You have made the decision to do battle with me and therefore to do battle with the entire black community . . . Black people of the world are united in common struggle which had its beginning with the exploitation of non-white people on a worldwide scale." As if to unveil his broader vision for the fight ahead, Baker then cited *Black Reconstruction in America*: "To quote from W. E. B. Du Bois, 'The emancipation of man is the emancipation of labor and the emancipation of labor is the freeing of that basic majority of workers who are yellow, brown, and black.'" Thanking the boss again, he ended with an ominous postscript: "P.S. You have lit the unquenchable spark."[29]

From there, the movement spread like wildfire to the other auto plants, each with its own acronym: ELRUM for the Eldon Avenue Revolutionary Union Movement and MARUM for the Mack Avenue Revolutionary Union Movement, and so forth. DRUM boycotted nearby saloons, organized workers in the alley where the crew drank between shifts, picketed UAW headquarters, and ran alternative slates of Black union officers against the Reuther faction. Though the

RUMs had the *Inner City Voice* as a common mouthpiece, in fact, said General Baker, they were largely a decentralized movement. In a retrospective interview, he said, "After that we got swamped. Workers were coming out of everywhere. We decided we can't handle this upsurge. What we can do is this: we got paper, we got ink, mimeograph, typewriters: you can use our equipment and you determine your own issues at your plant." He explained, "We didn't try to offer editorial leadership; we didn't and couldn't try to direct all that."[30]

Following on the heels of DRUM, and overlapping in local leadership at least in Detroit, was the Coalition of Black Trade Unionists (CBTU). Five Black labor leaders called the CBTU's inaugural convention in September 1972: William Lucy, secretary-treasurer of AFSCME; Charles Hayes, vice president of the Amalgamated Meatcutters and Butcher Workmen of North America; Nelson Jack Edwards, vice president of the UAW; William Simons, president of Local 6 of the American Federation of Teachers; and Cleveland Robinson, president of both the NALC and the Distributive Workers union. The convention, which took place in Chicago, drew 1,200 delegates from over two dozen unions. Though the meeting was called in part because the AFL-CIO decided to stay neutral in the 1972 presidential election without first consulting Black members, it was about much more that. Simons said in an interview that apart from expressing "displeasure to the position taken by George Meany and the executive council on the elections," the CBTU was "also concerned about the fact that much needs to be done in the labor movement to eradicate the racist practices, the discriminatory practices, which still exist within certain unions." Like the many Black labor groups before them, Simons added, "we felt that if we could organize, we would then be able to demonstrate that there are real concerns to which the labor movement is not addressing itself."[31]

Bayard Rustin had once championed precisely this kind of independent political action on the part of Black workers, but from his current perspective such a movement undercut the ongoing efforts of APRI and the AFL-CIO to consolidate the gains of the Negro-Labor alliance. He attacked the CBTU almost immediately after it was founded. In a letter to the editor of the *New York Times*, arguably the most public venue available for such a move, Rustin criticized the media for the "extensive coverage to the formation of a coalition of black trade unionists." He seemed to dismiss the coalition's concerns about race relations in organized labor by suggesting that "Black trade unionists are taking leadership positions in their unions, their communities, and in the political world with increasing frequency." Whatever issues remained would be taken care of by the A. Philip Randolph Institute, which, he noted, enjoyed "the support of the labor movement in general and . . . George Meany in particular in this effort." When the press asked William Lucy for a comment on Rustin's statement, he said, it was "apparently in accord with the viewpoint of the AFL-CIO leadership." Of the A. Philip Randolph Institute, Lucy rightly praised its important educational work, but added that it "was in danger of becoming counterproductive because of its unqualified defense of the status quo in the unions."[32]

Against the wishes of Black labor's centrist faction, now led by Rustin, the CBTU continued to organize and, indeed, hosted their second annual convention on May 25–27, 1973. Over 1,100 delegates from thirty-three international and other unions met in Washington, DC, to write and pass their by-laws and make plans for the coming year. Most organizations were affiliates of the AFL-CIO, and approximately two-fifths of the delegates were Black women. So as to make their purpose clear to people like Rustin, the leadership signed a statement on "The Need for a Coalition of Black Trade Unionists." To those familiar with the history of Black-led labor organizations, the statement would have sparked a sense of déjà vu. It read, "As black trade unionists, it is our challenge to make the labor movement more relevant to the needs and aspirations of black and poor workers. The CBTU will insist that black union officials become full partners in the leadership and decision-making of the American labor movement."[33]

.   .   .

In May 1979, just over a decade into the conflict between the CBTU and the APRI, A. Philip Randolph died. The world of organized labor witnessed an outpouring of gratitude for Black labor's Grand Old Man. President David Livingston of District 65, Cleveland Robinson's old union, said, "We mourn his death, but we remember his principled life and the struggles in which we joined him." Calling him the "Father of the Civil Rights Movement," the union recalled fondly, "many 65ers remember A. Philip Randolph as the man who walked our picket lines, visited our hall and expressed his solidarity in many warm and quiet ways. . . . To 65ers he was a special friend. A. Philip Randolph will not be forgotten." So deeply felt was his passing that Horace Sheffield, longtime leader of the TULC and former member of the NALC's militant faction, was determined to unite the APRI and the CBTU in his memory. The sentiment no doubt had to do with Randolph's evolving attitude toward the Black left. In his old age, he expressed disagreement with the Black Power movement, but never animosity. In fact, in an interview with *Ebony* magazine on the occasion of his eightieth birthday, Randolph extended an olive branch, saying, "The black militants of today are standing upon the shoulders of the 'new Negro radicals' of my day—the '20s, '30s and '40s. We stood upon the shoulders of the civil rights fighters of the Reconstruction era and they stood upon the shoulders of the black abolitionists." He explained, "I *love* the young black militants. I don't agree with all their methodology, and yet I can understand why they are in this mood of revolt, of resort to violence, for I was a young black militant myself, the angry young man of my day" [emphasis in original].[34]

Sheffield set to work mere weeks after Randolph's passing. At the June 1979 NAACP annual convention in Louisville, he called for the "merging of the two Black labor groups, the A. Philip Randolph Institute (APRI) and the Coalition of Black Trade Unionists (CBTU) and their allies, as the most significant and lasting tribute Black unionists and their allies could possibly make to Mr. Randolph's memory." A few months later, Sheffield followed up with William H. Oliver and Roosevelt Watts, who, in addition to being officials of the UAW and Transport Workers Union respectively, were also co-chairmen of the NAACP Ad Hoc Labor Committee. He cited two reasons for the merger: "(1) because it is what Mr. Randolph, who spent a lifetime of struggle trying to unite Black workers, would surely want us to do; and (2) because it will better enable us to marshal our forces in support of both the Black community and the labor movement . . . in the face of that growing 'anti-black anti-labor climate.'" He then sought the blessing of AFL-CIO president Lane Kirkland, who responded by saying that it seemed to him appropriate for the two groups "to sit down together and explore the possibility of resolving any differences that stand between them." Now all that remained was for the leaders of the two groups to agree to talks.[35]

CBTU made the first move. At the coalition's ninth annual convention, the membership paid tribute to Randolph's memory and resolved to begin talks with the institute. Noting that "A. Philip Randolph spent a lifetime of struggle trying to unite Black workers" and that "CBTU's primary objective is to organize Black workers into the trade union movement," the convention instructed "the President and Executive Board of CBTU to call for a meeting with the APRI leadership, to outline means for APRI and CBTU to discuss issues and programs that will protect and advance the interests of the Black and labor community."[36]

Rustin was more circumspect. The institute's leadership interpreted Sheffield's activity as an attempt to circumvent them to secure a merger. In a letter to Rustin and Norman Hill, the president and executive director of the APRI respectively, Sheffield assured the leaders that "There was certainly never any intent to bypass either of you in respect to this matter. I view both of you not only as fellow soldiers in the struggle, but genuine friends; and with Bayard, it's an association and friendship that dates back almost four decades." In not reaching out to the institute at the outset, however, Sheffield appears to have gotten off on the wrong foot. The suspicions only mounted from there. Even after the coalition's resolution calling for Black labor unity, Sheffield struggled to establish trust with the institute. In his last letter to Sheffield on the topic, Rustin asked whether Sheffield was calling for the merger "as an individual CBTU member or as a representative of the National CBTU leadership." Having had no correspondence with the coalition himself, Rustin said that he would "respond immediately to any official communication from the official CBTU leadership." Sheffield could only promise to convey his message to the CBTU board. Today, the A. Philip Randolph Institute and Coalition of Black Trade Unionists are both constituency groups in the AFL-CIO, but they remain separate organizations.[37]

· ● ·

The history of independent Black labor organizations from their beginnings in 1917 to their reincarnation after the March on Washington for Jobs and Freedom reflects the patterns we have returned to throughout this book. The first pattern has been that white workers and trade unionists have been inconsistent advocates of interracial solidarity. Throughout the period covered in these pages, the AFL has had a checkered history, sometimes forcefully advocating for interracial solidarity as they did in the aftermath of the 1963 March on Washington, but more often standing as the biggest obstacle to social change. Even the CIO, which had a far better track record on race than its rival federation prior to the merger, supported the National Negro Congress in the early drive to organize steel and other industries where Black workers predominated, only to freeze the NNC out once that drive came to fruition. As a merged body from 1955 onward, the AFL-CIO worked repeatedly to frustrate the advocates of interracial solidarity, though periodically the progressive remnants of the CIO, housed in the federation's industrial union department, rejoined the fight for racial justice.

The second pattern is that independent Black labor groups have been at the vanguard—the veritable Freedom Train—of interracial solidarity in the labor movement. In the second chapter, we saw the African Blood Brotherhood persuade the Communist movement and their unions to systematically attack the racial "chauvinism" of institutionalized labor. Similarly, though from a different politics of socialism and trade unionism, the Brotherhood of Sleeping Car Porters continually pushed the AFL to include their union as a bona fide affiliate and challenged the federation to tear down the color line in the trades. In the third chapter, we saw the rise of the National Negro Congress, which pressed the nascent CIO to organize Black workers into industrial unions, especially in the steel, auto, tobacco, and meat-packing industries. The 1941 March on Washington Movement then compelled the Roosevelt Administration to pass an executive order and establish a Fair Employment Practice Commission (FEPC) that could address the problem of employment discrimination in government, the defense industry, and unions. In the fourth chapter, we bore witness to the National Negro Labor Council's successive campaigns to push for the adoption of a model FEPC clause and then to integrate the retail, transportation, and manufacturing workforces, including in the South. The fifth chapter chronicled the efforts of the Negro American Labor Council to pressure the newly merged AFL-CIO to impose civil rights discipline on its local and state affiliates. And in this, the concluding chapter, we watched as the struggle of independent Black labor organizations continued in the Memphis and Charleston public sector strikes, the Dodge Revolutionary Union Movement, and the Coalition of Black Trade Unionists.

The third pattern is that factionalism between Black labor's Left and Centrist organizations—what I have called Black politics— propelled the historical development of the struggle to integrate the labor movement. This may seem a somewhat surprising finding to some, as one might assume that internal conflict in a social movement would simply tear it apart. But in fact, the ongoing conflict and consensus among these competing factions pushed Black labor from one phase of the struggle to the next. The conflict between the two brotherhoods in the 1920s not only shaped Randolph's insider approach to the AFL, but also set the stage for a concordat first at Harlem's United Front Conference in 1923 and then, perhaps more auspiciously, the formation of the National Negro Congress in the 1930s. The unification of the factions in the NNC produced some of the most significant progress toward interracial labor solidarity in the twentieth century, as seen in the organization of tens of thousands of Black workers into industrial unions. Randolph's break with the NNC in 1940, while leading to a weakening of the congress, also led to the formation of the March on Washington Movement in 1941, which secured the most significant commitment from the federal government to root out racism in industry and organized labor since Reconstruction. Factionalism persisted through the 1950s in the fight between the Negro Labor Committee-USA and the National Negro Labor Council, but the conflict also galvanized the NNLC to press forward with the cause of integration and shaped their decision to pursue their rival's main policy objective, namely, to install Fair Employment Practice Commissions in every union and level of government. As they did in the 1930s, the two factions unified again in the early 1960s to form the Negro American Labor Council. The ongoing conflict between the NALC's establishment and militant factions, in turn, led to the recuperation of the March on Washington as a tactic. The massive success of the 1963 March forced the AFL-CIO to impose civil rights discipline on its most intransigent local and state affiliates and, in turn, facilitated the passage of the Civil Rights Act in 1964 and Voting Rights Act in 1965. That historic coalition would divide into factions again after 1965, when DRUM and the CBTU rose up to challenge the status quo represented by Bayard Rustin and the A. Philip Randolph Institute. We must not diminish the seriousness of these internal debates or the betrayals that they entailed, but we must also acknowledge that an unintended consequence of these conflicts was tactical innovation. The shifts in tactics, from industrial organization to the March for example, caught the state and white organized labor off guard and heightened the pressure on these institutions to confront the problem of the color line. Put another way, it was the willingness of Black labor activists to engage in and navigate conflict among their own organizations and with the wider movement that impelled white labor leaders toward inclusion. Far from being only a weakness, then, factionalism was in part a strength.

The fourth pattern entails the relationship between Black labor and the state. The state continually undercut the dream of full citizenship in the labor movement. The FBI and CIA surveilled and infiltrated the brotherhoods of the 1920s. U.S. intelligence agencies also sowed mistrust in, and were partially responsible for destroying, the National Negro Congress, by cultivating spies who informed on their compatriots. The House Un-American Affairs Committee attempted to kill the National Negro Labor Council before it got off the ground, and although HUAC failed to do so, eventually the US Attorney General made the prospect of legal entanglements so daunting that the NNLC decided to disband instead of putting their membership in harm's way. Nor was the NALC immune to the state's counter-maneuvers. Though it enjoyed relatively more success and acceptance from the white establishment than previous

Black labor organizations, some of the NALC's top leaders were spies for the FBI.

But state repression, while ever present, fluctuated. It was heavier from 1947 to 1956, the high tide of McCarthyism, and lighter in the years before and after. What explains this variation? The historical evidence suggests that repression did not vary by party or by presidential attitudes toward the Communist Party. Both Democratic and Republican administrations prosecuted the Red Scare in equal measure, with the former destroying the National Negro Congress and the latter forcing the dissolution of the National Negro Labor Council. Relatively lighter periods of red-baiting occurred during both the Roosevelt administration, which relied politically on an alliance with the Communists in domestic and foreign policy, and the Kennedy administration, whose leading figures were inveterate Cold Warriors. Though a hard and fast rule is beyond the scope of this book, there is one correlation that is at least suggestive and grounds for future study. The most aggressive period of state repression occurred during factional splits in the Black labor movement, when the centrists became active agents of the Red Scare. Conversely, less aggressive periods were ones in which Black civil society was united and Black labor's competing factions defended each other against charges of subversion. We are left, therefore, with a searching paradox: that factionalism was both an engine of tactical innovation and, potentially, a precondition of state repression.

A fifth pattern is the activism and leadership of Black women. In the 1910s and 1920s Lucille Green Randolph and Grace Campbell were important figures in the Brotherhood of Sleeping Car Porters and African Blood Brotherhood, respectively. Thelma Dale and her all-woman staff played the leading role in the NNC during the Second World War. Black women were the prime movers behind the tobacco workers' campaign in the South, which was a partnership with the NNC's youth arm, the Southern Negro Youth Congress.

The organization and promotion of Black women was the strategic focus of the National Negro Labor Council, due in large part to the leadership of Vicki Garvin. The Negro American Labor Council was divided over the role that women should play in the national leadership, and its focus on Black women's integration into unions and the workforce was less than that of the NNLC before it. Indeed, the leadership of the 1963 March on Washington, which overlapped heavily with that of the NALC, included only two women, Anna Hedgeman and Dorothy Height, and the march program made a symbolic gesture of gratitude to Black women but featured no women speakers. After the march, the organization of Black women workers was central to the Charleston hospital workers' strike; the strike's symbolic leader was Coretta Scott King, and on the ground, the moving spirit of the struggle was Mary Moultrie. These five patterns—white inconsistency, Black leadership, factionalism, state repression, and Black women's activism—all shaped the trajectory of Black labor's struggle for interracial solidarity.

. . .

The middle decades of the twentieth century have much in common with our own time. Then, as now, the far right was in the ascendant. Nazism, fascism, and McCarthyism all emerged in the years covered in this book. Today, the far right is either the ruling or leading opposition party in the United States, Turkey, India, Brazil, and across Europe. The drift of the United States from an industrial to a service economy continues, and the size and shape of the labor movement has changed with it. The old private-sector industrial unions are now much smaller than they used to be. For example, from a high of 1.5 million members, the United Auto Workers now have 400,000 members, and most of them do not make cars. Recall that Ford's River Rouge Plant in Dearborn, Michigan once employed 80,000 workers by itself, and UAW Local 600, which represented those workers, was the largest local union in the entire world. Service and public sector unions are now far bigger than their industrial counterparts: AFSCME and the Teamsters each have over one million members; the American Federation of Teachers and Service Employees Internation Union each have upward of 2 million; and the National Education Association has a membership of 3 million. Finally, Black workers continue to face stark inequalities on the job market. According to a recent report of the Economic Policy Institute, the Black unemployment rate remains more than double that of whites in the American South, and Black workers, along with other minoritized working people, are still segregated into the lowest paid and most menial jobs in industries such as agriculture, childcare, and elder care.[38]

There are, however, two key differences between that time and ours. First, the U.S. labor movement is far weaker than it used to be. Automation, the outsourcing of union jobs overseas, union busting, and labor's own unwillingness and inability to organize unorganized workers, many of whom are women and people of color, have all contributed to labor's decline. Whereas about a third of all private-sector workers were union members at the midpoint of the twentieth century, by the 2010s just over one-tenth of the entire workforce—both private and public sector—were.[39] Importantly, this downward spiral occurred just as Black workers started to gain a foothold in unions that had once systematically excluded them. Second, if white men were once the most likely demographic to join a union, now Black people are. No population is more overrepresented in the private-sector labor movement than Black workers. This is especially true for Black women, whose unionization rate is double that of white women.[40]

The similarities and differences of the current moment present both challenges and opportunities. The challenges include the growing strength of anti-democratic forces, whose objective is to exclude and suppress those whom they see as a threat to what was once—in an alleged golden age—a traditional, wholesome, and homogenous society, where dominant groups enjoyed unchallenged supremacy. One opportunity for progressive forces is that a coalition of the excluded is potentially quite large—an overlapping alliance of women, people of color, workers, immigrants, and queer folk. Another opportunity is that Black trade unionists are arguably in a better position than ever before to assume leadership of unions and allied labor organizations.

To defeat the far right, who represent the greatest threat to Black workers and indeed the entire working class, we must take a page out of Black labor's playbook. Despite their suspicions of one another, the left and centrist factions of Black labor periodically put aside their differences to address the crisis of unemployment in their community. Randolph, a socialist and AFL insider, and John P. Davis, a communist, joined forces to break the color bar in organized labor so that Black workers would have a seat at the table as the New Deal and industrial unions expanded. They also understood that the racist and antiunion politics of the far right comprised the biggest obstacle to achieving their goal. Accordingly, they formed a popular front among themselves and white progressives to organize more Black workers and arrest the momentum of Nazism at home and abroad.

To assemble an analogous coalition today, we must rethink what the labor movement is. The history of independent Black labor organizations teaches us that unions are not the only groups that workers can form to effect social change. Of the seven Black-led groups discussed in preceding chapters, only one—the Brotherhood of Sleeping Car Porters—was a union, and even the BSCP operated for many years outside the official labor federations. And yet, the combined pressure of these successive organizations was able to push at least some sectors of the white-led labor movement toward inclusion and at the same time forge a vital link in the coalition against fascism.

In practice, the contemporary labor movement consists not only of unions, but also of worker centers, political parties, think tanks, professional associations, intellectuals, and cooperatives.

The time has come for our eclectic and multiracial labor movement to unite and align with other progressive forces. On August 3, 2022, Viktor Orbán, the head of the governing Far Right political party in Hungary, visited the Conservative Political Action Conference (CPAC) in Texas. He said, "Progressive liberals didn't want me to be here because . . . I'm here to tell you that we should unite our forces." Not content to win elections in individual countries, the enemies of democracy aspire to be a transnational political force, not unlike the Axis of the Second World War. This is a determined and well-resourced foe. They are the political descendants of those whom Black labor opposed in the middle of the twentieth century, and they are back.[41]

Fortunately, there are signs that the US labor movement is back, too. There are more petitions to the National Labor Relations Board for union elections than the board can handle. Workers are now organizing at major firms like Starbucks, Amazon, and Trader Joe's that for decades never knew unionization. Progressives are defeating their conservative counterparts in union leadership contests, most recently in the United Auto Workers and the Teamsters. There have been successful strikes across the economy, from education and hospitality to retail and manufacturing. A key dimension of this recent wave is the politics of intersectionality, a Black feminist ethic that sees the struggle for gender equity as inseparable from the fight for racial and economic justice. For example, the Fight for $15, which worked to establish a higher minimum wage in the fast food industry, was a partnership between the Service Employees International Union and the Movement for Black Lives. A new model called "Bargaining for the Common Good," which pushes for demands that benefit the entire community and not just the union membership, has underpinned some of the more recent and successful strikes in education, especially those of the Chicago Teachers Union and United Teachers Los Angeles. In 2020, after the murder of George Floyd, the Seattle Central Labor Council voted to expel the city's police union for its own problems with the excessive use of force. And Marcia Howard, a Black woman who has helped to maintain the occupation of George Floyd Square in Minneapolis, was elected vice president of the Minneapolis Federation of Teachers. She led a successful strike in the years following the 2020 uprising that centered an intersectional politics.[42]

Now some might suggest that intersectionality and fascism are effete academic terms that no worker could possibly understand. I beg to differ. In the 1940s, working-class people gave their lives to defeat fascism so that freedom might not perish from the earth. The notion that workers cannot sit still long enough to understand the threat of the far right, or that Black working-class women deserve to live in dignity, is not only empirically false, but also insulting. For several years, I co-taught a non-credit class for workers from across the University of Massachusetts–Amherst. Once I asked them why we never have conversations connecting gender, race, and class politics. One worker, a white man, said, "Because if we figured it out, they would be in big trouble." The solution is not to throw politics overboard, but to organize and lead with a vision of solidarity, one that can offer a coherent alternative to the politics of hate and division. One thing is for certain: any successful countermovement will benefit from the leadership and moral courage of Black workers. If we deal a generational defeat to the far right in our lifetime, then it will be because the Freedom Train made one more run.

Acknowledgments

This project began percolating between 2018 and 2022 when I was director of the UMass Amherst Labor Center. During my tenure, I encouraged a vision of solidarity that I hoped would speak to questions of gender and racial inequality and serve as an alternative agenda for the U.S. labor movement. Though most people were supportive, I encountered some principled opposition. I wondered about the source of the pushback and began reading books on the history of interracial solidarity. What surprised me most was that the main protagonists of these accounts were white activists in the CIO and Communist Party. Relatively few foregrounded the leadership of Black people. I then taught a graduate course on Black labor history. As my students and I worked our way through the syllabus, we came away with the same impression.

It was around that time that Naomi Schneider, executive editor of the University of California Press, posted a fateful tweet. She wrote that she wanted to publish more books on the labor movement and asked her followers if there were any authors they might recommend. A number of people recommended me. After some back and forth, Naomi generously offered me an advance contract, and I began the process of collecting, analyzing, and writing up the data that appear in this book.

Research grants allowed me to do this work. Many thanks to Aliqae Geraci of the Walter Reuther Library for the Sam Fishman Travel Award; Felicia Griffin-Fennell and Jamie Rowen for a grant from the Center for Justice, Law, and Societies (CJLS); and Jen Lundquist for the College of Social and Behavioral Sciences (SBS) Research Support Grant at UMass Amherst. The CJLS paid an undergraduate student, Xavier Aparicio, to collect and code the data for chapter 2. I then hired him with the SBS grant to work on chapter 3. Though this book bears only a vague resemblance to the one I laid out for Xavier in those early days, his excellent work and insight were instrumental to the development of the project as a whole.

These grants also allowed me to work with the excellent staff of four archives: the W. E. B. Du Bois Library at UMass Amherst; the Library of Congress Manuscript Division in Washington, DC; the Schomburg Center for Research in Black Culture in Harlem; and the Walter Reuther Library at Wayne State University in Detroit.

I am grateful for the support of my colleagues. The students, staff, and faculty of the Labor Center have been my rock since arriving in Amherst six years ago. I am particularly indebted to Jasmine Kerrissey for taking on the directorship of the Labor Center. Along the way, I have had the fortune of writing with fellow sociologists Fareen Parvez, Amy Schalet, and Ofer Sharone. I shudder to think what life would be like without the kindness and solidarity of Pawan Dhingra, Sanjiv Gupta, Moon-Kie Jung, Toussaint Losier, Sancha Medwinter, Brian Sargent, and Millie Thayer. Brian helped me reframe the contention among Black labor organizations as "Black politics." In addition, I developed my ideas in conversation with graduate students in the Labor Studies and Sociology programs, especially Swati Birla, Aaron Foote, Upasana Goswami, Venus Green, Salomi Jacob, Veda Kim, Mabrouka M'Barek, Kelly Miller, Esther Moraes, Brenda Quintana, Jordan Sanderson, Salman Sikandar, Anna Walden, and Tiamba Wilkerson. I hope they have learned as much from me as I have from them.

I have received excellent feedback at various stages of this project. Gracie Wooten, who was a member of the League of Revolutionary Black Workers and is still politically active, introduced me to Marian Kramer and the good people at the General Baker Institute in Detroit. They schooled me on the struggles of the 1960s and 70s and organized me to walk a picket line or two for water rights in Southeast Michigan. I tested out my theoretical framework at the University of California, Berkeley, Haverford College, and the Commonwealth Honors College at UMass Amherst. I am grateful to Mari Castañeda, Rici Hammer, Elise Herrala, and Michael Rodriguez-Muñiz for arranging those talks. While at Berkeley, Zophia Edwards of Johns Hopkins University observed that labor scholars miss the role of independent Black labor organizations because they focus too much on unions. I presented a condensed version of the book at Cornell ILR's Global Labor and Work Seminar. Special thanks to Tristan Ivory for the invitation, Santiago Anria and Christine Schmidt for organizing the talk, and many others who met with me in Ithaca, including Ghazah Abbasi, Kate Bronfenbrenner, Ian Greer, Deepa Kylasam Iyer, Youbin Kang, Or Shay, and Andrew Wolf.

Several people were kind enough to read the entire manuscript. José Itzigsohn, Michael Rodriguez-Muñiz, and Kim Voss read the book with care. They reminded me to define my terms, preview each chapter, and speak to academic audiences as well as to the public at large. Amel Ahmed and Leonardo Barbosa urged me to say flat-out that navigating internal conflict in social movement spaces is a strength, not a weakness. Two legends of the labor movement also read the book in draft form. Bill Fletcher, Jr., and Steven Pitts saved me from factual errors and pushed me to clarify my arguments. Steven interviewed me about the book for *Convergence Magazine* and the Block and Build podcast. Many thanks to Rishi Awatramani and Marcy Rein for coordinating logistics.

Last but not least, heartfelt thanks to my wife Emily Heaphy, our son Ellis, and our dog Phoenix for supporting me through another book project. Emily, who is a top-notch social scientist in her own right, read the introduction and conclusion and gave me important last-minute advice. My overall mood improved considerably when Michigan won the 2023 national championship in college football, but Emily, Ellis, and Phoenix still had to endure my absence and occasional crankiness. For their love and patience, they deserve pride of place at the end of this book.

Notes

Chapter 1

1. Michael Fletcher, "An Oral History of the March on Washington," *Smithsonian Magazine* (July 2013), https://www.smithsonianmag.com/history/oral-history-march-washington-180953863.

2. Lawton Johnson Travel Agency to Cleveland Robinson, July 20, 1963, BRP, Folder on "March on Washington Transportation memos including all unions attending," LoC; Al Lowenthal to all local IUE presidents, July 30, 1963, BRP, Folder on "March on Washington—Mobilization of Labor Unions—1963," LoC; Bayard Rustin to Whom it May Concern, August 20, 1963, BRP, Folder on "March on Washington—Mobilization of Labor Unions—1963," LoC; NJ Turnpike Authority to Bayard Rustin, August 21, 1963, BRP, Folder on "March on Washington—Mobilization of Labor Unions—1963," LoC.

3. Courtland Cox to Stokely Carmichael, August 18, 1963, BRP, Folder on "March on Washington Transportation memos including all unions attending," LoC; Leonard Farbstein, "ICC ASKED TO INVESTIGATE AUGUST 28th FREEDOM MARCH BUS CRISIS," August 27, 1963, BRP, Folder on "March on Washington Transportation memos including all unions attending," LoC.

4. Rachelle Horowitz to Bayard Rustin, "Planes Trains and Buses definitely coming to Washington," August 22, 1963, BRP, Folder on "March on Washington Transportation memos including all unions attending," LoC; Rachelle Horowitz to Bayard Rustin and Sy Posner, August 14, 1963, Folder on "March on Washington Transportation memos including all unions attending," LoC.

5. Fletcher, "An Oral History."

6. For an account of the labor roots of the march, see William P. Jones, *The March on Washington: Jobs, Freedom, and the Forgotten History of Civil Rights* (New York: Norton, 2013).

7. Philip S. Foner, *Organized Labor & The Black Worker, 1619-1981* (Chicago: Haymarket Books, [1974] 2017), 346; A.J. Muste to A. Philip Randolph, April 5, 1963, BRP, Folder on "March on Washington 1963—General Correspondence—March—June," LoC; Jones, *The March on Washington*.

8. Foner, *Organized Labor & The Black Worker*, 346; Rachelle Horowitz to Bayard Rustin and Sy Posner, August 19, 1963, BRP, Folder on "March on Washington Transportation memos including all unions attending," LoC; Tom Kahn, Letter to the Editor of the *New York Times* [in response to Arthur Bestor], July 22, 1963, BRP, "March on Washington, 1963—General Correspondence—July," LoC.

9. Marty Fassler, "Hill Lecture: Some of My Best Friends . . . " *The Justice* XV (17), March 12, 1963, HHP, Articles, 1956-1965, LoC; Foner, *Organized Labor*, 341-45; A. Philip Randolph, "Statement by A. Philip Randolph at Labor Dinner of NAACP Fifty-Second Annual Convention, Sheraton Hotel, Philadelphia, PA., July 14, 1961," APRP, Speeches and Writing File, July 14-Dec. 5, 1961, LoC.

10. Alabama Labor Council, "Special Convention of the Alabama Labor Council, AFL-CIO, Municipal Auditorium, 1930 8th Avenue, North, Birmingham, Alabama, 20th Street Entrance, Saturday, March 21, 1964," State AFL-CIO Proceedings, LoC; Foner, *Organized Labor*, 350-351; Mississippi AFL-CIO, "Proceedings of the Second Biennial Convention, Mississippi AFL-CIO, Heidelberg Hotel, Jackson, Miss., May 25-26-27, 1964," State AFL-CIO Proceedings, LoC.

11. Evelyn Nakano Glenn, *Unequal Freedom: How Race and Gender Shaped American Citizenship and Labor* (Cambridge: Harvard University Press, 2002), 79; Judith Stepan-Norris and Maurice Zeitlin, *Left Out: Reds and America's Industrial Unions* (Cambridge: Cambridge University Press, 2002), 258. For scholars who view the institutionalized labor movement as racially exclusionary, see also Aaron Brenner, Robert Brenner, and Cal Winslow, eds., *Rebel Rank and File: Labor Militancy and Revolt from Below During the Long 1970s* (New York: Verso, 2010); Dan Georgakas and Marvin Surkin, *Detroit, I do mind dying: A Study in Urban Revolution*, 2nd ed. (Boston: South End Press, 1998); Michael Goldfield, "Class, Race, and Politics in the United States: White Supremacy as the Main Explanation for the Peculiarities of American Politics from Colonial Times to the Present," *Research in Political Economy* 12 (1990): 83-127; Michael Goldfield, *The Color of Politics: Race and the Mainsprings of American Politics* (New York: New Press, 1997); Herbert Hill, "The Problem of Race in American Labor History," *Reviews in American History* 24, no. 2 (June 1996): 189-208; Gerald Hunt and David Rayside,

"Labor Union Response to Diversity in Canada and the United States," *Industrial Relations* 39, no. 3 (2000): 401–44; Richard Iton, *Solidarity Blues: Race, Culture, and the American Left* (Chapel Hill: University of North Carolina Press, 2000); Bruce Nelson, *Divided We Stand: American Workers and the Struggle for Black Equality* (Princeton: Princeton University Press, 2002); and David R. Roediger, *The Wages of Whiteness: Race and the Making of the American Working Class* (New York: Verso, 1991). For scholars who focus on the inclusiveness of organized labor in general or in select unions, see also Cliff Brown and John Brueggeman, "Mobilizing Interracial Solidarity: A Comparison of the 1919 and 1937 Steel Industry Labor Organizing Drives," *Mobilization* 2, no. 1 (1997): 47–70; Peter Cole, *Wobblies on the Waterfront: Interracial Unionism and Progressive-Era Philadelphia* (Urbana: University of Illinois Press, 2007); Toni Gilpin, *The Long Deep Grudge: A Story of Big Capital, Radical Labor, and Class War in the American Heartland* (Chicago: Haymarket Books, 2020); Michael Honey, "Anti-Racism, Black Workers, and Southern Labor Organizing: Historical Notes on a Continuing Struggle," *Labor Studies Journal* 25, no. 1 (2000): 10–26; Roger Horowitz, *'Negro and White, Unite and Fight!': A Social History of Industrial Unionism in Meatpacking* (Urbana: University of Illinois Press, 1997); Jake Rosenfeld and Meredith Kleykamp, "Organized Labor and Racial Wage Inequality in the United States," *American Journal of Sociology* 117, no. 5 (2012): 1460–1502; Maurice Zeitlin and L. Frank Weyher, "'Black and White, Unite and Fight': Interracial Working-Class Solidarity and Racial Employment Equality," *American Journal of Sociology* 107, no. 2 (2001): 430–67; Robert H. Zieger, *For Jobs and Freedom: Race and Labor in America since 1865* (Lexington: University Press of Kentucky, 2007).

12. For exceptions to this rule, see Erik S. Gellman, *Death Blow to Jim Crow: The National Negro Congress and the Rise of Militant Civil Rights* (Chapel Hill: University of North Carolina Press, 2012); Kimberley L. Phillips, *AlabamaNorth: African-American Migrants, Community, and Working-Class Activism in Cleveland, 1915–1945* (Urbana: University of Illinois Press, 1999); Mindy Thompson, "The Nation Negro Labor Council: A History," Occasional Paper No. 27 (New York: American Institute for Marxist Studies, 1978); Ernest Thompson and Mindy Thompson Fullilove, *Homeboy Came to Orange: A Story of People's Power* (New York: New Village Press, 2018).

13. Nell Irvin Painter, "The New Labor History and the Historical Moment," *Journal of Politics, and Culture, and Society* 2 (Spring 1989): 369–70; David Roediger, "'Labor in White Skin': Race and Working-Class History," in *Reshaping the U.S. Left*, ed. Mike Davis and Michael Sprinker (London: Verso, 1987), 288–89; Jenny Carson, *A Matter of Moral Justice: Black Women Laundry Workers and the*

Fight for Justice (Urbana: University of Illinois Press, 2021), 6–7. See also Rick Halpern, *Down on the Killing Floor: Black and White Workers in Chicago's Packinghouses, 1904–1954* (Urbana: University of Illinois Press, 1997), 2; and Hill, "The Problem of Race in American Labor History," 189.

14. Cedric de Leon, "Black from White: How the Rights of White and Black Workers Became 'Labor' and 'Civil' Rights after the U.S. Civil War," *Labor Studies Journal* 42, no. 1 (2016): 1–17.

15. I am referring here to the clash between the Black middle and working classes as well as the political conflict between an older generation of civil society actors and the so-called "New Negro" radicals of the 1920s and 1930s. For sources on these, see for example Robin D. G. Kelley, *Race Rebels: Culture, Politics, and the Black Working Class* (New York: Free Press, 1994); Phillips, *AlabamaNorth*, 11; Mark Solomon, *The Cry Was Unity: Communists and African Americans, 1917–1936* (Jackson: University Press of Mississippi, 1998), 6.

16. Venus Green and Cedric de Leon, "The Ruse of Recognition: Black Labor in the Afterlife of Slavery," *Sociology of Race and Ethnicity* (2024) https://doi.org/10.1177/23326492241247786; de Leon, "Black from White"; Foner, *Organized Labor & The Black Worker*, 4–5, 8–9, 11–12; Barbara S. Griffith, *The Crisis of American Labor: Operation Dixie and the Defeat of the CIO* (Philadelphia: Temple University Press, 1988); Sterling D. Spero and Abram L. Harris, *The Black Worker: The Negro and the Labor Movement* (New York: Columbia University Press, [1931] 1972), x, 7–9; Richard C. Wade, *Slavery in the Cities: The South, 1820–1860* (Oxford: Oxford University Press, 1967), 30, 33–35, 37.

17. Cedric Robinson, *Black Marxism: The Making of the Black Radical Tradition* (Chapel Hill: University of North Carolina Press, [1983] 2000).

18. Gellman, *Death Blow to Jim Crow*; M. Thompson, "The Nation Negro Labor Council: A History"; E. Thompson and Thompson Fullilove, *Homeboy Came to Orange*. Another book that features the National Negro Congress is Brian Dolinar, *The Black Cultural Front: Black Writers and Artists of the Depression Generation* (Jackson: University Press of Mississippi, 2012), though the book is concerned primarily with tracking the individual careers of Black artists and writers. Dolinar argues that far from stifling the latter, the left cultivated a vibrant community who saw their work as opening up a cultural front in the war against fascism.

19. Peter Cole, *Ben Fletcher: The Life and Times of a Black Wobbly* (Oakland: PM Press, 2021); Robin D. G. Kelley, *Hammer and Hoe: Alabama Communists during the Great Depression* (Chapel Hill: University of North Carolina Press, 1990); Robert Rodgers Korstad, *Civil Rights Unionism: Tobacco Workers and the Struggle for Democracy in the Mid-Twentieth Century South* (Chapel Hill: University of North

Carolina Press, 2003); Ruth Needleman, *Black Freedom Fighters in Steel: The Struggle for Democratic Unionism* (Ithaca: Cornell University Press, 2003). For the National Negro Congress and the organization of steel, see Michael Goldfield, *The Southern Key: Class, Race, and Radicalism in the 1930s and 1940s* (Oxford: Oxford University Press, 2020), 104.

20. W.E.B. Du Bois, *Black Reconstruction in America, 1860–1880* (New York: Atheneum, [1935] 1992).

21. Aldon Morris, *The Origins of the Civil Rights Movement: Black Communities Organizing for Change* (New York: Free Press, 1984); Aldon Morris, *The Scholar Denied: W.E.B. Du Bois and the Birth of Modern Sociology* (Oakland: University of California Press, 2015). Recent examples of Du Boisian sociology include José Itzigsohn and Karida Brown, *The Sociology of W.E.B. Du Bois: Racialized Modernity and the Global Color Line* (New York: NYU Press, 2020) and the many contributors to Aldon Morris, et al., eds., *The Oxford Handbook of W.E.B. Du Bois* (Oxford: Oxford University Press, 2022).

22. Contemporary labor scholars (broadly defined) who foreground the role of Black labor include Carson, *A Matter of Moral Justice*; Cole, *Wobblies on the Waterfront*; Foner, *Organized Labor and the Black Worker*; Gellman, *Death Blow to Jim Crow*; Georgakas and Surkin, *Detroit*; Kelley, *Hammer and Hoe*; Earl Lewis, *In Their Own Interests: Race, Class and Power in Twentieth-Century Norfolk, Virginia* (Berkeley: University of California Press, 1993); Mark Naison, *Communists in Harlem during the Depression* (Urbana: University of Illinois Press, [1983] 2005); Needleman, *Black Freedom Fighters in Steel*; Solomon, *The Cry Was Unity*; Joe William Trotter, Jr., *Workers on Arrival: Black Labor in the Making of America* (Oakland: University of California Press, 2019). An important tendency within this literature has been to highlight the role of Black trade unionists in what Jacquelyn Dowd Hall calls the "decisive first phase" of the "long civil rights movement." Some of the key works in this literature include Martha Biondi, *To Stand and Fight: The Struggle for Civil Rights in Postwar New York City* (Cambridge: Harvard University Press, 2003); Glenda Elizabeth Gilmore, *Defying Dixie: The Radical Roots of Civil Rights, 1919–1950* (New York: Norton, 2008); Jacquelyn Dowd Hall, "The Long Civil Rights Movement and the Political Uses of the Past," *Journal of American History* 91, no. 4 (March 2005): 1233–63; Michael Honey, *Southern Labor and Black Civil Rights: Organizing Memphis Workers* (Urbana: University of Illinois Press, 1993); Korstad, *Civil Rights Unionism*.

23. Justin McCarthy, "U.S. Approval of Labor Unions at Highest Point since 1965," *Gallup*, August 30, 2022, https://news.gallup.com/poll/398303/approval-labor-unions-highest-point-1965.aspx; National Labor Relations Board, "First

Three Quarters' Union Election Petitions Up 58%, Exceeding All FY21 Petitions Filed," https://www.nlrb.gov/news-outreach/news-story/correction-first-three-quarters-union-election-petitions-up-58-exceeding; Eric Blanc, *Red State Revolt: The Teachers' Strike Wave and Working-Class Politics* (New York: Verso, 2019); Tamara L. Lee, Sheri Davis-Faulkner, Naomi R. Williams, and Maite Tapia, *A Racial Reckoning in Industrial Relations: Storytelling as Revolution from Within* (Champaign: Labor and Employment Relations Association, 2022); Jane F. McAlevey, *No Shortcuts: Organizing for Power in the New Gilded Age* (Oxford: Oxford University Press, 2016); Joseph A. McCartin, Marilyn Sneiderman, and Maurice BP-Weeks, "Combustible Convergence: Bargaining for the Common Good and the #RedforEd Uprisings of 2018," *Labor Studies Journal* 45, no. 1 (2020): 97–113; Kim Moody, "Reversing the 'Model': Thoughts on Jane McAlevey's Plan for Union Power," *Spectre Journal* (November 8, 2020): 1–22.

24. Priscilla Murolo and A. B. Chitty, *From the Folks Who Brought You the Weekend* (New York: New Press, 2018), 235–36; Dan Clawson, *The Next Upsurge: Labor and the New Social Movements* (Ithaca: Cornell University Press, 2003); Cedric de Leon, "The Case for an Eclectic Mass Movement," *New Labor Forum* (Winter 2023): 80–86.

Chapter 2

1. Phyl Garland, "A. Philip Randolph: Labor's Grand Old Man," *The Crisis* (April 1969): 31–42, APRP, Box 43 Printed Matter 1969, LoC; Jervis Anderson, *A. Philip Randolph: A Biographical Portrait* (Berkeley: University of California Press, [1973] 1986). For an additional source on labor activism among African American migrants from the South, see Kimberley L. Phillips, *AlabamaNorth: African-American Migrants, Community, and Working-Class Activism in Cleveland, 1915–1945* (Urbana: University of Illinois Press, 1999).

2. Larry Tye, *Rising from the Rails: Pullman Porters and the Making of the Black Middle Class* (New York: Henry Holt and Company, 2004), 116–17.

3. Garland, "A. Philip Randolph."

4. Tye, *Rising from the Rails*, 118–19.

5. Tye, *Rising from the Rails*, 120.

6. Tye, *Rising from the Rails*, 122–23.

7. Anderson, *A. Philip Randolph*, 78.

8. Anderson, *A. Philip Randolph*, 79.

9. Anderson, *A. Philip Randolph*, 81.

10. A. Philip Randolph, "The Cause of and Remedy for Race Riots," *The Messenger* (September 1919): 14–21; A. Philip Randolph, "The Right and Left-Wing Interpreted," *The Messenger* (May 1919): 20–21; Jervis, *A. Philip Randolph*, 82.

11. Tye, *Rising from the Rails*, 2–3; Garland, "A. Philip Randolph"; Boston Citizens' Committee, "The Pullman Porters' Struggle," APRP, Folder on "BSCP 1926–1928," LoC; A. Philip Randolph, "Program of the Brotherhood of Sleeping Car Porters convention, Manhattan Casino, December 3, 1926," APRP, Folder on "BSCP 1926–1928," LoC.

12. Winston James, *Holding Aloft the Banner of Ethiopia: Caribbean Radicalism in Early Twentieth-Century America* (London: Verso, 1999), 157; Mark Solomon, *The Cry Was Unity: Communists and African Americans, 1917–1936* (Jackson: University Press of Mississippi, 1998), 5.

13. J.A. Zumoff, "The African Blood Brotherhood: From Caribbean Nationalism to Communism," *Journal of Caribbean History* 41, no. 1/2 (2007): 200–26; Solomon, *The Cry Was Unity*, 5.

14. James, *Holding Aloft the Banner of Ethiopia*, 158.

15. Solomon, *The Cry Was Unity*, 5; Zumoff, "The African Blood Brotherhood"; Carl Offord, "An Account of the African Blood Brotherhood: Interview with Cyril Briggs" (New York: Works Progress Administration, 1939), New York Public Library Digital Collections, https://digitalcollections.nypl.org/items/43869020-74fc-0133-591b-00505686a51c.

16. Cyril Briggs, "Deporting Aliens and Negroes," *The Crusader* 1, no. 8 (April 1919): 10; Cyril Briggs, "Make Their Cause Your Own," *The Crusader* 1, no. 11 (July 1919): 6.

17. Advertisement, *The Crusader* 2, no. 2 (October 1919): 27.

18. Tye, *Rising from the Rails*, 111, 131.

19. Randolph, "Program of the Brotherhood of Sleeping Car Porters convention"; Tye, *Rising from the Rails*, 131; Garland, "A. Philip Randolph."

20. Randolph, "Program of the Brotherhood of Sleeping Car Porters convention."

21. Tye, *Rising from the Rails*, 133.

22. A. Philip Randolph, "The Pullman Company and the Pullman Porter," *The Messenger* 7 (September 1925): 312–39.

23. Tye, *Rising from the Rails*, 131; A. Philip Randolph, "The Pullman Porters Fight and the Black Man's Burden," *Bulletin*, APRP, Folder on "BSCP 1926–1928," LoC.

24. Randolph, "Program of the Brotherhood of Sleeping Car Porters convention."

25. Boston Citizens' Committee, "The Pullman Porters' Struggle."

26. Boston Citizens' Committee, "The Pullman Porters' Struggle."

27. Solomon, *The Cry Was Unity*, 6–7, 12.

28. Cyril Briggs, "Africa for the Africans," *The Crusader* 3, no. 2 (October 1920): 8–9; Cyril Briggs, "The Salvation of the Negro," *The Crusader* 4, no. 2 (April 1921): 8–9.

29. Briggs, "Africa for the Africans"; Briggs, "The Salvation of the Negro"; Solomon, *The Cry Was Unity*, 13–14.

30. Cyril Briggs, "The Acid Test of White Friendship," *The Crusader* 4, no. 5: 8–9; Solomon, *The Cry Was Unity*, 16–17.

31. Offord, "An Account of the African Blood Brotherhood."

32. Cyril Briggs, "The African Blood Brotherhood," *The Crusader* 2, no. 10 (June 1920): 7, 22.

33. Offord, "An Account of the African Blood Brotherhood."

34. Commander, Tulsa Post, "The Tulsa Riot," *The Crusader* 4, no. 5 (July 1921): 5–6; Cyril Briggs, "The Tulsa Riot and the African Blood Brotherhood," *The Crusader* 4, no. 5 (July 1921): 10.

35. Solomon, *The Cry Was Unity*, 15, 20.

36. Solomon, *The Cry Was Unity*, 320n49; Cyril Briggs, "The Workers Party, Marcus Garvey, and the Negro," *The Crusader* 6, no. 1 (January-February 1922): 15.

37. "Memorandum to Mr. G.A. Kelly, General Solicitor," Pullman Company Archives, 06-01-04 Box 17 Folder 454, Newberry Library, https://web.archive .org/web/20180222225754/https://publications.newberry.org/pullman/items /show/223.

38. Tye, *Rising from the Rails*, 143.

39. Tye, *Rising from the Rails*, 149.

40. "7,000 Pullman Porters Ready for Strike Call," *New York Herald Tribune*, March 13, 1928, APRP, Folder on "BSCP 1926-1928," LoC; Philip S. Foner, *Organized Labor & The Black Worker, 1619-1981* (Chicago: Haymarket Books, [1974] 2017), 184; Tye, *Rising from the Rails*, 150.

41. "Pullman Porters Ready for Strike," *New York Times*, April 25, 1928, APRP, Folder on "BSCP 1926-1928," LoC; Anderson, *A. Philip Randolph*, 194.

42. Anderson, *A. Philip Randolph*, 197, 199-200.

43. Anderson, *A. Philip Randolph*, 202. .

44. Foner, *Organized Labor and the Black Worker*, 184; Anderson, *A. Philip Randolph*, 201. Brotherhood historian Larry Tye writes that Green wrote the tel-

egram at Randolph's urging and that Randolph furthermore used the telegram as a pretext to call off a strike he did not want (*Rising from the Rails*, 150).

45. Anderson, *A. Philip Randolph*, 201.

46. Foner, *Organized Labor and the Black Worker*, 184; Tye, *Rising from the Rails*, 150-11.

47. A. Philip Randolph, "Greetings to the Public from the Brotherhood," *Program of the Third Annual Ball of the Brotherhood of Sleeping Car Porters, Rockland Palace, 155th St. and 8th Ave, Friday Evening, December 7, 1928*, APRP, Folder on "BSCP 1926-1928," LoC; Anderson, *A. Philip Randolph*, 203; Tye, *Rising from the Rails*, 150.

48. Solomon, *The Cry Was Unity*, 28.

49. Solomon, *The Cry Was Unity*, 28.

50. "Report Made At: New York City, Date which made: 9/24/23, Period for which made: 9/22-23/23, Report made by: Earl E. Titus, Re: Radical Negro Activities," National Archives Folder: Casefile #61-23 on Cyril v. Briggs, Claude McKay, and the African Blood Brotherhood regarding government surveillance of African Americans; "Report Made At: New York City, NY, Date which made: 11/27/23, Period for which made: 11/23/23, Report made by: Earl E. Titus, Re: African Blood Brotherhood, Negro Radical Activities," National Archives Folder: Casefile #61-23 on Cyril v. Briggs, Claude McKay, and the African Blood Brotherhood regarding government surveillance of African Americans; "Report Made At: New York City, NY, Date which made: 11/30/23, Period for which made: 11/27/23, Report made by: Earl E. Titus, Re: African Blood Brotherhood, Negro Radical Activities," National Archives Folder: Casefile #61-23 on Cyril v. Briggs, Claude McKay, and the African Blood Brotherhood regarding government surveillance of African Americans. See also Solomon, *The Cry Was Unity*, 28-29.

51. William Monroe Trotter, "Colored Dead in Labor War in South," *Boston Guardian* (February 12, 1910): 3; "Report Made At: New York City, NY, Date which made: 8/16/23, Period for which made: 8/14/23, Report made by: Earl E. Titus, In Re: African Blood Brotherhood, Negro Radical Activities," National Archives Folder: Casefile #61-23 on Cyril v. Briggs, Claude McKay, and the African Blood Brotherhood regarding government surveillance of African Americans"; "Report Made At: New York City, Date which made: 9/24/23, Period for which made: 9/21/23, Report made by: Earl E. Titus, Re: Radical Negro Activities," National Archives Folder: Casefile #61-23 on Cyril v. Briggs, Claude McKay, and the African Blood Brotherhood regarding government surveillance of African Americans.

52. J.G. Tucker, "Special Report—Dec. 1, 1923," National Archives Folder: Casefile #61-23 on Cyril v. Briggs, Claude McKay, and the African Blood Brotherhood regarding government surveillance of African Americans.

53. "Report Made At: Chicago, Illinois, Date which made: Jan. 18, 1924, Period for which made: Jan. 15-16, 1923, Report made by: Earl E. Titus, Re: AFRICAN BLOOD BROTHERHOOD, Radical Negro Activities," National Archives Folder: Casefile #61-23 on Cyril v. Briggs, Claude McKay, and the African Blood Brotherhood regarding government surveillance of African Americans.

54. Solomon, *The Cry Was Unity*, 30-31.

55. Solomon, *The Cry Was Unity*, 32-33.

56. Mark Naison, *Communists in Harlem during the Depression* (Urbana: University of Illinois Press, [1983] 2005), 13; Solomon, *The Cry Was Unity*, 52.

57. Glenda Elizabeth Gilmore, *Defying Dixie: The Radical Roots of Civil Rights, 1919-1950* (New York: Norton, 2008), 51; Solomon, *The Cry Was Unity*, 52.

58. Solomon, *The Cry Was Unity*, 53.

59. Gilmore, *Defying Dixie*, 52.

60. Gilmore, *Defying Dixie*, 52, 56; Solomon, *The Cry Was Unity*, 54.

61. Gilmore, *Defying Dixie*, 53.

62. Gilmore, *Defying Dixie*, 53-54; Solomon, *The Cry Was Unity*, 55.

63. Gilmore, *Defying Dixie*, 54-55.

64. Gilmore, *Defying Dixie*, 56.

65. Gilmore, *Defying Dixie*, 56.

66. "Minutes of the Meetings of the Executive Council, American Federation of Labor, Washington, D.C. October 18-25, 1928," AFLR, LoC.

67. "Minutes of the Meetings of the Executive Council, American Federation of Labor, Washington, D.C. October 18-25, 1928," AFLR, LoC.

68. "Minutes of the Meetings of the Executive Council, American Federation of Labor, Washington, D.C. October 18-25, 1928," AFLR, LoC.

69. "Minutes of the Meetings of the Executive Council, American Federation of Labor, Washington, D.C. October 18-25, 1928," AFLR, LoC.

70. "Minutes of the Meetings of the Executive Council, American Federation of Labor, Washington, D.C. October 18-25, 1928," AFLR, LoC.

71. "Minutes of the Meetings of the Executive Council, American Federation of Labor, Roosevelt Hotel, New Orleans, Louisiana, November 1928," AFLR, LoC.

72. "Minutes of the Meeting of the Executive Council, American Federation of Labor, Alcazar Hotel, Miami, Florida, February 18-25, 1929," AFLR, LoC; "Minutes of the Meeting of the Executive Council, American Federation of Labor, Washington, D.C., May 5-12, 1930," AFLR, LoC; "Minutes of the Meetings of the Executive Council, American Federation of Labor, Whitcomb Hotel, San Francisco, California, September 28 to October 14, 1934," AFLR, LoC.

73. "Minutes of the Meetings of the Executive Council, American Federation of Labor, Whitcomb Hotel, San Francisco, California, September 28 to October 14, 1934," AFLR, LoC.

74. "Circular No. 384, Series 1934, Nov. 12 1934," Addendum to "Minutes of the Meeting of the Executive Council, American Federation of Labor, Washington, D.C., January 29 to February 14, 1935," AFLR, LoC.

75. "Minutes of the Meeting of the Executive Council, American Federation of Labor, Washington, D.C., January 29 to February 14, 1935," AFLR, LoC.

76. "Minutes of the Meeting of the Executive Council, American Federation of Labor, Atlantic City, NJ, August 5-16, 1935," AFLR, LoC.

77. "Minutes of the Meeting of the Executive Council, American Federation of Labor, Alcazar Hotel, Miami, Florida, January 15-29, 1936," AFLR, LoC.

Chapter 3

1. Mark Solomon, *The Cry Was Unity: Communists and African Americans, 1917-1936* (Jackson: University Press of Mississippi, 1998), 262-63.

2. Mark Naison, *Communists in Harlem during the Depression* (Urbana: University of Illinois Press, [1983] 2005), 52, 59-60. The party's intervention did not endear them to the NAACP, who took it as an intrusion on their turf, which included antilynching legislation and legal defense.

3. Naison, *Communists in Harlem during the Depression*, 154-55; Solomon, *The Cry Was Unity*, 219-21.

4. Solomon, *The Cry Was Unity*, 254; Robin D. G. Kelley, *Hammer and Hoe: Alabama Communists during the Great Depression* (Chapel Hill: UNC Press, 1990), 68-69.

5. Erik S. Gellman, *Death Blow to Jim Crow: The National Negro Congress and the Rise of Militant Civil Rights* (Chapel Hill: University of North Carolina Press, 2012), 13.

6. Gellman, *Death Blow to Jim Crow*, 13; Solomon, *The Cry Was Unity*, 234.

7. Gellman, *Death Blow to Jim Crow*, 14.

8. Solomon, *The Cry Was Unity*, 235.

9. Gellman, *Death Blow to Jim Crow*, 14.

10. "Statement of John P. Davis executive secretary of the Joint Committee on National Recovery, before the Complaint Hearing of the National Recovery Administration, February 28, 1934," NNC, Schomburg.

11. "Statement of John P. Davis."

12. Gellman, *Death Blow to Jim Crow*, 16; John P. Davis, "The Proposed Code of Fair Competition for the Steel Plate Fabricating Industry," NNC, Schomburg; John P. Davis, "Statement of the Joint Committee on National Recovery Concerning the Code of Fair Competition for the Shipping Industry," NNC, Schomburg.

13. John P. Davis, "A Survey of the Problems of the Negro Under the New Deal," *The Journal of Negro Education* 5, no. 1 (January, 1936): 3–12; Ralph Bunche, "A Critique of New Deal Social Planning as it Affects Negroes," *The Journal of Negro Education* 5, no. 1 (January, 1936): 59–65.

14. W.E. B Du Bois, "Social Planning for the Negro, Past and Present," *The Journal of Negro Education* 5, no. 1 (January, 1936): 110–25.

15. Mary Anderson, "The Plight of Negro Domestic Labor," *The Journal of Negro Education*, 5, no. 1 (January, 1936): 66–72.

16. A. Philip Randolph, "The Trade Union Movement and the Negro," *The Journal of Negro Education*, 5, no. 1 (January, 1936): 54–58.

17. Jervis Anderson, *A. Philip Randolph: A Biographical Portrait* (Berkeley: University of California Press, 1986), 229–230.

18. Anderson, *A. Philip Randolph*, 231.

19. Anderson, *A. Philip Randolph*, 230.

20. Gellman, *Death Blow to Jim Crow*, 23–24.

21. Anderson, *A. Philip Randolph*, 231.

22. Gellman, *Death Blow to Jim Crow*, 25; "The Official Proceedings of the National Negro Congress, February 14–15–16 1936, Chicago," NNC, Schomburg, p. 9.

23. "The Official Proceedings of the National Negro Congress," p. 9.

24. "The Official Proceedings of the National Negro Congress," p. 9.

25. "The Official Proceedings of the National Negro Congress," pp. 12–13; Gellman, *Death Blow to Jim Crow*, 69.

26. "The Official Proceedings of the National Negro Congress," pp. 17–19.

27. "The Official Proceedings of the National Negro Congress," pp. 21–22; Keith Gilyard, *Louise Thompson Patterson: A Life of Struggle for Justice* (Durham: Duke University Press, 2017).

28. Gellman, *Death Blow to Jim Crow*, 28.

29. Gellman, *Death Blow to Jim Crow*, 28–29.

30. Gellman, *Death Blow to Jim Crow*, 29.

31. John P. Davis, "PROPOSED PLAN FOR ORGANIZATION OF NEGRO STEEL WORKERS IN YOUNGSTOWN, O. Submitted by the National Negro Congress to Steel Workers Organizing Committee of the Committee for Industrial Organization," June 10, 1936, NNC, Schomburg. For another example of one of

Davis's proposals see "Memorandum. To: John Brophy, Committee for Industrial Organization. From: John P. Davis, National Negro Congress. Subject: Proposal for Initiation of National Organizing Campaign for Tobacco Workers," May 18, 1937, NNC, Schomburg.

32. John Brophy to Adolph Germer, June 11, 1936, APRP, LoC; Gellman, *Death Blow to Jim Crow*, 35.

33. Gellman, *Death Blow to Jim Crow*, 36, 39–40.

34. Gellman, *Death Blow to Jim Crow*, 36, 38–39, 41, 43–46.

35. V. R. Tompkins to John P. Frey, Feb. 23, 1937, APRP, LoC; V. R. Tompkins to John P. Frey, March 2, 1937, APRP, LoC; Gellman, *Death Blow to Jim Crow*, 42–43.

36. "Proceedings of Second Congress . . . 1937, Nat'l Negro Congress Box 11," NNC, Schomburg.

37. "Oral Interview, C. LeBron Simmons, Norman McRae, Interviewer, 1969," Black Workers in the Labor Movement oral histories, WRL.

38. "Memorandum. To: John Brophy, Committee for Industrial Organization. From: John P. Davis, National Negro Congress. Subject: Proposal for Initiation of National Organizing Campaign for Tobacco Workers," May 18, 1937, NNC, Schomburg; John P. Davis, "ANALYSIS OF QUESTIONNAIRES IN FIVE PLANTS IN THE TOBACCO INDUSTRY," [c. 1935], NNC, Schomburg.

39. Gellman, *Death Blow to Jim Crow*, 76, 79, 81–86, 93, 96.

40. Gellman, *Death Blow to Jim Crow*, 88, 104; Gilyard, *Louise Thompson Patterson*.

41. Gellman, *Death Blow to Jim Crow*, 51–53; see also Roger Horowitz, *'Negro and White, Unite and Fight!': A Social History of Industrial Unionism in Meatpacking* (Urbana: University of Illinois Press, 1997), 4, 5, 8; and Rick Halpern, *Down on the Killing Floor: Black and White Workers in Chicago's Packinghouses, 1904–1954* (Urbana: University of Illinois Press, 1997), 3, 121, 137, 160. Horowitz presents a more nuanced version of the inclusion school in labor historiography, such that Black workers are not merely the passive beneficiaries of the white left. For Horowitz the presence of Black workers shaped militant industrial, left-led unionism as much as white militants cultivated the support of Black workers. These, together with the structural class conflict endemic to the industry itself, led to the rise of interracial class-based unionism. Halpern, too, straddles the debate between inclusion and exclusion by suggesting that white and Black packinghouse workers thought in both race and class terms in periods of workplace division and solidarity. That said, Horowitz does not mention the role of the National Negro Congress in organizing the meatpacking industry, while Halpern mentions the NNC only in passing.

42. 1937 speech: "Proceedings of Second Congress . . . 1937, Nat'l Negro Congress Box 11," NNC, Schomburg.

43. "Speech by President John L. Lewis of the CIO, delivered at the opening session of the National Negro Congress in Washington, D.C." (April 26, 1940), NNC, Schomburg; Gellman, *Death Blow to Jim Crow*, 151.

44. A. Philip Randolph, "The World Crisis and the Negro People Today," "Third National Negro Congress, April 26, 27, 28, 1940, United States Department of Labor Auditorium, Washington, D.C." April 26, 1940, NNC, Schomburg.

45. Anderson, *A. Philip Randolph*, 235; Gellman, *Death Blow to Jim Crow*, 153

46. "Report of John P. Davis National Secretary of the National Negro Congress, Saturday, April 27, at 11:30 P.M.," NNC, Schomburg.

47. Report of the Resolutions Committee, "Third National Negro Congress, April 26, 27, 28, 1940, United States Department of Labor Auditorium, Washington, D.C.," April 26, 1940, NNC, Schomburg; Anderson, *A. Philip Randolph*, 237.

48. Anderson, *A. Philip Randolph*, 237.

49. Anderson, *A. Philip Randolph*, 237.

50. Anderson, *A. Philip Randolph*, 238.

51. Anderson, *A. Philip Randolph*, 241–42.

52. Anderson, *A. Philip Randolph*, 244.

53. Anderson, *A. Philip Randolph*, 245.

54. Anderson, *A. Philip Randolph*, 247–48.

55. Anderson, *A. Philip Randolph*, 249.

56. Anderson, *A. Philip Randolph*, 249.

57. Anderson, *A. Philip Randolph*, 249–50.

58. Anderson, *A. Philip Randolph*, 251–52.

59. Anderson, *A. Philip Randolph*, 255.

60. Lerone Bennett, Jr., "The Day They Didn't March," *Ebony*, February 1977, APRP, folder "Biographical File, Printed Matter, Undated," LoC.

61. Bennett, "The Day They Didn't March."

62. Bennett, "The Day They Didn't March."

63. Bennett, "The Day They Didn't March."

64. Bennett, "The Day They Didn't March."

65. Bennett, "The Day They Didn't March."

66. John P. Davis to Edward E, Strong, May 27, 1941, NNC, Schomburg.

67. John P. Davis to Edward E, Strong, May 27, 1941, NNC, Schomburg.

68. John P. Davis to "Congressman," May 27, 1941, NNC, Schomburg; John P. Davis to James Carey, August 28, 1941, NNC, Schomburg; James Carey to John P. Davis, September 9, 1941, NNC, Schomburg.

69. John P. Davis to Frank Bender, September 5, 1941, NNC, Schomburg; Frank Bender to John P. Davis, September 8, 1941, NNC, Schomburg.

70. Gellman, *Death Blow to Jim Crow*, 47-49.

71. "Oral Interview, C. LeBron Simmons, Norman McRae, Interviewer, 1969," Black Workers in the Labor Movement oral histories, WRL. For the CIO's complex relationship to civil rights, see also Marshall F. Stevenson, Jr., "Challenging the Roadblocks to Equality: Race Relations and Civil Rights in the CIO, 1935-1955," Center for Labor Research Report No. WP-006 (Columbus: Ohio State University, 1991).

72. Gellman, *Death Blow to Jim Crow*, 143-144; "Minutes of the NNC Board," May 24, 1942, NNC, Schomburg.

73. Dayo F. Gore, *Radicalism at the Crossroads: African American Women Activists in the Cold War* (New York: NYU Press, 2011), 24.

74. Gore, *Radicalism at the Crossroads*, 26-27; Gellman, *Death Blow to Jim Crow*, 168-69.

75. Gellman, *Death Blow to Jim Crow*, 196-97.

76. Ben Davis, "Negro Organizations—1945," *Congress View* 2, no. 11 (February 1945), NNC, Schomburg.

77. "Minutes of the National Board Meeting—National Negro Congress," January 14, 1945, NNC, Schomburg.

78. Gellman, *Death Blow to Jim Crow*, 207-208; "Sketch, Doxey A. Wilkerson," *Congress View* 3, no. 5 (August 1945), NNC, Schomburg.

79. Gellman, *Death Blow to Jim Crow*, 209; Gore, *Radicalism at the Crossroads*, 41-42; *Congress View* 3, no. 9 (December 1945).

80. "Memo to: Council Members and National Board Members of the National Negro Congress," December 10, 1946, NNC, Schomburg; "Action Program for 1947," *Action* (January 2, 1947), NNC, Schomburg; "The Truman-Schwellenback Statements—A Danger to Peace and Democracy," *Action* (March 14, 1947), NNC, Schomburg.

81. Gellman, *Death Blow to Jim Crow*, 255, 260-61.

82. "National Negro Congress—Special Committee Meeting—National Board," July 7, 1947, NNC, Schomburg.

Chapter 4

1. Thompson and Thompson Fullilove, *Homeboy Came to Orange: A Story of People's Power* (New York: New Village Press, 2018), 3-4.

2. Thompson and Thompson Fullilove, *Homeboy Came to Orange*, 4.

3. Thompson and Thompson Fullilove, *Homeboy Came to Orange*, 5.

4. Thompson and Thompson Fullilove, *Homeboy Came to Orange*, 6–8.

5. Thompson and Thompson Fullilove, *Homeboy Came to Orange*, 10–11.

6. Thompson and Thompson Fullilove, *Homeboy Came to Orange*, 12.

7. Thompson and Thompson Fullilove, *Homeboy Came to Orange*, 15; "RE-PORT ON UPW WORK IN THE SOUTH," EGP, Box 9, Folder 2, Schomburg. All quotations from the EGP are courtesy of Marie Louise Guinier.

8. Mindy Thompson, "The National Negro Labor Council: A History," Occasional Paper No. 27, New York: American Institute for Marxist Studies, 1978), 4–5, 7–8; Thompson and Thompson Fullilove, *Homeboy Came to Orange*, 16; "THE GUINIER CASE. STATEMENT OF DANIEL ALLEN, SECRETARY-TREASURER, NEW YORK DISTRICT, STATE, COUNTY AND MUNICIPAL WORKERS OF AMERICA," August 22, 1941, NNC, Schomburg; George B. Murphy Jr. to Ewart Guinier, July 19, 1941, NNC, Schomburg; John P. Davis to Ewart Guinier, October 22, 1941, NNC, Schomburg; Erik S. Gellman, *Death Blow to Jim Crow: The National Negro Congress and the Rise of Militant Civil Rights* (Chapel Hill: University of North Carolina Press, 2012), 260; Ewart Guinier, "Remarks at Plenary Session, Sunday, October 28, 1951, Cincinnati Founding Convention, National Negro Labor Council," EGP, Box 9, Folder 14, Schomburg.

9. Thompson, "The National Negro Labor Council," 7; Guinier, "Plenary Remarks."

10. Jervis Anderson, *A. Philip Randolph: A Biographical Portrait* (Berkeley: University of California Press, [1973] 1986), 135; Mark Solomon, *The Cry Was Unity: Communists and African Americans, 1917–1936* (Jackson: University Press of Mississippi, 1998), 5; Andrew E. Kersten, *A. Philip Randolph: A Life in the Vanguard* (Lanham: Rowman and Littlefield, 2007), 28; J.G. Tucker, "Special Report—June 17, 1922," National Archives Folder: Casefile #61-23 on Cyril v. Briggs, Claude McKay, and the African Blood Brotherhood regarding government surveillance of African Americans.

11. Mark Naison, *Communists in Harlem during the Depression* (Urbana: University of Illinois Press, [1983] 2005), 39.

12. Naison, *Communists in Harlem during the Depression*, 141, 143, 176.

13. Naison, *Communists in Harlem during the Depression*, 150.

14. Naison, *Communists in Harlem during the Depression*, 181, 198, 262–63; Solomon, *The Cry Was Unity*, 287.

15. Naison, *Communists in Harlem during the Depression*, 245–46, 287, 292, 309.

16. Anderson, *A. Philip Randolph*, 268; Naison, *Communists in Harlem during the Depression*, 310.

17. Frank Crosswaith and A. Philip Randolph, "The Negro Labor Committee, USA," January 31, 1950, CIO Secretary-Treasurer records Part 2, Box 151, Folder 18, WRL.

18. "Negro Labor Committee USA to Philip Murray," April 25, 1950, CIO Secretary-Treasurer records Part 2, Box 151, Folder 18, WRL.

19. William Green to Frank Crosswaith, Chairman; A. Philip Randolph, Vice-Chairman, Negro Labor Committee, USA, April 20, 1950, CIO Secretary-Treasurer records Part 2, Box 151, Folder 18, WRL.

20. "Letter from William R. Hood, Chairman, Continuations Committee of National Trade Union Conference for Negro Rights to Walter P. Reuther, President of UAW-CIO," August 1, 1950), UAW President's office, WPRP, Box 348, Folder 10, WRL; M. Thompson, "The National Negro Labor Council," 8.

21. M. Thompson, "The National Negro Labor Council," 8.

22. Thompson and Thompson Fullilove, *Homeboy Came to Orange*, 16.

23. Thompson and Thompson Fullilove, *Homeboy Came to Orange*, 16.

24. Speech of Ewart Guinier, June 30, 1950, EGP, Box 9, Folder 14, Schomburg.

25. Letter from William R. Hood, Chairman, Continuations Committee of National Trade Union Conference for Negro Rights to Walter P. Reuther, President of UAW-CIO, August 1, 1950, UAW President's office, WPRP, Box 348, Folder 10, WRL.

26. Ewart Guinier, "For a Grass-roots FEPC," *March of Labor* (February 1951), EGP, Box 9, Folder 14, Schomburg.

27. Dayo F. Gore, "From Communist Politics to Black Power: The Visionary Politics and Transnational Solidarities of Victoria 'Vicki' Ama Garvin," in *Want to Start a Revolution? Radical Women in the Black Freedom Struggle*, ed. Dayo F. Gore, Jeanne Theoharis and Komozi Woodard (New York: NYU Press, 2009), 74–76.

28. Gore, "From Communist Politics to Black Power," 76–77; Dayo F. Gore, *Radicalism at the Crossroads: African American Women Activists in the Cold War* (New York: NYU Press, 2011), 35; "Vicki Garvin—Black Activist and Internationalist Passes," *Anti-Imperialist News* (June 12, 2007), accessed March 20, 2024, http://freedom archives.org/pipermail/news_freedomarchives.org/2007-June/002169.html.

29. Vicki Garvin, "Union Leader Challenges Progressive America," *Freedom* (November 1950), VGP, Box 2, Folder 13, Schomburg. All quotations from the Vicki Garvin Papers are courtesy of Lincoln Bergman and Miranda Bergman. M. Thompson, "The National Negro Labor Council," 11.

30. Judith Stepan-Norris and Maurice Zeitlin, *Left Out: Reds and America's Industrial Unions* (Cambridge: Cambridge University Press, 2002), 95; M. Thompson,

"The National Negro Labor Council," 10; William R. Hood, "For these things we fight," (1951), ETP, Box 1, Folder 7, Schomburg. All quotations from the Ernest Thompson collection are courtesy of Dr. Joseph Wilson.

31. M. Thompson, "The National Negro Labor Council," 10; Thompson and Thompson Fullilove, *Homeboy Came to Orange*, 21.

32. M. Thompson, "The National Negro Labor Council," 10; Thompson and Thompson Fullilove, *Homeboy Came to Orange*, 22.

33. M. Thompson, "The National Negro Labor Council," 13.

34. M. Thompson, "The National Negro Labor Council," 12–13.

35. M. Thompson, "The National Negro Labor Council," 13, 16.

36. "Proceedings of Founding Convention of the National Negro Labor Council," October 27 and 28, 1951, VGP, Box 2, Folder 11, Schomburg.

37. "Proceedings of Founding Convention."

38. M. Thompson, "The National Negro Labor Council," 20–21.

39. M. Thompson, "The National Negro Labor Council," 20–21.

40. "Address of William R. Hood, President, National Negro Labor Council," October 27, 1951, HNP, Box 4, Folder 10, WRL.

41. "Address of William R. Hood."

42. "Address of William R. Hood."

43. "Address of M.E. Travis, Secretary-Treasurer, International Union of Mine, Mill and Smelter Workers, National Negro Labor Council, Cincinnati, Ohio, October 28, 1951," HNP, Box 4, Folder 10, WRL.

44. "Founding convention resolutions: 'Resolution on Jobs; 'Economic Equality for Negro Women'; 'Resolution on FEPC,'" 1951, HNP, Box 4, Folder 10, WRL.

45. "Founding convention resolutions."

46. Vicki Garvin, "Labor Council links Fight of Negro People and Unions," *Freedom* I, no. 10 (October 1951), HNP, Box 4, Folder 10, WRL.

47. M. Thompson, "The National Negro Labor Council," 29.

48. M. Thompson, "The National Negro Labor Council," 29.

49. James B. Carey, "Negro Labor Committee, USA," CIO Executive Minutes, 1952, pages 70–71, WRL.

50. "TO: ALL INTERNATIONAL UNION OFFICERS, EXECUTIVE BOARD MEMBERS, DEPARTMENT HEADS, AND ADVISORY COUNCIL MEMBERS ON ANTI-DISCRIMINATION, RE: THE NATIONAL NEGRO LABOR COUNCIL AND LOCAL COUNCILS," January 23, 1952, UAW Washington Office Leg. Dept, Donald Montgomery records, Box 25, Folder 10, WRL.

51. "To James B. Carey, CIO Sec-Tr," 1952, CIO Secretary-Treasurer records, Part 2, Box 151, Folder 18, WRL; "Constitution and By-Laws" (Negro Labor

Committee, USA), March 1, 1952, CIO Secretary-Treasurer records, Part 2, Box 151, Folder 18, WRL.

52. M. Thompson, "The National Negro Labor Council," 34–35.

53. "Negro Labor Council Launches Job Program in New York City," Greater New York Negro Labor Council Press release, March 11, 1952, EGP, Box 9, Folder 14, Schomburg.

54. "Minutes, Meeting of the Negro Labor Committee, USA, held at The Amalgamated Bldg., 333 S. Ashland Blvd., Chicago Illinois," July 19, 1952, CIO Secretary-Treasurer records, Part 2, Box 151, Folder 18, WRL.

55. M. Thompson, "The National Negro Labor Council," 31.

56. M. Thompson, "The National Negro Labor Council," 31–33.

57. M. Thompson, "The National Negro Labor Council," 53–54.

58. "Program of the Second Annual Convention of the NNLC, Cleveland Ohio," November 21–23, 1952, ETP, Box 1, Folder 7, Schomburg; Thompson and Thompson Fullilove, *Homeboy Came to Orange*, 27.

59. "Program of the Second Annual Convention."

60. Thompson and Thompson Fullilove, *Homeboy Came to Orange*, 27.

61. "Program of the Second Annual Convention."

62. "Program of the Second Annual Convention."

63. "Program of the Second Annual Convention."

64. "Program of the Second Annual Convention.".

65. "Program of the Second Annual Convention."

66. Thompson and Thompson Fullilove, *Homeboy Came to Orange*, 27, 29.

67. "NLC Lays Plans to End Hotel Jimcrow." *The Daily Worker*, September 27, 1953, EGP, Box 9, Folder 14, Schomburg; "Program of the Third Annual Convention of the NNLC, Chicago," Dec. 3–5, 1953, ETP, Box 1, Folder 7, Schomburg.

68. "Labor Lowers the Boom on Jim Crow; NNLC, Key Unions Hold Anti-Bias Conferences," *Freedom*, September 1953, EGP, Box 9, Folder 14, Schomburg.

69. Coleman Young, "Keynote Address, Third Annual Convention, National Negro Labor Council, Chicago, Illinois, December 4, 5, 6, 1953, December 4, 1953, EHP, Box 16, Folder 18, WRL.

70. "Let freedom ride the rails," 1954, VGP, Box 2, Folder 12, Schomburg.

71. "Let freedom ride the rails."

72. Thompson and Thompson Fullilove, *Homeboy Came to Orange*, 30; M. Thompson, "The National Negro Labor Council," 59–61.

73. M. Thompson, "The National Negro Labor Council," 63; Toni Gilpin, *The Long Deep Grudge: A Story of Big Capital, Radical Labor, and Class War in the American Heartland* (Chicago: Haymarket Books, 2020), 164.

74. M. Thompson, "The National Negro Labor Council," 64.

75. Young, "Keynote Address, Third Annual Convention"; M. Thompson, "The National Negro Labor Council," 64.

76. M. Thompson, "The National Negro Labor Council," 68; "Give us this day our daily bread," ca. 1954, ETP, Box 1, Folder 7, Schomburg.

77. M. Thompson, "The National Negro Labor Council," 71.

78. "Give us this day our daily bread"; M. Thompson, "The National Negro Labor Council," 70.

79. M. Thompson, "The National Negro Labor Council," 72; Thompson and Thompson Fullilove, *Homeboy Came to Orange*, 33.

80. M. Thompson, "The National Negro Labor Council," 73-74.

81. Negro Trade Unionist Committee, "*NEGRO WORKERS—DANGER AHEAD*," (Fall 1955), VGP, Box 2, Folder 12, Schomburg; Negro Trade Unionist Committee, "DELEGATES TO THE CONVENTION," Fall 1955, VGP, Box 2, Folder 12, Schomburg.

82. M. Thompson, "The National Negro Labor Council," 74.

83. M. Thompson, "The National Negro Labor Council," 75; "The National Negro Labor Council Reunion, June 4-5, 1993, Cobo Center, Detroit, Michigan," VGP, Box 2, Folder 18, Schomburg.

84. M. Thompson, "The National Negro Labor Council," 76.

85. "Vicki Garvin, NNLC Reunion, Detroit, Mich., June 4-5, 1993," VGP, Box 2, Folder 18, Schomburg.

86. M. Thompson, "The National Negro Labor Council," 79-80.

87. M. Thompson, "The National Negro Labor Council," 78.

88. VGP, Box 2, Folder 18, Schomburg.

Chapter 5

1. A. Philip Randolph, "The Negro and CIO-AFL Merger," *Chicago Defender*, August 13, 1955, in *For Jobs and Freedom: Selected Speeches and Writings of A. Philip Randolph*, ed. Andrew E. Kersten and David Lucander (Amherst: University of Massachusetts Press, 2014), 86-87.

2. Jervis Anderson, *A. Philip Randolph: A Biographical Portrait* (Berkeley: University of California Press, [1973] 1986), 298.

3. Anderson, *A. Philip Randolph*, 299.

4. Anderson, *A. Philip Randolph*, 299-300.

5. Anderson, *A. Philip Randolph*, 300-1.

6. Anderson, *A. Philip Randolph*, 301.

7. Anderson, *A. Philip Randolph*, 302.

8. Anderson, *A. Philip Randolph*, 303.

9. "Statement by A. Philip Randolph to the Steering Committee of the Proposed National Negro Labor Council, Hotel Carnegie, Cleveland, Ohio, November 14, 1959," APRP, "Speeches and Writings File (2), Sept. 7–Dec. 4, 1959," LoC.

10. "Statement by A. Philip Randolph."

11. "Summary of Proceedings—The Founding Convention of the Negro American Labor Council," May 27-28-29, 1960, RBP, Box 1, "NALC" folder, WRL.

12. "Summary of Proceedings—The Founding Convention."

13. "Summary of Proceedings—The Founding Convention."

14. "Summary of Proceedings—The Founding Convention"; William P. Jones, "The 'Void at the Center of the Story': The Negro American Labor Council and the Long Civil Rights Movement," in *Reframing Randolph: Labor, Black Freedom, and the Legacies of A. Philip Randolph*, ed. Andrew E. Kersten and Clarence Lang (New York: NYU Press, 2015), 231; William P. Jones, *The March on Washington: Jobs, Freedom, and the Forgotten History of Civil Rights* (New York: Norton, 2013), 137.

15. "Summary of Proceedings—The Founding Convention"; Judith Stepan-Norris and Maurice Zeitlin, *Talking Union* (Urbana: University of Illinois Press, 1996), 153; "The National Negro Labor Council Reunion, June 4–5, 1993, Cobo Center, Detroit, Michigan," VGP, Box 2, Folder 18, Schomburg, courtesy of Lincoln Bergman and Miranda Bergman.

16. "Summary of Proceedings—The Founding Convention"; Jones, "The 'Void at the Center of the Story,'" 231.

17. "Summary of Proceedings—The Founding Convention"; Jones, "The 'Void at the Center of the Story,'" 232; Jones, *The March on Washington*, 138.

18. "Minutes, EXECUTIVE BOARD MEETING, NEGRO AMERICAN LABOR COUNCIL, Room 532, Statler-Hilton Hotel, Detroit, Michigan, Monday, May 30, 1960- 10:20 a.m.," RBP, Box 1, "NALC" folder, WRL; "Minutes, NEGRO AMERICAN LABOR COUNCIL National Executive Board Meeting Conrad Hilton Hotel—Chicago, Ill. July 30, 1960- 11:30 A.M.-5:00 P.M, RBP, Box 1, "NALC" folder, WRL.

19. Anderson, *A. Philip Randolph*, 306.

20. "Time for Action—Resolution" [passed at Workshop on Race Bias in Trade Unions], February 17-18, 1961, RBP, Box 1, "NALC" folder, WRL; Jones, *The March on Washington*, 140-41.

21. Jones, *The March on Washington*, 141-44.

22. Jones, *The March on Washington*, 145–46.

23. Jones, *The March on Washington*, 146–47.

24. Anderson, *A. Philip Randolph*, 307.

25. Anderson, *A. Philip Randolph*, 308.

26. Jones, *The March on Washington*, 147.

27. Jones, *The March on Washington*, 149.

28. "A. Philip Randolph to the NY NALC," May 28, 1962, APRP, Folder on "Negro American Labor Council—General, 1960–1968," LoC.

29. Jones, *The March on Washington*, 156.

30. Letter from A. Philip Randolph to David Dubinsky, August 20, 1962, APRP, Folder: "Negro American Labor Council-General, 1960-1968," LoC; Letter from David Dubinsky to A. Philip Randolph, September 14, 1962, APRP, Folder: "Negro American Labor Council - General, 1960-1968," LoC; Letter from A. Philip Randolph to David Dubinsky, September 25, 1962, APRP, Folder: "Negro American Labor Council-General, 1960-1968," LoC.

31. Jervis Anderson, *A. Philip Randolph*, 309; A. Philip Randolph to David Dubinsky, August 20, 1962, APRP, Folder on "Negro American Labor Council—General, 1960–1968," LoC; David Dubinsky to A. Philip Randolph, September 14, 1962, Folder on "Negro American Labor Council—General, 1960–1968," LoC; A. Philip Randolph to David Dubinsky, September 25, 1962, Folder on "Negro American Labor Council—General, 1960–1968," LoC.

32. "Proceedings: Third Annual Negro American Labor Council convened at 10:40am, Saturday November 10, 1962 in the Main Ballroom of the Sheraton Atlantic Hotel at 34th Street and Broadway, in New York City," November 1962, APRP, Folder on "Negro American Labor Council Convention" (Folder 4), LoC.

33. "Proceedings: Third Annual Negro American Labor Council."

34. "Proceedings: Third Annual Negro American Labor Council."

35. "Proceedings: Third Annual Negro American Labor Council."

36. "Proceedings: Third Annual Negro American Labor Council."

37. "Proceedings: Third Annual Negro American Labor Council."

38. "Proceedings: Third Annual Negro American Labor Council."

39. "Proceedings: Third Annual Negro American Labor Council"; Jones, *The March on Washington*, 158.

40. Jones, *The March on Washington*, 159–60.

41. Jones, *The March on Washington*, 60–61.

42. Bayard Rustin, "The Negro in 1943," Folder on "Articles on Civil Rights, 1940s-1950s," Box 39, BRP, LoC; Bayard Rustin, "In Apprehension How Like a God!" William Penn Lecture, 1948, Delivered at Arch Street Meeting House,

Philadelphia," Folder on "Articles on Civil Rights, 1940s-1950s," Box 39, BRP, LoC.

43. Anderson, *A. Philip Randolph*, 323.

44. Anderson, *A. Philip Randolph*, 323-24.

45. Anderson, *A. Philip Randolph*, 324; Tom Kahn, Letter to the Editor of the *New York Times* [in response to Arthur Bestor], July 22, 1963, BRP, Folder on "March on Washington, 1963—General Correspondence—July," LoC.

46. A. Philip Randolph to Roy Wilkins, March 25, 1963, BRP, Folder on "March on Washington, 1963—General Correspondence—March-June," LoC.

47. A. Philip Randolph to Roy Wilkins, March 25, 1963; Anderson, *A. Philip Randolph*, 322-23; A. Philip Randolph to Martin Luther King, Dorothy Height, and Rosa Gragg, March 26, 1963, BRP, Folder on "March on Washington, 1963—General Correspondence—March-June," LoC.

48. James Farmer to A. Philip Randolph, BRP, Folder on "March on Washington, 1963—General Correspondence—March-June," LoC; Whitney Young to A. Philip Randolph, April 2, 1963, BRP, Folder on "March on Washington, 1963—General Correspondence—March-June," LoC; A. Philip Randolph to Whitney Young, April 3, 1963, BRP, Folder on "March on Washington, 1963—General Correspondence—March-June," LoC; Whitney Young to A. Philip Randolph, April 13, 1963, BRP, Folder on "March on Washington, 1963—General Correspondence—March-June," LoC.

49. "Meeting on Emancipation March on Washington at 217 West 125ᵗʰ Street, Wednesday April 10, 1963, 2:30pm," April 10, 1963, BRP, Folder on "March on Washington, 1963—General Correspondence—March-June," LoC.

50. "Report to National Executive Board," [n.d.], BRP, Folder on "March on Washington, 1963—General Correspondence—July," LoC.

51. Bayard Rustin, "Labor" [n.d.], BRP, Folder on "March on Washington Proposed Plans—1963" LoC.

52. "Report to National Executive Board," BRP, Folder on "March on Washington, 1963—General Correspondence—July," LoC; Jones, *The March on Washington*, 171.

53. Philip S. Foner, *Organized Labor & The Black Worker, 1619-1981* (Chicago: Haymarket Books, [1974] 2017), 348.

54. A. Philip Randolph to Walter Reuther, June 28, 1963, BRP, Folder on "March on Washington, 1963—General Correspondence—March—June," LoC; A. Philip Randolph to Walter Reuther, BRP, Folder on "March on Washington, 1963—General Correspondence—July" LoC; Water Reuther to A. Philip Randolph, BRP, Folder on "March on Washington, 1963—General Correspondence—July," LoC.

55. A. Philip Randolph to Leon Davis, BRP, Folder on "March on Washington, 1963—General Correspondence—March—June," LoC; Alex Sirota to James Farmer, July 30, 1963, BRP, Folder on "March on Washington—Mobilization of Labor Unions—1963," LoC.

56. Jones, *The March on Washington*, 168–69.

57. Jones, *The March on Washington*, 169–70.

58. Memo to James Farmer, Martin Luther King, John Lewis, A. Philip Randolph, Roy Wilkins, Whitney Young, BRP, Folder on "March on Washington Proposed Plans—1963," LoC.

59. Jones, *The March on Washington*, 170–71, 179; Bayard Rustin to A. Philip Randolph, August 9, 1963, BRP, Folder on "March on Washington Transportation memos including all unions attending," LoC.

60. Memo from Rachelle Horowitz to Bayard Rustin, August 8, 1963, BRP, Folder on "March on Washington Transportation memos including all unions attending," LoC; Memo from Rachelle Horowitz to Bayard Rustin and Sy Posner, August 14, 1963, BRP, Folder on "March on Washington Transportation memos including all unions attending," LoC; Memo from Rachelle Horowitz to Bayard Rustin, "Planes Trains and Buses definitely coming to Washington," August 22, 1963, BRP, Folder on "March on Washington Transportation memos including all unions attending," LoC; Jones, *The March on Washington*, 179.

61. Al Lowenthal to all IUE Locals, BRP, Folder on "March on Washington—Mobilization of Labor Unions—1963," LoC.

62. Jones, *The March on Washington*, 181.

63. "Proposed Plans for March," Memo to James Farmer, Martin Luther King, John Lewis, A. Philip Randolph, Roy Wilkins, and Whitney Young," BRP, Folder on "March on Washington Proposed Plans—1963," LoC.

64. "Proposed Plans for March."

65. "Proposed Program—Lincoln Memorial," BRP, Folder on "1963 March on Washington—Program," LoC.

66. "March on Washington for Jobs and Freedom; Part 6 of 17," Open Vault from WGBH, https://openvault.wgbh.org/catalog/A_CB387942466C46F6BAE-6528BAFD53055. Retrieved November 29, 2023.

67. "March on Washington for Jobs and Freedom; Part 6 of 17."

68. "March on Washington for Jobs and Freedom; Part 6 of 17."

69. "Special Convention of the Alabama Labor Council, AFL-CIO, Municipal Auditorium, 1930 8th Avenue, North, Birmingham, Alabama, 20th Street Entrance, Saturday, March 24, 1964," State AFL-CIO Proceedings, LoC.

70. "Special Convention of the Alabama Labor Council."

71. "Proceedings of the Second Biennial Convention, Mississippi AFL-CIO, Heidelberg Hotel, Jackson, Miss., May 25–26–27, 1964," State AFL-CIO Proceedings, LoC.

72. "Proceedings of the Second Biennial Convention."

73. Foner, *Organized Labor and the Black Worker*, 350–51.

74. Foner, *Organized Labor and the Black Worker*, 353-54.

Chapter 6

1. Philip S. Foner, *Organized Labor & The Black Worker, 1619-1981* (Chicago: Haymarket Books, [1974] 2017), 370, 374.

2. Bayard Rustin to George Meany, June 7, 1965, BRP, LoC; George Meany to Bayard Rustin, June 21, 1965, BRP, Folder on "A. Philip Randolph Institute, Miscellaneous, 1965-1976," LoC; "Catalyst: The A. Philip Randolph Institute Sparks A 'Political' Attack on Slums and Poverty," p. 7, BRP, Folder on "A. Philip Randolph Institute, Miscellaneous, 1965-1976," LoC; "Meeting on Emancipation March on Washington at 217 West 125ᵗʰ Street, Wednesday April 10, 1963, 2:30pm," April 10, 1963, BRP, Folder on "March on Washington, 1963—General Correspondence—March-June," LoC.

3. "Catalyst," 7–8.

4. Bayard Rustin to George Meany, December 6, 1965, BRP, Folder on "A. Philip Randolph Institute, Miscellaneous, 1965-1976," LoC; Bayard Rustin to George Meany, May 3, 1967, BRP, Folder on "A. Philip Randolph Institute, Miscellaneous, 1965-1976," LoC.

5. Foner, *Organized Labor and the Black Worker*, 370, 374.

6. Foner, *Organized Labor and the Black Worker*, 371, 372–73.

7. Foner, *Organized Labor and the Black Worker*, 371.

8. Foner, *Organized Labor and the Black Worker*, 372, 373.

9. "Dr. Martin Luther King, Jr. Speech at 1199—March 10, 1968," https://www.youtube.com/watch?v=f_jYt9EXu-8; Foner, *Organized Labor and the Black Worker*, 376.

10. Foner, *Organized Labor and the Black Worker*, 374-75, 377.

11. J. Edwin Stanfield, "In Memphis: More Than a Garbage Strike," Special Report, Southern Regional Council, Atlanta Georgia, 1968, Box 31 Administrative Files, Whitney Young Papers, Columbia University, reprinted in *Black Workers: A Documentary History from Colonial Times to the Present*, ed. Philip S. Foner and Ronald L. Lewis (Philadelphia: Temple University Press, 1989), 585–603.

12. Stanfield, "In Memphis."

13. Stanfield, "In Memphis."

14. Foner, *Organized Labor and the Black Worker*, 377; Stanfield, "In Memphis."

15. Foner, *Organized Labor and the Black Worker*, 382–83.

16. Foner, *Organized Labor and the Black Worker*, 384.

17. Murray Seeger, "Carolina Strike United Rights, Labor Groups," *Los Angeles Times* (April 4, 1969) in Foner and Lewis, *Black Workers*, 604–9.

18. Seeger, "Carolina Strike"; Foner, *Organized Labor and the Black Worker*, 389.

19. Seeger, "Carolina Strike"; Mary A. Moultrie, Letter 4, "Letters from the Charleston Strikers: What the Strike Meant," in Foner and Lewis, *Black Workers*, 615.

20. Coretta Scott King, Roy Wilkins, A. Philip Randolph, Whitney Young, Roy Innis, Bayard Rustin, Dorothy I. Height, and George A. Wiley, "National Organizing Committee Hospital and Nursing Home Employees, District 1199 Archives," in Foner and Lewis, *Black Workers*, 610–11.

21. Foner, *Organized Labor and the Black Worker*, 394.

22. Erica Chenoweth, "Rustin's Legacy of Civil Resistance in the US," in *Bayard Rustin: A Legacy of Protest and Politics*, ed. Michael G. Long (New York: NYU Press, 2024), 20; Jonathan Eig, "Rustin and King: Stony the Road They Trod," in Long, *Bayard Rustin*, 85; John D'Emilio, "Troubles I've Seen: Rustin and the Price of Being Gay," in Long, *Bayard Rustin*, 141.

23. Albert Shanker to Bayard Rustin, September 9, 1967, BRP, Folder on "UFT strike," LoC; "New York Association of Black School Supervisors and Administrators, Press Release, 12 noon, For Tues. Sept. 17," BRP, Folder on "UFT strike," LoC.

24. Bayard Rustin, "An Appeal to the Community from Black Trade Unionists," *New York Post*, Sept. 19, 1968, BRP, Folder on "UFT strike," LoC.

25. Edward Urquhart to Bayard Rustin, September 19, 1968, BRP, Folder on "UFT strike," LoC; B. Louis to Bayard Rustin, September 19, 1968, BRP, Folder on "UFT strike," LoC.

26. Bayard Rustin, "The Effect of the Negro Revolt on American Institutions," *YWCA Magazine*, June 1968, BRP, Folder on "Trade unionists and labor issues," LoC; Bayard Rustin, "The Failure of Black Separatism," *Harper's Magazine*, January 1970, BRP, Folder on "Trade unionists and labor issues," LoC.

27. "Tom of the Month," *Inner City Voice*, Vol. 1, No. 8 (June 1968): 3, HHP, LoC.

28. "Black Workers Uprising," *Inner City Voice*, Vol. 1, No. 8 (June 1968): 3, HHP, LoC.

29. Dan Georgakas and Marvin Surkin, *Detroit, I do mind dying: A Study in Urban Revolution* (Chicago: Haymarket Press, [1975] 2012), 21–22.

30. Interview with General Baker, Tape OH 732_General Baker_1-22-10, Coalition of Black Trade Unionists collection, WRL.

31. Jacoby Sims, "A Giant Step Toward Unity," *Daily World*, February 10, 1973, in Foner and Lewis, *Black Workers*, 662.

32. Foner, *Organized Labor and the Black Worker*, 432-33.

33. Foner, *Organized Labor and the Black Worker*, 432-33.

34. Phyl Garland, "A. Philip Randolph: Labor's Grand Old Man," *The Crisis* (April 1969): 31-32, APRP, Box 43 Printed Matter 1969, LoC; "District 65 Remembers A. Philip Randolph," *The Distributive Worker* (May 1979): 1-2, APRP, Box 43 Printed Matter 1969, LoC.

35. Horace Sheffield to William H. Oliver and Roosevelt Watts, December 7, 1979, BRP, Folder on "CBTU," LoC; Lane Kirkland to Horace Sheffield, February 4, 1980, BRP, Folder on "CBTU," LoC.

36. "BLACK LABOR ORGANIZATIONAL UNITY: APRI AND CBTU," BRP, Folder on "CBTU," LoC.

37. Horace Sheffield to Bayard Rustin and Norman Hill, January 18, 1980, BRP, Folder on "CBTU," LoC; Horace Sheffield to Bayard Rustin, May 8, 1980, BRP, Folder on "CBTU," LoC.

38. UAW, "Who We Are," https://uaw.org/about/, accessed December 15, 2023; AFSCME, "We Are AFSCME," https://www.afscme.org/about/we-are-afscme, accessed December 15, 2023; Stepan-Norris and Zeitlin, *Left Out*, 95; AFT, "About Us," https://www.aft.org/about, accessed December 15, 2023; "About SEIU," https://www.seiu.org/about, accessed December 15, 2023; "Teamsters Structure," https://teamster.org/about/teamsters-structure, accessed December 15, 2023; "Rooted in Racism and Economic Exploitation: The Southern Economic Model" (Washington, DC: Economic Policy Institute, 2023).

39. Judith Stepan-Norris and Jasmine Kerrissey, *Union Booms and Busts: The Ongoing Fight over the U.S. Labor Movement* (Oxford: Oxford University Press, 2023), 7.

40. Jake Rosenfeld, *What Unions No Longer Do* (Cambridge: Harvard University Press, 2014), 100-3.

41. David Smith, "Orbán urges Christian nationalists in Europe and US to 'unite forces' at CPAC," *The Guardian*, August 4, 2022, https://www.theguardian.com/world/2022/aug/04/viktor-orban-cpac-speech.

42. Cedric de Leon, "The Case for an Eclectic Mass Movement," *New Labor Forum* 32, no. 1 (2023): 80-86. For guidance on how to rethink the labor movement through an intersectional lens, please read Stacy Davis Gates, Sheri Davis, Marilyn Sneiderman, and Alisha Volante, "Critical Race Feminism and Common

Good Unionism," *Nonprofit Quarterly* (September 28, 2022), https://nonprofit-quarterly.org/critical-race-feminism-and-common-good-unionism; Tamara L. Lee, Sheri Davis-Faulkner and Naomi R. Williams, eds., *A Racial Reckoning in Industrial Relations: Storytelling as Revolution from Within* (Champaign: Labor and Employment Relations Association, 2022); Tamara L. Lee and Maite Tapia, "Confronting Race and Other Social Identity Erasures: The Case for Critical Industrial Relations Theory," *ILR Review* 74, no. 3 (2021): 637–62; Erica Smiley and Sarita Gupta, *The Future We Need: Organizing for a Better Democracy in the Twentieth-First Century* (Ithaca: Cornell University Press, 2022); Maite Tapia, Tamara L. Lee, and Mikhail Filipovitch, "Supra-Union and Intersectional Organizing: An Examination of Two Prominent Cases in the Low-Wage US Restaurant Industry," *Journal of Industrial Relations* 59, no. 4 (2017): 487–509.

Bibliography

Archival Sources

Library of Congress, Manuscript Division (LoC)

A. Philip Randolph Papers (APRP)
American Federation of Labor Records (AFLR)
Bayard Rustin Papers (BRP)
Herbert Hill Papers (HHP)
State AFL-CIO Proceedings

Schomburg Center for Research in Black Culture

Ernest Thompson collection, courtesy of Dr. Joseph Wilson (ETP)
Ewart Guinier papers, courtesy of Marie Louise Guinier (EGP)
National Negro Congress records (NNC)
Vicki Garvin papers, courtesy of Lincoln Bergman and Miranda Bergman (VGP)

Walter Reuther Library, Wayne State University (WRL)

Black Workers in the Labor Movement oral histories
CIO Secretary-Treasurer Records
Coalition of Black Trade Unionists Collection
Erma Henderson Papers (EHP)
Donald Montgomery Records
Harold Norris Papers (HNP)

Robert Battle Papers

Walter P. Reuther Papers (WPRP)

W. E. B. Du Bois Library, University of Massachusetts Amherst

Boston Guardian

Digital Collections and Sources

American Federation of State, County and Municipal Employees. [n.d.]. "We Are AFSCME." https://www.afscme.org/about/we-are-afscme. Accessed December 15, 2023.

American Federation of Teachers. [n.d.]. "About Us." https://www.aft.org/about. Accessed December 15, 2023.

The Crusader. 1918–1922. https://www.marxists.org/history/usa/pubs/crusader/index.htm.

Fletcher, Michael. 2013. "An Oral History of the March on Washington." *Smithsonian Magazine* (July). https://www.smithsonianmag.com/history/oral-history-march-washington-180953863. Accessed November 1, 2023.

Gates, Stacy Davis, Sheri Davis, Marilyn Sneiderman, and Alisha Volante. 2022. "Critical Race Feminism and Common Good Unionism." *Nonprofit Quarterly* (September 28). https://nonprofitquarterly.org/critical-race-feminism-and-common-good-unionism. Accessed December 17, 2023.

International Brotherhood of Teamsters. [n.d.]. "Teamsters Structure." https://teamster.org/about/teamsters-structure. Accessed December 15, 2023.

King, Martin Luther, Jr. 1968. "Dr. Martin Luther King, Jr. Speech at 1199—March 10, 1968." https://www.youtube.com/watch?v=f_jYt9EXu-8. Accessed December 8, 2023.

McCarthy, Justin. 2022. "U.S. Approval of Labor Unions at Highest Point since 1965." *Gallup* (August 30). https://news.gallup.com/poll/398303/approval-labor-unions-highest-point-1965.aspx. Accessed December 16, 2023.

The Messenger. 1917–1928. https://www.marxists.org/history/usa/pubs/messenger/index.htm. Accessed August 7, 2023.

National Educational Association. [n.d.]. "About NEA." https://www.nea.org/about-nea. Accessed December 15, 2023.

National Labor Relations Board. 2022. "First Three Quarters' Union Election Petitions Up 58%, Exceeding All FY21 Petitions Filed." https://www.nlrb

.gov/news-outreach/news-story/correction-first-three-quarters-union
-election-petitions-up-58-exceeding. Accessed November 1, 2023.

Offord, Carl. 1939. "An Account of the African Blood Brotherhood: Interview
with Cyril Briggs." New York: Works Progress Administration. New York
Public Library Digital Collections. https://digitalcollections.nypl.org
/items/43869020–74fc-0133–591b-00505686a51c. Accessed July 10, 2023.

Service Employees International Union. [n.d.]. "About SEIU." https://www
.seiu.org/about. Accessed December 15, 2023.

Smith, David. 2022."Orbán urges Christian nationalists in Europe and US to
'unite forces' at CPAC." *The Guardian* (August 4). https://www.theguardian
.com/world/2022/aug/04/viktor-orban-cpac-speech. Accessed December
16, 2023.

S.n. "Memorandum to Mr. G.A. Kelly, General Solicitor." Pullman Company
Archives, 06–01–04 Box 17 Folder 454, Newberry Library. https://web.archive.
org/web/20180222225754/https://publications.newberry.org/pullman/items
/show/223. Accessed August 14, 2023.

United Auto Workers. [n.d.]. "Who We Are." https://uaw.org/about. Accessed
December 15, 2023.

U.S. Department of Justice. Casefile #61 -23: Cyril v. Briggs; African Blood
Brotherhood; Claude McKay; Third Communist Party Internationale,
Department of Justice-Bureau of Investigation Surveillance of Black
Americans, Freedom of Information Act Retrievals, National Archives,
Washington, D.C.; Washington Federal Records Center, Suitland, Maryland;
Federal Records Centers in Ft. Worth, Texas and Bayonne, New Jersey; and
from the Federal Bureau of Investigation, Freedom of Information Act
Office. https://blackfreedom.proquest.com/casefile-61–23-cyril-v-briggs-
african-blood-brotherhood-claude-mckay-third-communist-party-
internationale-department-of-justice-bureau-of-investigation-surveillance-
of-black-americans-freedom. Accessed July 12, 2023.

WGBH Boston. 1963. "March on Washington for Jobs and Freedom; Part 6 of
17" (November 29), Open Vault from WGBH. https://openvault.wgbh.org
/catalog/A_CB387942466C46F6BAE6528BAFD53055. Accessed November
1, 2023.

Secondary Sources

Anderson, Jervis. [1973] 1986. *A. Philip Randolph: A Biographical Portrait.*
Berkeley: University of California Press.

Anderson, Mary. 1936. "The Plight of Negro Domestic Labor." *The Journal of Negro Education* 5, no. 1: 66–72.

Biondi, Martha. 2003. *To Stand and Fight: The Struggle for Civil Rights in Postwar New York City*. Cambridge: Harvard University Press.

Blanc, Eric. 2019. *Red State Revolt: The Teachers' Strike Wave and Working-Class Politics*. New York: Verso.

Brenner, Aaron, Robert Brenner, and Cal Winslow, eds. 2010. *Rebel Rank and File: Labor Militancy and Revolt from Below During the Long 1970s*. New York: Verso.

Brown, Cliff, and John Brueggeman. 1997. "Mobilizing Interracial Solidarity: A Comparison of the 1919 and 1937 Steel Industry Labor Organizing Drives." *Mobilization* 2, no. 1: 47–70.

Browne, Simone. 2015. *Dark Matters: Surveillance of Blackness*. Durham: Duke University Press.

Bunche, Ralph. 1936. "A Critique of New Deal Social Planning as it Affects Negroes." *The Journal of Negro Education* 5, no. 1: 59–65.

Carson, Jenny. 2021. *A Matter of Moral Justice: Black Women Laundry Workers and the Fight for Justice*. Urbana: University of Illinois Press.

Chenoweth, Erica. 2024. "Rustin's Legacy of Civil Resistance in the US." In *Bayard Rustin: A Legacy of Protest and Politics*, edited by Michael G. Long. New York: NYU Press.

Clawson, Dan. 2003. *The Next Upsurge: Labor and the New Social Movements*. Ithaca: Cornell University Press.

Cole, Peter. 2007. *Wobblies on the Waterfront: Interracial Unionism and Progressive-Era Philadelphia*. Urbana: University of Illinois Press.

———. 2021. *Ben Fletcher: The Life and Times of a Black Wobbly*. Oakland: PM Press.

Davis, John P. 1936. "A Survey of the Problems of the Negro Under the New Deal." *The Journal of Negro Education* 5, no. 1: 3–12.

de Leon, Cedric. 2016. "Black from White: How the Rights of White and Black Workers Became 'Labor' and 'Civil' Rights after the U.S. Civil War." *Labor Studies Journal* 42, no. 1: 1–17.

———. 2023. "The Case for an Eclectic Mass Movement." *New Labor Forum* 32, no. 1: 80–86.

D'Emilio, John. 2024. "Troubles I've Seen: Rustin and the Price of Being Gay." In *Bayard Rustin: A Legacy of Protest and Politics*, edited by Michael G. Long. New York: NYU Press.

Dolinar, Brian. 2012. *The Black Cultural Front: Black Writers and Artists of the Depression Generation*. Jackson: University Press of Mississippi.

Du Bois, W. E. B. [1935] 1992. *Black Reconstruction in America, 1860–1880*. New York: Atheneum.

———. 1936. "Social Planning for the Negro, Past and Present." *The Journal of Negro Education* 5, no. 1: 110–25.

Eig, Jonathan. 2024. "Rustin and King: Stony the Road They Trod." In *Bayard Rustin: A Legacy of Protest and Politics*, edited by Michael G. Long. New York: NYU Press.

Foner, Philip S. [1974] 2017. *Organized Labor & The Black Worker, 1619–1981*. Chicago: Haymarket Books.

Foner, Philip S., and Ronald L. Lewis, eds. 1989. *Black Workers: A Documentary History from Colonial Times to the Present*. Philadelphia: Temple University Press.

Gellman, Erik S. 2012. *Death Blow to Jim Crow: The National Negro Congress and the Rise of Militant Civil Rights*. Chapel Hill: University of North Carolina Press.

Georgakas, Dan, and Marvin Surkin. 1998. *Detroit, I do mind dying: A Study in Urban Revolution*. 2nd ed. Boston: South End Press.

Gilmore, Glenda Elizabeth. 2008. *Defying Dixie: The Radical Roots of Civil Rights, 1919–1950*. New York: Norton.

Gilpin, Toni. 2020. *The Long Deep Grudge: A Story of Big Capital, Radical Labor, and Class War in the American Heartland*. Chicago: Haymarket Books.

Gilyard, Keith. 2017. *Louise Thompson Patterson: A Life of Struggle for Justice*. Durham: Duke University Press.

Glenn, Evelyn Nakano. 2002. *Unequal Freedom: How Race and Gender Shaped American Citizenship and Labor*. Cambridge: Harvard University Press.

Goldfield, Michael. 1990. "Class, Race, and Politics in the United States: White Supremacy as the Main Explanation for the Peculiarities of American Politics from Colonial Times to the Present." *Research in Political Economy* 12: 83–127

———. 1997. *The Color of Politics: Race and the Mainsprings of American Politics*. New York: New Press.

———. 2020. *The Southern Key: Class, Race, and Radicalism in the 1930s and 1940s*. Oxford: Oxford University Press.

Gore, Dayo F. 2009. "From Communist Politics to Black Power: The Visionary Politics and Transnational Solidarities of Victoria 'Vicki' Ama Garvin." In *Want to Start a Revolution? Radical Women in the Black Freedom Struggle*, edited by Dayo F. Gore, Jeanne Theoharis, and Komozi Woodard. New York: NYU Press.

———. 2011. *Radicalism at the Crossroads: African American Women Activists in the Cold War*. New York: NYU Press.

Green, Venus, and Cedric de Leon. 2024. "The Ruse of Recognition: Black Labor in the Afterlife of Slavery." *Sociology of Race and Ethnicity*. https://doi.org/10.1177/23326492241247786.

Griffith, Barbara S. 1988. *The Crisis of American Labor: Operation Dixie and the Defeat of the CIO*. Philadelphia: Temple University Press.

Hall, Jacquelyn Dowd. 2005. "The Long Civil Rights Movement and the Political Uses of the Past." *Journal of American History* 91, no. 4: 1233–63.

Halpern, Rick. 1997. *Down on the Killing Floor: Black and White Workers in Chicago's Packinghouses, 1904–1954*. Urbana: University of Illinois Press.

Hill, Herbert. 1996. "The Problem of Race in American Labor History." *Reviews in American History* 24, no. 2: 189–208.

Honey, Michael. 1993. *Southern Labor and Black Civil Rights: Organizing Memphis Workers*. Urbana: University of Illinois Press.

———. 2000. "Anti-Racism, Black Workers, and Southern Labor Organizing: Historical Notes on a Continuing Struggle." *Labor Studies Journal* 25, no. 1: 10–26.

Horowitz, Roger. 1997. *'Negro and White, Unite and Fight!': A Social History of Industrial Unionism in Meatpacking*. Urbana: University of Illinois Press.

Hunt, Gerald, and David Rayside. 2000. "Labor Union Response to Diversity in Canada and the United States." *Industrial Relations* 39, no. 3: 401–44.

Iton, Richard. 2000. *Solidarity Blues: Race, Culture, and the American Left*. Chapel Hill: University of North Carolina Press.

Itzigsohn, José, and Karida Brown. 2020. *The Sociology of W. E. B. Du Bois: Racialized Modernity and the Global Color Line*. New York: NYU Press.

James, Winston. 1999. *Holding Aloft the Banner of Ethiopia: Caribbean Radicalism in Early Twentieth-Century America*. London: Verso.

Jones, William P. 2013. *The March on Washington: Jobs, Freedom, and the Forgotten History of Civil Rights*. New York: Norton.

———. 2015. "The 'Void at the Center of the Story': The Negro American Labor Council and the Long Civil Rights Movement." In *Reframing Randolph: Labor, Black Freedom, and the Legacies of A. Philip Randolph*, edited by Andrew E. Kersten and Clarence Lang. New York: NYU Press.

Kelley, Robin D. G. 1990. *Hammer and Hoe: Alabama Communists during the Great Depression*. Chapel Hill: University of North Carolina Press.

———. 1994. *Race Rebels: Culture, Politics, and the Black Working Class*. New York: Free Press.

Kersten, Andrew E. 2007. *A. Philip Randolph: A Life in the Vanguard*. Lanham: Rowman and Littlefield.

Korstad, Robert Rodgers. 2003. *Civil Rights Unionism: Tobacco Workers and the Struggle for Democracy in the Mid-Twentieth Century South*. Chapel Hill: University of North Carolina Press.

Lee, Tamara L., Sheri Davis-Faulkner, Naomi R. Williams, and Maite Tapia. 2022. *A Racial Reckoning in Industrial Relations: Storytelling as Revolution from Within*. Champaign: Labor and Employment Relations Association.

Lee, Tamara L., and Maite Tapia. 2021. "Confronting Race and Other Social Identity Erasures: The Case for Critical Industrial Relations Theory." *ILR Review* 74, no. 3: 637–62.

Lewis, Earl. 1993. *In Their Own Interests: Race, Class and Power in Twentieth-Century Norfolk, Virginia*. Berkeley: University of California Press.

McAlevey, Jane F. 2016. *No Shortcuts: Organizing for Power in the New Gilded Age*. Oxford: Oxford University Press.

McCartin, Joseph A., Marilyn Sneiderman, and Maurice BP-Weeks. 2020. "Combustible Convergence: Bargaining for the Common Good and the #RedforEd Uprisings of 2018." *Labor Studies Journal* 45, no. 1: 97–113.

Moody, Kim. 2020. "Reversing the 'Model': Thoughts on Jane McAlevey's Plan for Union Power." *Spectre Journal* (November 8): 1–22.

Morris, Aldon. 1984. *The Origins of the Civil Rights Movement: Black Communities Organizing for Change*. New York: Free Press.

———. 2015. *The Scholar Denied: W. E. B. Du Bois and the Birth of Modern Sociology*. Oakland: University of California Press.

Morris, Aldon, Walter Allen, Cheryl Johnson-Odim, Dan S. Green, Marcus Anthony Hunter, Karida Brown, and Michael Schwartz, eds. 2022. *The Oxford Handbook of W. E. B. Du Bois*. Oxford: Oxford University Press.

Murolo, Priscilla, and A. B. Chitty. 2018. *From the Folks Who Brought You the Weekend*. New York: New Press.

Naison, Mark. [1983] 2005. *Communists in Harlem during the Depression*. Urbana: University of Illinois Press.

Needleman, Ruth. 2003. *Black Freedom Fighters in Steel: The Struggle for Democratic Unionism*. Ithaca: Cornell University Press.

Nelson, Bruce. 2002. *Divided We Stand: American Workers and the Struggle for Black Equality*. Princeton: Princeton University Press.

Painter, Nell Irvin. 1989. "The New Labor History and the Historical Moment." *Journal of Politics, Culture, and Society* 2 (Spring): 367–70.

Phillips, Kimberley L. 1999. *AlabamaNorth: African-American Migrants, Community, and Working-Class Activism in Cleveland, 1915–1945*. Urbana: University of Illinois Press.

Randolph, A. Philip. 1936. "The Trade Union Movement and the Negro." *The Journal of Negro Education* 5, no. 1: 54–58.

———. [1955] 2014. "The Negro and CIO-AFL Merger," *Chicago Defender*, August 13, 1955. In *For Jobs and Freedom: Selected Speeches and Writings of A. Philip Randolph*, edited by Andrew E. Kersten and David Lucander. Amherst: University of Massachusetts Press.

Robinson, Cedric. [1983] 2000. *Black Marxism: The Making of the Black Radical Tradition*. Chapel Hill: University of North Carolina Press.

Roediger, David R. 1987. "'Labor in White Skin': Race and Working-Class History." In *Reshaping the U.S. Left*, edited by Mike Davis and Michael Sprinker. London: Verso.

———. 1991. *The Wages of Whiteness: Race and the Making of the American Working Class*. New York: Verso.

Rosenfeld, Jake. 2014. *What Unions No Longer Do*. Cambridge: Harvard University Press.

Rosenfeld, Jake, and Meredith Kleykamp. 2012. "Organized Labor and Racial Wage Inequality in the United States." *American Journal of Sociology* 117, no. 5: 1460–1502.

Smiley, Erica and Sarita Gupta. 2022. *The Future We Need: Organizing for a Better Democracy in the Twentieth-First Century*. Ithaca: Cornell University Press.

S.n. 2023. "Rooted in Racism and Economic Exploitation: The Southern Economic Model." Washington, DC: Economic Policy Institute.

Solomon, Mark. 1998. *The Cry Was Unity: Communists and African Americans, 1917–1936*. Jackson: University Press of Mississippi.

Spero, Sterling D., and Abram L. Harris. [1931] 1972. *The Black Worker: The Negro and the Labor Movement*. New York: Columbia University Press.

Stepan-Norris, Judith, and Jasmine Kerrissey. 2023. *Union Booms and Busts: The Ongoing Fight over the U.S. Labor Movement*. Oxford: Oxford University Press.

Stepan-Norris, Judith, and Maurice Zeitlin 1996. *Talking Union*. Urbana: University of Illinois Press.

———. 2002. *Left Out: Reds and America's Industrial Unions*. Cambridge: Cambridge University Press.

Stevenson, Marshall F., Jr. 1991. "Challenging the Roadblocks to Equality: Race Relations and Civil Rights in the CIO, 1935-1955." Center for Labor Research Report No. WP-006. Columbus: Ohio State University.

Tapia, Maite, Tamara L. Lee, and Mikhail Filipovitch. 2017. "Supra-Union and Intersectional Organizing: An Examination of Two Prominent Cases in the Low-Wage US Restaurant Industry." *Journal of Industrial Relations* 59, no. 4: 487-509.

Thompson, Ernest, and Mindy Thompson Fullilove. 2018. *Homeboy Came to Orange: A Story of People's Power.* New York: New Village Press.

Thompson, Mindy. 1978. "The National Negro Labor Council: A History." Occasional Paper No. 27. New York: American Institute for Marxist Studies.

Trotter, Joe William, Jr.. 2019. *Workers on Arrival: Black Labor in the Making of America.* Oakland: University of California Press.

Tye, Larry. 2004. *Rising from the Rails: Pullman Porters and the Making of the Black Middle Class.* New York: Henry Holt and Company.

Wade, Richard C. 1967. *Slavery in the Cities: The South, 1820-1860.* Oxford: Oxford University Press.

Zeitlin, Maurice, and L. Frank Weyher. 2001. "'Black and White, Unite and Fight': Interracial Working-Class Solidarity and Racial Employment Equality." *American Journal of Sociology* 107, no. 2: 430-67.

Zieger, Robert H. 2007. *For Jobs and Freedom: Race and Labor in America Since 1865.* Lexington: University Press of Kentucky.

Zumoff, J.A. 2007. "The African Blood Brotherhood: From Caribbean Nationalism to Communism." *Journal of Caribbean History* 41, no. 1-2: 200-26.

Index

Bray, James A., 78
Bridges, Harry, 145, 235
Briggs, Cyril, 8, 11, 17, 22, 25, 28–33, 38–45, 51–56, 59, 66–67, 69, 72, 76, 136, 141; "Africa for the Africans," 38–39; "The Salvation of the Negro," 38–39; "Security of Life for Poles and Serbs, Why Not for Colored Nations?," 31
Brooklyn Naval Clothing Supply Depot, 114
Brophy, John, 117–18
Brophy memo, 117–18
Brotherhood of Dining Car Employees, 49
Brotherhood of Railway Clerks, 201
Brotherhood of Sleeping Car Porters (BSCP), 21–22, 28, 33, 65, 78, 88, 172, 266, 269
Browder, Earl, 115–16
Brown, Edgar, 99
Brown, John, 156
Brown, Mayme, 114
Brown, Sterling: "Strong Men," 155
Brown, Theodore, 200
Brown, Viola, 10, 168, 174–75
Brownell, Attorney General Herbert, 179–80, 183
Bunche, Ralph, 76–77, 81, 98, 100–101, 118
Burch, Jack, 152
Burton, Charles Wesley, 81–82
Business Week, 250
Byrd, Mabel, 73, 75

Campbell, Grace, 29, 32, 51–52, 67, 125, 266
Campbell, Jessie Scott, 114
capitalism, 8, 10, 29, 31, 76; advent of colonial, 38; imperialism and, 32, 55. *See also* imperialism

Capital Transit Company workers' strike, 117
Carey, James, 110, 153, 161, 162, 176, 181, 202, 229
Carmichael, Stokely, 2–3, 216
Carson, Jenny, 6
Carter, Elmer, 78
Carter, R.A., 78
Cayton, Revels, 116–17, 119–20
Central Intelligence Agency (CIA), 265
Charleston, 249–50
Charleston hospital workers' strike (1969), 20, 239, 249–52, 267
Chase, Stuart, 61
Chi, C.T., 56
Chicago, 49, 56, 59, 61, 80–82, 88, 89, 94–95, 103, 117, 121, 140, 145, 148, 164, 167, 171, 199, 213, 258
Chicago Defender, 57, 185, 196
Chicago Teachers Union, 271
Chinese Students Alliance, 56
Churchill, Winston, 114
Civil Rights Act (1964), 4–5, 235–36, 240, 265
Civil Rights Congress (CRC), 91, 118, 164
Civil Rights Movement, 15, 200; leaders of the, 104; role of Black trade unionists in the, 200–201, 280n22; support of trade unionists for the, 207, 233–34. *See also* law
Clark, Sheriff Jim, 235
Clawson, Dan, 17
Cleveland, 87, 165–67
Coalition of Black Trade Unionists (CBTU), 20, 239, 258–62, 264–65; "The Need for a Coalition of Black Trade Unionists," 259–60
coal mining, 71–72; Southern workers in, 71

Ingersol, Minneola, 88
Ingersoll, Robert, 28
Inner City Voice, 255, 258
International Association of Machinists, 60, 101, 119
International Labor Defense (ILD), 69–70, 72, 82, 116
International Ladies Garment Workers Union (ILGWU), 4, 96, 141, 143, 203–6, 217, 220–21, 226–29
International Longshore and Warehouse Union (ILWU), 145, 153, 160, 179, 182, 235
International Longshoremen's Association (ILA), 140, 186
International Union of Electrical, Radio and Machine Workers of America (IUE), 1, 138, 176, 181, 202, 226–27, 229
International Union of Mine, Mill and Smelter Workers (Mine Mill), 145, 153, 157, 161, 182
International Uplift League, 53
interracial solidarity, 5, 7, 9, 13, 16, 17, 26, 38, 41, 44, 65, 66, 76, 78, 84, 86, 111, 119–20, 157, 168, 181, 236–39, 221, 228, 229, 235, 245, 262, 267. *See also* Black labor; white labor
intersectionality, 10, 85, 270–71
Interstate Commerce Commission (ICC), 1–2
I. N. Vaughan and Company, 92
Irish Republican Army, 40

Jackson, Attorney General Robert H., 108
Jackson, Augusta, 94
Jackson, Congressman Donald L., 165
Jackson, James, 83, 93
Jackson County Emergency Union, 233–34

Jennings, L. Joy, 195, 213
Jett, Jenny, 114
Jett, Maude, 114
Jett, Ruth, 114
Jim Crow, 153, 157, 166–71, 175; in the army, 31; in the South, 31; in trade unions, 4, 76, 78, 139, 178, 189–90, 255. *See also* racial segregation; racism
Johnson, Arnold P., 142
Johnson, Clyde, 71
Johnson, Henry, 88, 90, 94–95
Johnson, James Weldon, 53, 214
Johnson, President Lyndon, 232, 238, 242, 249
Joint Committee on National Recovery (JCNR), 74–75; "The Position of the Negro in Our National Economic Crisis" (conference), 75
Jones, Quincy, 226
Jones, T. O., 247, 249

Kahn, Tom, 3, 216
Kansas City, 45, 49, 101
Kelley, Robin D.G., 15
Kennedy, President John F., 15, 198–99, 217, 224, 228, 232, 238, 266
King, Coretta Scott, 249, 267
King, Jr., Martin Luther, 3, 11, 17, 194, 197–98, 202, 216–20, 223, 229, 235, 239, 244–56
Kirkland, Lane, 261
Knights of Labor, 10, 13
Korstad, Robert Rodgers, 15
Ku Klux Klan, 157, 179–80

Labor's Non-Partisan League (LNPL), 96, 99–100; antiwar position of the, 99–100
LaGuardia, Mayor Fiorello, 105-7, 143

Founded in 1893,
UNIVERSITY OF CALIFORNIA PRESS
publishes bold, progressive books and journals
on topics in the arts, humanities, social sciences,
and natural sciences—with a focus on social
justice issues—that inspire thought and action
among readers worldwide.

The UC PRESS FOUNDATION
raises funds to uphold the press's vital role
as an independent, nonprofit publisher, and
receives philanthropic support from a wide
range of individuals and institutions—and from
committed readers like you. To learn more, visit
ucpress.edu/supportus.

www.ingramcontent.com/pod-product-compliance
Lightning Source LLC
Chambersburg PA
CBHW020822270326
41928CB00006B/414